Checks Unbalanced

CHECKS

UNBALANCED

The Quiet Side of Public Spending

HERMAN B. LEONARD

Basic Books, Inc., Publishers   *New York*

Table 6.3, "Tax-Exempt and Taxable Bond Yields, 1978–1982, is reprinted by permission from the Government Finance Officers Association.

Library of Congress Cataloging-in-Publication Data
Leonard, Herman B.
   Checks unbalanced.
   Bibliography: p. 265.
   Includes index.
   1.   United States—Appropriations and expenditures.
I.   Title.
HJ2051.L46   1986   336.3′9′0973   85–43103
ISBN   0–465–00973–5 (cloth)
ISBN   0–465–00974–3 (paper)

To Kathryn Anne Angell

No money shall be drawn from the Treasury, but in consequence of Appropriations made by Law, and a regular Statement and Account of the Receipts and Expenditures of all public Money shall be published from time to time.

—Constitution of the United States, Article I, Section IX, Clause 7

Contents

Preface

THIS BOOK has two purposes. Its chief aim is to explore the patterns shared by the major forms of nonappropriated public spending. It also provides descriptions of the history and workings of these "quiet" spending programs. The programs are all fascinating in their own right, and together they tell a rich story.

Because I had to learn about a collection of programs, this book relies more than most on help from colleagues, associates, friends, and assistants. Help came in many forms: through random hallway conversations, organized seminars, and formal written comment and criticism at various stages in the organizing and drafting stages of this work. Some may not have realized how much I was learning from what they said. Others may have noticed the odd habit I developed of pulling out a small notepad to take down thoughts they inspired or contributed. A surprisingly high fraction of those notes are represented somewhere in what follows.

I cannot thank by name all of those who have helped me during this project, but I hope they will know how grateful I am for ideas, images, words, support, and encouragement. I especially want to thank Karl Case, Hale Champion, James Chan, Regina Herzlinger, Robert Klitgaard, Helen Ladd, Richard Musgrave, Richard Ravitch, Peter Rousmaniere, and Tom Schelling, all of whom have stimulated my interest in these subjects and have helped me to understand them better. I am deeply indebted to Graham Allison, Francis Bator, Judy Doneiko, John Donahue, Barbara Dyer, Howard Frant, Steven Kelman, Martin Kessler, Charles Kireker, Winthrop Knowlton, Shelley Metzenbaum, Mark Moore, Richard Neustadt, Mary O'Keeffe, Robert Pollard, Don Price, Robert Reich, Elisabeth Rhyne, Raymond Vernon, and Richard Zeckhauser. Each read one or more drafts of the manuscript and commented extensively on both substance and presentation. The manuscript has been thoroughly rewritten in response to their generous and constructive criticism. I have learned a great deal from each of them and have taken many of their suggestions about which ideas to pursue and how to develop them, about what could safely be omitted, and about more graceful wording.

I was ably assisted in this project. My work was supported in part by the Japanese Corporate Associates Program of the John F. Kennedy School of Government, Harvard University, and I am grateful for their help. Work on various portions of this book was also supported by a grant to the Kennedy School from the Alfred P. Sloan Foundation to "establish an intellectual beachhead in the field of public management," and I greatly appreciate both the assistance and the foundation's willingness to support research in this area. Robert Rodriguez assembled many of the source materials used in this project. Mary Naus gave me encouragement and efficient administrative assistance. Edward McAdams meticulously retyped the barely legible edited versions that began to pile up toward the end. Karen Skelton provided expert help in tracking down references and additional information as the project moved toward completion. Nancy Gibson read the first draft of the manuscript and suggested many ways to make the language more vivid. This book is much the better for their time, effort, good humor, patience, and their skilled management of the author. I am deeply grateful to all of them.

My greatest debt is to Susan Bender. She read each draft (often several times) and proposed reams of changes in substance and in presentation. No detail was too small, nor any bold idea for improvement too sweeping. She looked—and she forced me to look—with care at every sentence, every paragraph, every argument. Her criticism was good-natured, kind, and diplomatic—but determined. Her suggestions were always good—and often sparkling. This would quite literally have been a different book without her help.

Throughout this project, my family has been wonderful. They have given me support, encouragement, and many helpful suggestions. They had faith —and they gave me faith—that I would finish. Both of my parents read an early draft, made many useful suggestions, and pointed out numerous editorial problems while there was still time to fix them. My wife was encouraging, hopeful, supportive—and resolute. Gently, but firmly, she kept letting me know that I should press on, so that one day I would be done.

This project has been a pleasure and a privilege. I want to thank all of the people who have helped to make it so, from the research to the writing and production. The John F. Kennedy School of Government has provided an intellectual home in which I could develop this work, first as separate projects and then as one. I am grateful for its creative climate and its willingness to schedule my teaching to facilitate this research. I also want to express appreciation to Martin Kessler and the staff of Basic Books, who have made even the final preparation and production enjoyable.

Checks Unbalanced

Introduction

AVOIDANCE AND OBFUSCATION are not often found on the list of civilized arts, but the march of progress has made both essential in the modern world. Civilized people go to great lengths to avoid having to confront unpleasant news and uncomfortable feelings. We help others avoid collisions with what they would prefer not to know—and what *we* would prefer they not know—through elaborate subterfuges.

When we hide our private business, as a matter of personal privilege and social convention, we deal with the consequences, good and bad, alone. But when we practice avoidance and obfuscation in public affairs, the consequences reach us all. A civilized penchant to look away—the willingness of some to hide and of others to tolerate the hiding of the public's business—is on its face antithetical to our society's fundamental governing precept: government by the informed consent of the governed.

Yet avoidance and obfuscation of the public's financial business are a national pastime approaching an art form. We carefully avoid noticing over $1 trillion in accumulated government liabilities to government retirees and $4 trillion to current and future social security recipients. We hide over $300 billion in annual federal spending and unmeasured billions in state spending by carrying it out on the tax side of the budget. We roll subsidies and loans together into complex bundles that make it hard to discern what —or how much—was given away. We studiously look the other way while public infrastructure systems crumble into disrepair, then seek off-budget "creative financing" schemes to renew the cycle of construction and decay. We engage in modern shell games to lure firms into one state rather than another, and fund the inducements through low-visibility tax abatements.

We stand by while a variety of entrenched spending programs quietly distribute public resources.

The last decade has seen a concerted struggle to bring all forms of government spending under control. After decades of uninterrupted growth of public responsibilities, tax burdens, and spending, Americans in the late 1970s and early 1980s asked searching questions about the conduct of government, its efficiency, and its role in their lives. They reassessed their expectations—and aspirations—about what government could do for them. They devised new approaches for making government more attentive to the public interest. The view that government served the interests of the few at the expense of the many was asserted in forceful frustration. It became popular to argue that government should be "disentangled from its connection with special interests and made responsive to genuine public opinion. . . . It then becomes an instrument of civilization and of humanity." These words for our time were written in 1912 by the then newly elected President Woodrow Wilson.[1] Keeping government attentive to the business of the wider public interest, and not to narrowly defined special interests, is a timeless task—and, therefore, always timely. Currently, stress at all levels of government and the historic federal budget deficit create incentives to find alternative spending routes. Opportunities for quiet spending are particularly attractive. Taming the incentives to exploit them is therefore a particularly urgent task today.

How can elected and appointed government officials be induced to look beyond the narrow interests—including their own—that constantly nominate themselves as worthy of government largess? Ideally, public officials should be fully answerable to the public at large. Decisions would require financially informed public consent. Public consent means, at a minimum, tolerance or acquiescence, continuing allegiance and willingness to be governed. Full financial information means a complete understanding, within the bounds of existing knowledge, of what a given program entails and of what its costs and effects are. No one can ever give a precise account, in advance, of every aspect of program cost, operation, and impact. We would be satisfied if the public had knowledge of the best available description (including uncertainties) of a program, thoroughly understood this knowledge, and gave its authorization.

This is not an operational standard. Yet this ideal does identify the two basic ingredients of financial accountability—systems of information and tests of consent.

The framers of our Constitution erected structures incorporating both ingredients, making much of the conduct of government highly visible.

Introduction

Reluctant to concentrate too much authority in any one place, they created multiple opportunities for interested review. First, systems of information ensure public knowledge. The public at large can obtain descriptions of government activities, lists of available resources, and analyses of performance. The interested citizen or commentator can examine the process through a variety of windows; each sheds light on a different facet of what the government does. Collectively, the views through these windows provide a reasonably comprehensive collage of government affairs.

Many of the government's financial activities are particularly visible. Budgets are public. They are the progeny of considered debate within (and between) the executive and legislative branches. Public hearings are commonplace. Reams of information are available to those who choose to look. Many people do. Official auditors certify the accuracy of financial statements. Official agencies, like the Congressional Budget Office for the federal government and offices of legislative analysis in many states, provide analysis and commentary. Self-appointed private groups summarize and highlight the flood of data flowing forth on the government's financial affairs. Interested and informed members of the press and academic communities concentrate on understanding and disseminating information about the public's finances. Taxpayers themselves can and do examine some of the descriptions and analyses of government activities that appear daily.

Second, specified tests of consent probe public authorization. Constitutional, statutory, and customary rules mandate how direct spending by public entities will be deliberated, authorized, recorded, and revealed. Short of the ballot box, the standard test of approval for public spending is whether a designated fraction of legislators approve an appropriation. Spending programs must compete with each other for limited funds made available through an explicit tax system. The appropriations process ensures that the flow of funds is visible—that basic spending information is easily available. Taxation or borrowing is a prerequisite to spending; funds must be provided and then explicitly appropriated before they are disbursed. Furthermore, authority to use the public's money is subjected to a series of "checks and balances." These tests of consent are points of contact with specified actors who have explicit powers to approve, disapprove, expedite, or obstruct and who can legitimately claim to represent interests of some part of the public.

The appropriations process is the operational answer we have given to the question of how to assure reasonable financial accountability to the many and conflicting interests of the public. Yet some financial activity avoids the tests built into the appropriation process. Published descriptions of government financial activities generally trace only the actual cash receipts and disbursements of the Treasury. Not every authorized commitment of public resources results in an immediate cash expenditure; not every promise made or favor granted by the government can be measured in monetary terms. Governments at all levels have developed mechanisms that transfer resources outside the spotlight of traditional financial disclosure. These transfers are forms of spending. They use public resources, presumably for public ends. But they escape, in remarkably varied ways, the scrutiny characteristic of the traditional public appropriations process.

This book is about spending by public organizations that is *not* carried out through the standard appropriations process. It examines "quiet" or "low-profile" spending—unappropriated disbursements of public resources —at all levels of government. Any use of public financial resources without appropriation is defined as a form of "quiet" spending. This makes it relatively straightforward to determine whether any given spending program is "quiet." It leaves open, however, the question of how to define "spending." All government actions use public resources; the appropriations process is designed to consider only those parts of government actions that use *financial* resources. If we are to focus on programs for which treatment through an appropriations process is practical, we will have to limit the definition of spending.

The narrowest definition of spending equates it with the direct disbursement of financial claims—checks written on the public treasury. A sizable volume of unappropriated public spending fits into this very restricted conception of spending. But this excludes many uses of financial resources by public organizations that are spending by any reasonable interpretation. When a public organization promises to make a future payment, the promise is a form of spending whether the payment is scheduled for next year or for tomorrow. When the organization consumes physical assets it owns to generate current services, it is spending no less than if the asset consumed were held in the form of dollars. The government spends when public financial liabilities increase or when the value of publicly owned capital assets declines. Spending thus includes (1) directly disbursing financial claims, in particular, money; (2) taking on liability for future payment; and (3) consuming assets. When it happens without appropriation, we define it as quiet spending.

A wide variety of public programs operate in the realm of quiet public spending. This book concentrates on the major examples—programs involving the most spending, the farthest removed from public scrutiny, posing the deepest accountability challenge.

The Major Forms of Quiet Spending

PAYMENT WITH A PROMISE: PUBLIC-EMPLOYEE RETIREMENT SYSTEMS

Public organizations routinely promise to provide retirement incomes to their employees. These promises are not fully backed by any governmental IRA; insufficient assets have been set aside to finance them. Federal public pension systems have accumulated a bill for over $1 trillion; state and local government pension systems also face sizable quietly accumulated debts. The components of public-employee retirement systems that have been most scrutinized—for example, fraudulent disability payments—involve only a small fraction of the commitments. The bulk of the funding provides for the regular retirement income of former public servants. These systems pay out billions of dollars each year for services received long ago. Almost all are funded on a "pay-as-you-go" basis: current tax payments finance the retirement of employees who provided public services to an earlier generation of taxpayers. Meanwhile, we continue to promise current public employees that they, too, will receive pensions—and we continue to set aside little or no money to pay for them, preferring to rely on the taxes collected from later taxpayers. The difference between the value of the promises we give to current employees and the amount we set aside to redeem those promises constitutes a large and growing public liability. As such, it is one of the largest forms of quiet public spending.

CASCADING LIABILITIES: THE SOCIAL SECURITY SYSTEM

The nation's largest public retirement system, the social security system, is also funded on a pay-as-you-go basis. It collects earmarked tax revenues and pays retirement and health benefits to retirees. Payments flow through a series of trust funds, which ostensibly balance inflows of taxes against outflows of benefits. The system grew steadily from its inception during the Great Depression until impending cash crises threatened to bankrupt the trust funds in the late 1970s and again in the early 1980s. These crises spurred considerable public debate, and the system's hidden liabilities were suddenly on display. The immediate cash crisis was alleviated, but cash solvency hides a continuing vast transfer of funds from each generation to its predecessor. In much the same way as public-employee retirement systems, the social security system involves vast quiet spending—in spite of the success of recent reforms designed to make it "solvent."

UNAPPROPRIATED SUBSIDIES: FEDERAL LOANS AND LOAN GUARANTEES

When a public organization makes or guarantees a loan to a private entity, the borrower often reaps a subsidy. The government's interest rate is generally below market rates for the level of risk; the net cost of the loan or guarantee thus depends on the interest rate (or guarantee premium) relative to the riskiness of the loan. Risk is intangible; it is hard to assess in monetary terms. The amount of the subsidy is therefore difficult to pinpoint. Nonetheless, the extension of subsidized credit amounts to a direct disbursement of current funds. There is no explicit consideration or appropriation of this subsidy component of below-market loans or loan guarantees. The value of liabilities accepted exceeds the value of assets obtained; quiet spending is taking place.

SPENDING THROUGH TAXES: SUBSIDIES THROUGH TAX EXPENDITURES

A reduction in taxes has the same impact on the budget deficit (or, less frequently these days, budget surplus) as additional spending has. From the perspective of budget balance, tax breaks are simply another form of spending. They are quite direct; they are current and denominated in dollars. A dollar not received by the Treasury might just as well be a dollar received and then spent; the public is spending current resources just as much as if the funds were first raised through taxation and then paid out as grants. This view of tax breaks has led to their being relabeled "tax expenditures." The only difference between the direct grant form and the tax expenditure form is that tax expenditures do not have to run through the appropriations process—that is, the only difference is that tax expenditures are *quiet* spending.*

ASSET SPEND-DOWN: PUBLIC DISINVESTMENT

When an individual draws funds out of a savings account and uses them to purchase services for current consumption, it qualifies as spending. The public owns a substantial savings account in the form of physical assets built

*Tax expenditures crop up in so many forms and places that it will take us three chapters to treat them fully.

8

through public investments over the years—waterways, roads, bridges, dams, buildings, machinery. Our society has been systematically drawing down this savings account for years. This is a form of public spending. But our accounting systems hardly notice. Public accounting systems were designed mainly to track cash disbursements, so their concern with capital assets is mainly with the management and efficient use of the money spent, not with recording the value of the assets purchased. At all levels of government, accounting records almost entirely ignore what assets are owned, their state of repair, and their value. These systems therefore imply that it costs nothing to use existing assets. Indeed, they suggest the opposite: by cataloging the costs of maintenance as a current expense, they make it seem cheaper to use up assets than to keep them in good repair. This form of quiet spending proceeds by default. It corrodes public assets *unless* active direct spending counterbalances it—which makes this perhaps the quietest spending of all.

FINANCING CONFUSION: THE ART AND CRAFT OF PUBLIC LEASING

A debt is a debt is a debt—or is it? When it's in the form of a lease, we sometimes pretend it isn't. Public borrowing transfers costs to future taxpayers—a tempting option for taxpayers in every generation. As a consequence, public appropriations processes generally take great pains to scrutinize borrowing carefully. At the state and local levels, borrowing often requires a special bond resolution or direct voter approval. But some forms of borrowing escape attention. Long-term rentals by public organizations —public leases—are not generally subject to the same stringent scrutiny as bond issues. Recently, they have become a popular form of borrowing, at least in part because they obfuscate the liability the public is accepting. Building up public liabilities by promising future payments is a form of spending. When, as with most public leases, there is no explicit long-term appropriations commitment, leasing is quiet spending.

A variety of programs avoid the regular appropriations process. Most public retirement systems fund current pension payments through the appropriations process, but these pay-as-you-go charges are only a small fraction of the total system liability. Funds for credit programs likewise must be appropriated, but substantial subsidies are hidden within loan disbursements and receipts. Tax expenditures are entirely removed from the appropriations process. State economic development programs obscure much of their cost through tax expenditure mechanisms. Private use tax-exempt bonds are issued at the state level, but subsidies for their interest payments are financed—without appropriations—at the federal level. Allowing fixed assets to deteriorate (by not maintaining them) frees scarce funds that can be appropriated for other purposes. Leasing is often used precisely to escape the capital budgeting appropriations process.

Part I of this book examines these forms of quiet spending, concentrating on the most important forms of each. Public pensions at all levels of government, the social security system, and federal credit programs are reviewed in some detail. Some state and local governments operate special credit programs, but they are generally small, and data on them are so diffuse that they cannot be treated here. Federal tax expenditure programs are reviewed relatively comprehensively. Again, data on state programs are not reliable, though there is sufficient research on state economic development programs conducted through tax expenditures to permit discussion of them. A prime *state* economic development program operated through a *federal* tax expenditure—the industrial development bond program—is reviewed in depth. Consumption—through deterioration—of public assets is treated only with reference to infrastructure assets. Uses of other public assets—military hardware, land, mineral resources, and so on—are omitted, again for lack of reliable data. The obfuscation of public debt liabilities through leasing is discussed, though once again data on the extent of spending involved are impossible to construct.

Many other uses of public authority might conceivably be defined as quiet spending. The largest in dollar terms are entitlement programs like Medicaid and welfare. Arguably, these programs commit future resources for which no funds have been set aside, much as pensions do. The form of this commitment is materially different from that of pensions, however. Each year's entitlement spending is debated on its own terms, not simply paid as promised in years long past. Even without any contract ensuring that public employees receive retirement incomes, or fixing public pension benefits, the commitment to pay "earned" pension benefits nevertheless differs from the commitment to fund most "unearned" entitlements. It seems more in keeping with the stated character of these programs to treat entitlement programs as current spending financed by current revenues.

Spending by public authorities—like water and sewer commissions and port, turnpike, and public power authorities—could also be viewed as quiet public spending. Public authorities annually spend billions of dollars raised through "user" fees. This spending is excluded here on the basis that it is not supposed to be authorized through a legislative appropriations process. Public authorities have deliberately been sheltered from the appropriations process—excused from it by duly constituted legislative authority. However, many authors have emphasized the lack of public control and accountability exercised over the spending by public authorities, and this spending could be put under the rubric of quiet spending.[2]

Regulation—the imposition of rules or mandates that require individuals, firms, or other governments, to spend—is arguably one of the most pervasive and expensive forms of public intervention in the economy. It could be classified as quiet public spending: we can think of the resources the government forces others to expend as having been taxed away and then spent by the public on the required equipment, procedures, or activities. Regulation reaches into practically every corner of society, from product safety standards for children's toys to acid rain reducing scrubbers on industrial smokestacks. It is too sweeping a subject to be covered here. Though it could be included in the category of quiet spending, it is excluded on the grounds that it stretches the meaning of "spending" too far.[3]

Another form of low-profile spending, much discussed but rarely examined, is inefficiency in the conduct of government. When work is duplicated, or capacity sits idle, or excessively high prices are paid for items or services purchased by the government, funds are siphoned off without providing corresponding benefits. Waste has a low profile because it is difficult to separate from legitimate expense. Many regard this as one of the principal accountability problems of government. But it is an accountability problem of appropriated spending, not a form of quiet spending.

The quiet spending treated here provides a reasonably comprehensive look at public spending programs conducted without the benefit of appropriations review. Precisely because these programs have been so unobtrusive for so long, no reliable data exist on the extent of spending through some of these avenues. Too little is known about the scope of state and local tax expenditures to permit estimates of their dollar magnitude. Even a narrowed focus on state tax expenditures for economic development provides only a general sense of the scale of spending. The lack of asset records at all levels of government prohibits assessment of the annual costs of deterioration. Moreover, the boundaries of quiet spending—whether it includes public authorities, regulation, and entitlements, for example—are debatable. There is little to be gained, therefore, by trying to estimate the total annual flow of quiet spending. Rough estimates of the quiet spending examined here, however, show it to be quite substantial. Federal tax expenditures are on the order of $300 billion annually. Social security has averaged roughly $100 billion per year. When credit subsidies and civil service, military, and other federal retirement programs are added, the annual total is easily over $500 billion. This very rough estimate suggests that quiet federal spending is more than half the size of appropriated federal spending.

Why Is Quiet Spending Important?

Granted that quiet spending is a sizable phenomenon, why is it important? Direct forms of public spending involve larger sums, however much we stretch the definition of quiet spending. Nothing guarantees that even programs for which appropriated funds are supplied actually serve the general public and its interests. Why then do quiet spending programs deserve special attention?

The fundamental issue is whether quiet spending conforms to our general expectations about how government spending decisions will be made. Our systems of public financial decision, management, and review rest upon statutory and constitutional directives about the form of scrutiny that will be applied to spending decisions. The presumption is that decisions to spend will be made through appropriations. To the framers of those directives, that presumption was far from idle. Their forebears in the English Parliament had fought for two centuries to wrest control of spending from the monarchy. Years of bitter experience told them that incomplete or unbalanced control was utterly inadequate. Their solution was a comprehensive appropriations process. A fundamental component of that process is competition among programs for scarce public funds. Each program battles with others for a limited supply of public resources. Decisions to spend are balanced by the reality that funds must come from somewhere—from other programs or from additional taxes or borrowing. These decisions are forced into a constrained arena. Whether this generates good decisions—or even whether this is a fair characterization of most appropriations processes—is beside the point. The appropriations process is the established, generic test, the gauntlet that spending programs are expected to run to gain approval to use scarce public funds.

Quiet spending programs directly offend the established appropriations order. They depart from the logic of appropriations review, of informed consent. They live outside the requirement that they confront other spending priorities. Spending is obscured. Since cost is not necessarily apparent, quiet programs are less likely to be forced to show that their benefits exceed their costs. While the appropriations process does not force a cost-benefit analysis for each program considered within it, it does impose the competitive check; each program must compete either against other programs or against the pressure to hold down total spending. Competition in the appropriations process forces deliberative choice. This choice is the operational surrogate for informed consent, and it confers legitimacy. Quiet programs tend to escape these balancing pressures. This consistent evasion of the appropriations process makes these programs harder to review, assess, and challenge.

They share other characteristics as well. First, there is a dearth of comprehensible information about the current financial costs of most low-profile programs. In part, this is what we mean by low-profile. But even when basic figures do exist—for programs like pensions and tax expenditures—they are hard for anyone other than experts to understand. Couched in technical language, they often rest on a detailed set of assumptions about our economic future, and sometimes baffle even the experts.

It is not that information about these programs is hidden; in many cases there simply is none. For most quiet spending programs there are no well-defined standards for a sensible, comprehensive, and comprehensible financial characterization. Accountants and actuaries have been struggling for years—sometimes with each other—to find understandable ways to present the current cost and condition of public pension systems. There are no standards for developing inflation-adjusted (or nominal, for that matter) estimates of public asset depreciation. Estimation of the subsidy in credit programs is rudimentary, in spite of the advanced state of knowledge in theoretical finance: government loans and loan guarantees are complicated and not easy to value. There is no strong consensus on how leases should be analyzed and how much more they cost than alternative forms of borrowing. In spite of repeated attempts to construct them, fully convincing measures of the actual revenue losses from tax expenditures do not exist.

A second common feature of low-profile programs is their financial complexity. With direct expenditure programs, even if the benefits cannot be assessed, the number of dollars spent is reasonably clear. By contrast, assessing low-profile spending leads to a maze of analytical questions. Sometimes—with tax expenditures, for example—it takes mild mental gymnastics to understand how the activity represents spending. The base from which to measure is unclear—from what reference tax system can tax expenditures be measured? What would be the cost of funds to borrowers in federal credit programs (from which we should measure the subsidy provided)? What is the real cost of capital obtained by the government through a sale-leaseback? How much do we give away by providing state investment tax credits? It is nearly impossible to determine definitively how much some quiet programs spend.*

*In fairness, this is also difficult for some direct spending programs. We know the budgeted costs, but not the actual resource costs—what economists call the opportunity costs—of direct government spending. This problem applies to quiet spending as well. At least for direct expenditure programs we have one reasonably well-defined cost figure from which to work.

Complexity serves two purposes. It may provide a justification for conducting the program quietly; the claim is that it must be custom-tailored to serve its prescribed function. Complexity also makes the program more difficult to understand, thereby shielding it from effective attention. This ha been called the "billion-dollar-headache syndrome"—if it is too much of a headache to figure out what is going on, the program may be left alone.

A third characteristic common to many quiet spending programs is that they are not subject to regular review once they are in place. Pensions are determined as a fraction of salaries; the form of the pension plan is reviewed only rarely. Tax expenditures, once authorized, spend money every year without reauthorization. Infrastructure assets deteriorate unless positive— and visibly costly—action is taken to maintain them.

Avoiding regular review may mean that the scale of spending receives only shallow scrutiny. Federal pension systems quietly spend approximately $40 billion annually. Few appropriated programs of that magnitude receive as little conscious attention. Unfunded promises to future social security recipients have quietly committed an average of $100 billion annually for the last forty years. The social security program receives a great deal of attention, but debate centers on its cash spending, not on its hidden spending. Uncounted billions in quiet annual depreciation of the nation's inventory of physical assets receive little attention when compared with the scrutiny accorded even small appropriated programs like Aid to Families with Dependent Children, which spends less than $10 billion annually.

The lack of required balancing and review may also impair management incentives. Public estimates—based only on direct pension spending—understate the cost of public-employee retirement, underestimating the true cost of labor to public organizations. Labor-saving investments will thus be undervalued. The failure to track (or even acknowledge) the value of public assets encourages penny-wise and pound-foolish maintenance strategies for public capital. There is, of course, no magic in the appropriations process that guarantees efficient, accountable use of public funds, but oversight and competition at the least encourage efficiency.

In sharp contrast to the irregular review of quiet programs, direct expenditure programs are held up for debate in each budget cycle. In a system of governance where the mechanisms of accountability are integrated into the system of decision making, accountability tests are most forcefully applied when a decision is required. Quiet spending that continues so long as no decision is made to stop it—as many quiet spending programs do— thus operates beyond the reach of much of the established accountability structure.

Introduction

A fourth element common to most quiet spending programs is a disconnection between those who receive benefits and those who pay. Pensions chronologically disconnect those who receive from those who pay, making future taxpayers pay for current services. Industrial development bonds shift the bill for state and local projects to federal taxpayers. Leasing moves costs from local taxpayers to the federal Treasury. This is not unique to quiet spending programs; much direct spending also spreads costs widely. But in quiet spending programs this disconnection seems more deliberate, more a part of the purpose.

Finally, low-profile programs seem to involve spending without paying; public resources are disbursed without an explicit offset in any payment account. A promise made to a current employee that he or she will receive a pension fifteen years from now, part of it in return for services this year, is not registered as payment. The benefits purchased with money we would have spent on maintenance seem free, because the payment—a deteriorating infrastructure—is not noted in any explicit account. Tax expenditures, which reward selected activities, have no tangible cost. Low-profile programs use real public resources, but they don't make us feel as though money is being spent. In the language of accounting, there are credits (purchases of services, transfers of resources, provision of benefits—spending) but no debits (recognition of costs, allowance for future disbursements—payment). It is not that these programs are costless. Rather, the problem is our awareness; we simply note the benefits and ignore the expense. These programs all represent checks written on the public treasury, unbalanced by any requirement to provide funds.

The quiet programs we examine are remote from, or only partially included in, the traditional appropriations process. They tend to spend large amounts of public resources with low levels of scrutiny. They avoid competition with other programs. They are financially complicated. It is difficult to obtain truly descriptive information about them; costs and expenses are often obscured. No appropriate standards have been prescribed for what comprehensive information about them should look like. Many continue to spend unless specifically halted. They often impose costs on taxpayers at a place, time, or level of government removed from the beneficiaries. They spend public resources but try to avoid the pinch of payment.

The common features of these programs assault the basic prerequisite of accountability. Accountability requires the financially informed consent of the governed; these programs are hard pressed to achieve it. It is difficult to find, generate, understand, or utilize information about them because of their financial complexity. The public is not now aware and cannot readily be made aware of the nature of these programs; it is difficult to see how they can be fully accountable.

This doesn't imply that all quiet spending is worse than all appropriated spending. It does suggest, however, that making a quiet program noisier may make it better. Quiet spending programs pose a challenge: what other test can substitute for the appropriations process and achieve a similar degree of accountability?

There can never be any operational test for whether a public action is truly in the general interest of all citizens, in the "public interest."[5] Accountability must therefore be viewed as a characteristic of a decision, a characteristic conferred by the process through which the decision was reached. In our constitutional order, financial accountability might be thought of as produced by the decision-making processes through which society grants financially informed consent for the use of public financial resources. The process's cornerstones must therefore be (1) systems of information about expected program costs and effects and (2) prescribed forms of consent or authorization.[6]

Since there can be no definitive test of whether any particular spending program—quiet or appropriated—is in "the" public interest (taken as the interest of the whole), there is little point in joining that debate here. We can never answer these questions satisfactorily; each observer must ultimately form a personal judgment. It is not the purpose of this work to advance any particular conclusion about whether the forms or examples of spending discussed here are in the public interest. We merely assert that governmental practice should be kept reasonably close to the defined constitutional norm. Quiet spending programs cannot pass that test today.

This book explores how the accountability of quiet spending programs could be strengthened. This is an operational question, and it will bend to analysis and data. The accountability of quiet spending programs can potentially be enhanced, however well or poorly they now serve the public interest. Available information can be improved. Consent may be made more direct by bringing the programs closer to or under the aegis of the appropriations process. The accuracy, scope, reliability, and usefulness of information can be examined with relative objectivity. Methods for extending the reach of the appropriations process can also be defined and studied. The decision process itself can be improved either by upgrading the available information or by changing the form in which authorization must be granted. These are unambiguous tasks, and we don't need to wait for a resolution of abstract political theories of accountability before getting started on them.

Examining Quiet Spending Programs Together

Each of the quiet spending programs examined here has been discussed before. Usually, each one is treated as if it were a distinct phenomenon, arising as a unique pathology, each escaping the appropriations process in its own special way and for its own singular reasons.

This misses a fundamental feature of quiet spending. The common traits of quiet spending suggest a common pattern; these programs are not unique departures from the established norm. Their existence is no accident. Each reflects powerful forces intrinsic to our systems of financial decision making. Most are conscious evasions, carefully crafted to avoid the competitive appropriations arena. Proponents argue that, for a variety of reasons specific to each program, each deserves special dispensation and privilege. All seek that privilege in the same form: being exempted from having to confront other programs in an appropriations fight.

One way to characterize the forces that create quiet spending programs is in the language of the principal-agent model developed by economists. Political scientists have long observed narrow interest groups and broad public attitudes competing for attention from elected representatives. Economists tend to shy away from political phenomena, but recently they have shown considerable interest in a conception of economic interactions that views them more like political contests. This approach—the principal-agent model—observes that in many important transactions, we (the principals) engage others (the agents) to work for us. We cannot perfectly observe their work, because we are busy or because we do not have the expertise to evaluate the service received. Real-estate brokers, lawyers, and doctors are hired agents who do things for us that we often cannot fully evaluate. In the management of these principal-agent relationships, economics tells us to look at incentives; political science warns us that the principals are not well-informed about what their agents are doing.[7]

The basic question addressed by the agency model is how the relationship can be structured to produce what the principal wants. The model examines the principal's ability to establish efficient incentives and then monitor the activities of the agent. Monitoring enforces the structure of incentives created by the contracts. Incentives and monitoring—the agent's inducements and the principal's access to accurate information about the agent's activities—are the key accountability issues.

The agency approach tackles the problem that the agent's interests are not perfectly aligned with the principal's. Contracts are structured to make the agent's interests coincide, as much as possible, with those of the principal. A monitoring system is designed to enforce the bargain. In a world where monitoring is imperfect, however, the agent will sometimes be able to improve his or her own position at the expense of the principal. Agency theory explores how such conflicts of interest can be minimized, but often they cannot be eliminated.*

Few agency relationships are as important as the one between citizens and their government in a democratic republic, and few are fraught with such deep conflicts of interest.[8] The structures of checks and balances create and enforce the system of incentives by which the interested principals attempt to extract the best possible performance from their governmental agents.

But who are the principals? On whose behalf is government conducted —who are the supposed, and who are the actual, beneficiaries? Economists often view government officials as agents for taxpaying principals. Constitutionally, however, taxpaying has not been a qualification for voting since early in the nineteenth century. And voting has never been a qualification for citizenship. According to the democratic theory that legitimates our system, "we the people" are the principals, taxpaying or not, voting or not, citizens or not. So, if elective-office holders are "agents," they must be presumed to represent all the people in their districts, active or not.†
Agency theory presumes that the agents act on incentives: they work for their principals and incidentally for themselves—that is, for reelection. Agency theory thus identifies various constituencies affecting the design and choice of spending programs. For each activity of government, we expect a "benefit" constituency—those who benefit most directly from a given program—to advance its case. There may also be an "employment" constituency—a collection of contractors, suppliers, and employees whose livelihood flows in part from the government's provision. There is always a "payer" constituency, though its members may not always know who they are. Finally, public officials, who derive their political clout from helping some or all of the other constituencies, have a direct interest in the outcome of the debate. These interests often—perhaps *usually*—conflict. None is

---

*Potential conflicts of interest that remain—an accountant turning a blind eye to deceptive reporting in order to maintain a lucrative account, for example, or a bond salesman misrepresenting a credit rating to close a deal—deeply concern professional groups. In professions based on agency relationships, a central function of professional societies is to develop and enforce codes of ethics and conduct that seek to minimize conflicts of interest and to punish agents who act in their own interest rather than in that of their principals.

†Elected officials are not, of course, the only agents. They in turn hire others and delegate power to them. Agency theory scrutinizes these agency relationships as well.

inherently less legitimate than the others. The agency approach pays close attention to how programs affect the interests of each possible constituency. Whose interests predominate? Does the balance seem right? Agency theory nominates these as central concerns.

Agency theory suggests that the political interests of the agents—and not just the interests of the benefit, payer, and employment constituencies—may be steering the ship. We might prefer that, when given the choice, elected officials would choose to serve broad rather than narrow interests. But the elective system often forces them to serve narrow, articulate interests in order to survive. The agents have a need and right to advance their political interests. If they don't, who will? And if they don't, who next will represent the constituency or support the beneficiaries? Getting elected is prerequisite to serving principals. The problem is not that agents work for themselves—it is to make sure that when they are working for themselves they are working for us. Agency theory indicates the importance of examining quiet spending programs to see whose interests they are really serving. Is it the stated beneficiaries, or is it primarily the narrow political interests of the agents who established it?

From the perspective of agency theory, quiet spending is an expected result of intrinsic incentives rather than an irritating and randomly occurring pathology. Various groups seek to advance particular interests, which they always represent as, and which sometimes are, more general interests as well. They pressure their agents for performance, by which they mean the successful advancement of their politically expressed desires. Within the appropriations process, elected officials—the agents in this story—juggle mutually counterbalancing pressures to fund programs while holding taxes down. They naturally seek ways to meet the expressed political demands of their constituencies while avoiding the pressures that come from raising taxes or reducing other spending. Quiet spending avenues meet these joint requirements. The restraints of the appropriations process thus produce a steady pressure to innovate outside it.

Since the appropriations process exists precisely to avoid an unstructured free-for-all over intangible public resources, spending through a quiet channel almost always comes with a story about why this form of spending is particularly important and deserving of special privilege. Each program can describe why forcing it to compete with other programs would put it at an unfair disadvantage. This is a "parasol" approach to government spending: collectively, we demand sunshine, but individually we prefer parasols to protect our favorite spending initiatives from the intense sunshine demanded by others.

The Broader Challenge

The universal plea for parasols should be seen as an expected, recurring, intrinsic manifestation of the pressure to meet political demands through the least politically expensive channels. Quiet spending programs are thus a natural outgrowth of the agency structure of government. They are an enduring feature of the public financial landscape, worthy of careful study individually and as a wider phenomenon. They do not arise by accident, nor will they fade away by attrition or disuse. Since they avoid our standard accountability test, an obvious question is how the accountability of each might be strengthened, regardless of how well they currently serve the public interest. Our system must provide sufficient control of government financial activities to nurture broad tolerance or active support from a duly informed electorate. Ultimately, we return to the generic problems: what data are needed, in what form, provided to whom, held against what tests of assent? To raise the level of scrutiny accorded a particular quiet spending program, should we require more and better information about it or bring it toward the brighter arena of the appropriations process? Short of the appropriations hearing room, does any body of information have the same clout in the decision making? Although improved information may be an inadequate substitute for the appropriations process, more information is still generally better than less.

Part I (chapters 1 through 8) of this book focuses on individual quiet spending programs. Their shared patterns raise broader questions for the accountability of spending decisions. Part II examines two general approaches to balancing the forces of spending and restraint for quiet spending programs. The first approach advocates better accounting, budgeting, reporting, and disclosure—raising the profile of spending by making information more intelligible, comprehensive, and available. Chapter 9 discusses accounting and accountants as a crucial part of that process. There is ample room for improvement in the accounting we currently carry out for public organizations. It does not follow, however, that better accounting is the best route to higher levels of accountability. The accounting profession is not inclined—and may not be able—to expand its professional domain enough to close the existing informational gaps.

The second approach—born of frustration with the failures of the first —is to impose simple, broad limits on governmental discretion. These usually take the form of tax and expenditure limits or balanced-budget requirements or both. Chapter 10 discusses the limitation approach; chapter considers the proposal to require a balanced federal budget through constitutional amendment. The central question is whether these approaches improve accountability and raise the profile of hidden spending. The imposition of broad limitations does seem to enhance the sensitivity and perhaps the responsiveness of public officials, but many forms of quiet spending are not captured within the imposed limits.

If these approaches will provide little (or insufficient) help, what else can we do to enhance financial accountability? Throughout the discussion of the examples of quiet spending in chapters 1 through 8, specific suggestions are made for improving the accountability of individual programs. If we believe that there should be less hidden spending—either that it should be less hidden or that there should be less spending—how might we move to control it? The conclusion offers a few broader suggestions. Some are traditional; some are largely speculative. The thrust is to accept the existence of pressures to obscure spending as an enduring feature of modern government. It is not the fault of its elected or appointed officials, and not necessarily always a problem. But if we want to reduce, balance, or limit spending, both program-specific and more general suggestions are worth pursuing.

The phenomenon of quiet spending poses deep challenges for the accountability of other uses of government resources. We might expect accountability in the financial realm to be easier to characterize and to construct than in other, less well-defined uses of public authority like police power, diplomacy, and military force. But even financial accountability is elusive. The forces we find that strengthen it may therefore have broader application in increasing accountability outside the realm of financial concerns as well as inside it.

The kinds of spending referred to here as quiet or low-profile are often identified by more pejorative labels. A common term—"off-budget"—is not descriptive of most of the programs discussed here, because it generally refers only to direct expenditure programs that do not appear in ordinary budget documents. Many commentators exhibit a distinct policy bias against quiet spending programs. The presumption is that these programs have been extended beyond what taxpayers desire because what they spend doesn't feel like "real" money. This work attempts to avoid this bias. It looks at major forms of quiet spending, describes their structure, and inquires about their accountability. It is consciously sympathetic to two aspects of these programs. First, all are legally authorized. Some are more in line with systems of checks and balances than others, but all have been duly (though not necessarily explicitly) established through the legislative process. Second, these programs are not accidental. They result from real pressures felt by those who establish or use them and from real incentives

created by our political system. They were established and are administere
by officials who believe, for the most part, that they are worthwhile. The
officials may be proven wrong, but they are not knaves. We cannot assun
that low-profile spending is wrong or self-serving or not in the publ
interest. But we can usefully examine how we might bring it closer to th
established constitutional order.

PART I

THE MAJOR FORMS

OF

QUIET SPENDING

Chapter 1

Public Pension Systems

THE PILGRIMS at Plymouth left a culture of flinty perseverance that saw them through the raw cold of New England winters. They handed down a spirit of single-mindedness in which lay the seeds of an independence movement that would flower in the balmy days of spring a century and a half later. Some of the houses they built stand to this day. They created a vision of what life on these shores could be, forged in the warmth of summer heat and tempered in the cool, crisp realism of New England fall. They left a storehouse of knowledge about how to keep that vision—and themselves and their offspring—alive and growing.

They also left the first major program of nonappropriated government spending. In 1636, the Pilgrims established a relief program for soldiers disabled in the defense of the colony. The program was duly authorized by a governmental authority sanctioned by an interested public. No one made —or, at least, no one left us a record of—any estimates of how much the program would cost, but it was not authorized accidentally and it enjoyed support within the small community. No one seems to have been particularly concerned that the program authorized expenditures far into the future for which funds would have to be supplied later.

Almost from the earliest days of government in this country, then, pensions for public servants have been an accepted form of compensation. Those who followed the Pilgrims developed more general income supplements in response to the economic distress of particular groups that had served the public. In 1818, Congress established a system of pensions for needy Revolutionary War veterans. Since only a small fraction of the veterans were still alive, the program was not very expensive. True to the pattern of public pensions since, the program was extended in 1832 to cover veterans without respect to need.

From these modest roots, public pension programs have grown steadily and quietly to command sizable fractions of our national resources. In 1982, federal retirement programs alone covered nearly 5 million active employees in over 30 separate plans. In 1980, state and local government retirement programs covered nearly 12 million additional employees under 6,600 separate plans.[1] About 4 million former employees receive retirement benefits under these plans, and annual benefit payments to former public employees exceed $40 billion.

Public pensions are big business. A great many people receive them; an even larger number anticipate them. Public pension funds hold over $250 billion in assets. While some of these are invested in simple "index" funds requiring little active management, over half of the total is in securities portfolios that are actively invested by trustees and the brokers and financial consultants they hire. Public pension funds represent a large fraction of the wealth of the employees who expect to receive them, constitute a considerable bloc of concentrated financial clout, and are a source of prodigious amounts of income for accountants, portfolio managers, and other professional money handlers.

Not the least of the interested parties is the taxpayer—if interest is defined as financial involvement rather than as active attention. A variable, but generally small, fraction of the assets held by these funds comes from employee contributions; the rest is the public's money, compensating public servants for services taxpayers have already received. Retirement payments from these funds have increased, and taxpayers are concerned by the increasing pension flows from already strained treasuries. Recurrent scandals, particularly concerning the abuses of disability pensions, have raised taxpayer awareness of public-employee retirement systems as a public financial concern.

But as taxpayers we are much more deeply involved in public pensions than most of us know. Pensions are a form of compensation for employees. A pension is a component of the bargain between employer and worker. In return for work during a career of public service, employees receive payments beyond the years of active service. Employees want to work only for a limited portion of their lives and still receive income to maintain a reasonable standard of living past retirement and into old age. The payment for thirty-five years of work is spread over those thirty-five years and perhaps an additional fifteen years of retirement.[2] This arrangement provides security to an employee who otherwise faces the problem of receiving, paying taxes on, and then investing—and worrying about losing—funds for retirement.

Pensions imply that part of the cost of current services is deferred for payment at a later time. The thirty-five years of work cost fifty, not thirty-five, years of payments; call it salary or call it pension, it is compensation for the same thirty-five years of service. Retirement incomes are part of the cost borne by the employer, and in public pension systems ultimately by the taxpayer. We should be aware of the full cost of work we choose to have done in the public sector. Just as important, we should be aware of the full benefit when we decide to make an investment that will reduce the amount of public-employee labor we use. The value of future pension payments we make pursuant to work performed now should properly be regarded as part of the current cost of government.

Generally speaking, it is not. The cost of future pension benefits for current services has traditionally been ignored in describing current costs. Instead, only the current payment of benefits—to former employees, for services they rendered long ago—has typically been included in reckonings of the current cost of government. Such a system is known as a pay-as-you-go funding approach. It is a form of public borrowing. Current taxpayers are borrowing a part of the services of current public servants, promising to pay them later in the form of pensions. The large and, of late, rapidly increasing liability for retirement payments in recognition of current services is cheerfully handed on to future taxpayers, only some of whom were also the beneficiaries of the services when they were rendered.

In a nation born of a revolution against taxation without representation, we might expect that public borrowing for the purpose of passing burdens to future taxpayers would be suspect. When the public sector borrows money, particularly at the state and local level, it explicitly reviews whether the benefits of the intended expenditure will be felt over a long period. A higher level of scrutiny and accountability is generally considered more equitable for decisions that defer costs to future taxpayers, who cannot represent themselves at the time of the decision.* Many jurisdictions require approval of each new bond issue in a special voter referendum. Held against that standard, the degree of public scrutiny and oversight of the implicit borrowing through extensions of public pension promises is indefensibly low.

---

*This is more true of state and local than of federal borrowing, which is often a result as much of macroeconomic policy as of a considered decision to defer payments.

How Large Is Pension Borrowing?

If governments put aside enough money each year so that, with accumulated interest, they would be able to pay the pension benefits their employees earned that year, no pension liability would remain. Such fully funded pension systems are paid for on a current basis: the amount paid in each year matches the liability incurred on behalf of services rendered in that year. Taxpayers in each year pay the full salary and pension cost of the benefits they choose to have produced for them. Fully funded systems, rare though they may be, are a baseline against which to view the performance of other systems.

We can ask two questions of a system that is not fully funded. First, what payment would be required this year if it *were* fully funded—that is, what would be the full funding payment that would have to be made this year if prior payments were up to date? This amount, often referred to as the normal cost, is frequently expressed as a fraction of current salary payments. For example, we might find that a given pension system had a full-funding rate of 25 percent of salary. In order to make a current payment that would, with interest, provide enough money to pay for the pension benefits earned annually, an amount equal to 25 percent of salary payments would have to be set aside.

Second, how far behind has the fund fallen? That is, how much more money would the fund have (together with accumulated interest) if it had always been funded on a full-funding basis? Or, equivalently, how much more would the fund have to have in assets in order to be able to make all future pension payments required of it, if it is fully funded in the future? How much, in short, would we need to "catch up"? This "unfunded liability" of the pension fund denotes the accumulated implicit debt of the fund —the amount future taxpayers will have to pay in exchange for services already rendered by current and former government workers.* Unfunded liability is a *current* concept; it measures how far out of balance the fund's existing liabilities and assets are. It does not incorporate *future* underfunding or other departures from full-funding management.†

*There is no inviolate reason why borrowing should not be carried out through the pension system. If, for example, workers earned pensions by building bridges that future taxpayers will use, there is no inherent inequity in the pension borrowing process. What is important is that the implicit borrowing be explicitly recognized.

†It is common in some estimates of legislative impact and some studies of the social security system, for example, to calculate the additional amount of money the system would need to cover its obligations if it were to be operated indefinitely under current law. This would accrue into today's debt the liability for planned future underfunding. The unfunded liability concept

These two central characteristics of pension funds—normal cost and unfunded liability—are simple in concept. They are hard to assess, however, because they require projections about an uncertain future. Estimating the full-funding rate, for example, requires us to assess how much current employees earn in a given year in the form of pension rights. But in most public-employee pension systems, retirement income—and, therefore, this year's accrual toward it—depends on salary in the final year or years of service and on the total number of years of service. In addition, we cannot calculate what pension rights an employee has earned in a particular year (or estimate their cost) without knowing how long he or she will live in retirement or what rate of interest will be earned on funds set aside today to meet these future obligations. To estimate the cost of pension liabilities, we must collect data on anticipated career patterns, project salary trajectories, predict future economic variables (including the rate of return expected on invested pension assets), and then simulate the future of the pension system.

The estimation process is further complicated by additional choices about how to recognize pension obligations public sector workers have earned. In many public pension systems, workers are not vested—that is, they do not have specific legal entitlements until they reach retirement age. For example, an Army lieutenant colonel who qualifies for a $30,000 pension by retiring with twenty years of service would receive no retirement income if he or she retired with nineteen years. A strict legal construction of these systems would regard such an employee as earning the entire pension in the twentieth year of service. This approach, known as the accrued vested benefits method, is based on the view that employment can be terminated by the employer at any time, so that workers should be seen as having earned only what they are explicitly and legally entitled to. It is widely applied to retirement plans in the private sector, where workers can in fact be terminated more easily.

In the public sector, however, it is out of place. Public workers do not stay in their jobs strictly at the pleasure of their employer. (Indeed, it is arguable whether private workers do either, but the case that public workers do would be even harder to make.) Moreover, viewing the claims of public workers as accruing at the instant of actual vesting (very late in the career under many plans) understates the magnitude of the public's accumulating obligation.* The use of the accrued benefits method leads to a relatively

---

used here does not accrue such future errors into the estimate of today's liability. It includes only underfunding that has already taken place.

*The individual worker can reasonably assess the value of claims as zero until they are vested. Indeed, there is evidence that workers do have low valuations of their pensions in the

small estimate of the obligation to employees since the entitlement to benefits generally climbs steeply in the last few years of work.

For public plans in which the workers often have (or seem to have) rights akin to tenure in their jobs, and often considerable political clout as well, the alternative is to view the pension rights as accruing over the employee's working life. Such "projected-benefits" approaches use recent history to predict the future work experience of current employees—how many will retire at what ages, how salaries will rise, and so on. Pension obligations commensurate with these historical career profiles are then calculated. Finally, an appropriate time pattern is chosen to spread this obligation over the employee's career. A common choice, the entry age normal method, accrues the obligation as a level fraction of the employee's projected salary. Thus, if after twenty years of work the employee has earned half a lifetime's salary, then he or she will have accrued half of the value of the pension obligation as well. This method, which still accrues a sizable fraction of the pension obligation late in the worker's career (because salaries tend to be higher in those years) appropriately defines the full-funding rate for the pension system. The funding rate is that fraction of salary which, if set aside for each employee each year, would, together with accumulated interest, provide a fund adequate to pay the retirement benefits.

Even the entry age normal projected-benefits approach presents many complicated estimation problems. Assumptions must be made about rates of promotion, retirement, disability, death, and salary increase, about future rates of return on the assets invested in the pension fund, and about future rates of inflation. These predictions, which are usually based on recent plan experiences, are difficult to make, and the results must always be used with caution. On the other hand, assuming away future salary increases or inflation or improvements in mortality rates amounts to ignoring what can be a substantial portion of the pensions problem. Such obfuscation is not uncommon. Congress, for example, instructs its actuary for the Civil Service Retirement System to treat all future salary increases as discretionary —that is, to assume that Congress will not approve any. Since civil service pensions depend on salary in the final three years of work, this dramatically reduces—and substantially distorts—the estimated liability.

---

early years. See, for example, James E. Pesando, "The Usefulness of the Wind-Up Measure of Pension Liabilities: A Labour Market Perspective" (Working Paper no. 1559, National Bureau of Economic Research, Cambridge, Mass., February 1985). However, using such low estimates is ill-advised in estimating aggregate system liabilities. The fraction of nonvested benefits that will become vested can be accurately estimated. Ignoring this as a component of the aggregate liability makes little sense.

Public Pension Systems

FEDERAL RETIREMENT SYSTEMS

The federal government administers numerous retirement programs for its employees. In 1983 it had thirty-eight plans, most of which were for small and specialized categories of workers. The two largest plans, covering the great majority of all federal employees, are the Civil Service Retirement System (CSRS) and the Military Retirement System (MRS). The CSRS covers about 2.8 million employees and provides annual benefits of $20 billion to about 1.4 million former workers. The MRS covers about 2.1 million active workers and annually pays benefits of $18 billion to another 1.3 million retirees.

These two plans offer very generous benefits, compared with those of retirement programs administered by private firms.* Both of the plans, like most public sector plans, are defined-benefit plans: their rules are written in terms of the benefits they will provide, typically as a fraction of final salary (or the average salary over the final few years), the fraction depending on the number of years of service.† Under CSRS rules, an employee with thirty years of service can retire at age fifty-five and receive a lifetime retirement pension equal to 56 percent of his or her average salary in the highest-paid three years of work. These are usually the last three years. With inflation and normal longevity increases, the three-year salary average tends to be a little over 90 percent of the salary in the final year. Thus, the CSRS permits a civil servant to end a thirty-year career in the government at age fifty-five with a retirement salary of over half of his or her final year's salary. This pension is paid for life—an expected span of about twenty years for someone retiring voluntarily at fifty-five. Moreover, *the pension is fully indexed to the cost of living,* so that its purchasing power is fixed. Finally, under current law there is no offset to this payment for current retirees for receipts under the Social Security program; former federal employees are free to take jobs covered by the Social Security system and qualify for independent benefits under that program.‡

The MRS provides even more generous benefits. Retirement is available after twenty years of service, regardless of the person's age. The pension is

*The Report of the President's Private Sector Study on Cost Containment, the "Grace Commission" report, is highly critical of federal retirement programs, noting that they provide benefits three to six times more generous than those of even high-quality private pension programs.

†The alternative form of plan, called a defined-contribution plan, is like an IRA or Keogh plan. Here, the employer (and possibly the employee) contributes to a fund for each employee, such as a bank account. The annual contribution is specified; the eventual payout is not—it depends on the earned rate of return. These plans have many desirable accountability features and will be discussed in more detail later.

‡Recent revisions in the social security program specify the social security entitlements of new federal workers, so that when they retire the two systems will no longer be independent.

2.5 percent of the three-year salary average for each year of service (with a maximum of 75 percent), so a veteran of twenty years of service can receive an immediate pension of half of his or her base pay. An armed services employee who serves for thirty years receives a pension equal to the maximum 75 percent of base pay. Because of the early age at which many employees enter the armed services and the relatively short career required before immediate pension benefits are payable, many former servicepeople receive retirement benefits for more years than they worked. Like the CSRS, and unlike any major pension system in the private sector, the MRS fully indexes retirement benefits to the cost of living. The value of retirement benefits often exceeds the total value of base pay received over the working career.

Neither of these systems is fully funded. The military system has traditionally not been funded at all. In 1984, Congress passed legislation that puts it on an "accrual" basis, which means that it will shift from a pay-as-you-go basis to a fund that collects employer contributions and pays benefits. Debate continues about how the existing unfunded liability—the amount by which the fund is currently behind—can (or whether it should) be made up.

The CSRS is partly funded from employee contributions (currently, 7 percent of payroll). The remainder is paid through a matching employer contribution and a supplemental appropriation added by Congress in 1969 because the program was inadequately funded and the fund in danger of being exhausted. The supplemental appropriation is considered an "interest payment" replacing the additional interest earnings the fund would have if it were closer to being fully funded and therefore had a larger asset base. It is not regarded as part of the cost of federal compensation; only the employer contribution appears in agency budgets, as a part of the cost of the federal work force.

The annual cost of these systems, computed on a fully funded basis, is impressive. The full-funding rate for most private plans is in the range of 5 to 15 percent of payroll. For the federal civilian retirement plan, it is about 36 percent of payroll, and for the military plan it is about 58 percent.[3] The employees pay 7 percent of their salaries to the CSRS, leaving the government liability at 29 percent of the payroll. The current recognized employer contribution is 7 percent. The remaining 22 percent is deficit financing: a liability to future retirees is accumulating, to be paid by future taxpayers. *No* funds have been set aside to pay for future *military* retirement benefits; the government pays recipients each year. It is responsible for a pension bill more than half the size of the entire payroll.

These accumulating liabilities appear in startling relief when we examine the unfunded liabilities of these systems. In September of 1982, the CSRS had assets of about $100 billion against already accumulated liabilities of about $675 billion; the net unfunded liability was $575 billion. The MRS had no assets, and a net unfunded liability of $525 billion.[4] These two systems constitute a liability for future taxpayers *similar in character and magnitude to the explicitly recognized national debt.* *

These implicit public debts constitute a very large fraction of the net worth of government employees. The unfunded liability of the CSRS for current employees is $211,000 per employee. The pension system thus amounts to a bank account, with an average balance over $200,000, on behalf of each current federal worker. Similarly, the average future military retiree will receive $93,000 in benefits already accrued.†

These liabilities also place a large burden on the taxpayers who will pay them. The combined unfunded liabilities of the CSRS and MRS amount to an implicit debt of over $5,000 for every adult in the United States.

STATE AND LOCAL PENSION PLANS

Public pension plans have long been used by state and local governments as a form of employee compensation. Before the turn of the century, pension plans were set up for police, fire fighters, and teachers in many major cities. Nearly 90 percent of the plans now in force in major cities predate 1930.[5] In this century, the growth in scope, location, and dollar magnitudes has been steady and rapid. Beneficiaries of state and local plans rose from about 200,000 at the end of World War II to over 2 million in 1977. Benefit payments rose from less than $200 million in 1945 to more than $12 billion in 1980.[6] Over 5000 separate plans now cover a total of about 12 million employees, over 10 million of them in plans administered by state governments. State and local pension plans hold assets of over $200 billion. Their investment practices and returns are a big business and a matter of considerable financial interest. Over half of these assets are invested in corporate stocks and bonds.[7]

The funding situation for state and local pension plans is even more precarious than that of the federal government's; the federal government has recourse to a more extensive and stronger tax base than do most state

---

*Some argue that the national debt should not be a matter of concern, that it is a debt of taxpayers to each other, and not a net burden. Where some receive and others pay, however, there are distributional consequences. And to the extent that the system defers payment for services already rendered, it obscures part of the cost of government services.

†The average accrued unfunded liability for the military system is held down by the fact that most employees will leave the service before they qualify for any benefits. Fewer than 15 percent of all armed services employees ever collect pensions. The average unfunded liability to those who will collect is thus considerably higher than the overall average.

and local governments, even controlling for scale. In many jurisdictions, the shadow cast by the unfunded liabilities of pension systems has begun to have a material impact on credit ratings. Rating agencies like Standard & Poor's or Moody's and securities analysts who study the reliability of tax-exempt debt recognize little difference between the taxpayers' obligations under pension plans and their explicitly noted obligations under bond covenants.[8] It is not obvious what order of precedence these claims would be given if, for example, a major city entered receivership.

A number of recent studies have examined the financial integrity of state and local pension funds. Estimates that are both consistent and comprehensive are extremely difficult to come by, since there are no firm universal accounting guidelines for public pension plans.* Different jurisdictions value their plans by means of different actuarial methods, economic assumptions, and funding concepts. They report at different times. Some include future inflation and salary increases in their projections of future benefit payments, while others do not project benefits at all, computing only accrued vested benefits.[9] In spite of these difficulties, a discernible pattern of substantial underfunding emerges in state and local plans.

The most comprehensive recent study of state and large local retirement plans is a survey conducted by Frank Arnold in 1983. His study covered all 144 state-administered plans and a sample of local plans with more than five hundred members, including plans of the twenty largest cities. Using plan descriptions for information about benefit formulas, aggregated actuarial data to project future plan experience, and a variety of alternative sets of economic assumptions, Arnold estimated the unfunded liabilities of the plans in his sample.[10] In light of the difficulties of assembling data for all plans, and of the fact that the aggregated actuarial data will not fit any plan perfectly, these results must be used with some caution. Arnold assumes a relatively high rate of interest to be earned on fund assets (three percentage points above the rate of inflation); using a lower real rate of interest would result in larger unfunded liabilities, so these estimates are probably on the low side. They do, however, provide a sense of the financial condition of state and local pension plans, and they represent one of the few attempts to conduct a comprehensive study on the basis of data for individual plans.

Arnold concluded that state-administered plans are substantially underfunded. Total liabilities (on a projected-benefits basis) for these plans in 1978 were $295 billion; their assets were $125 billion. Assets cover less than 45 percent of liabilities. Collective unfunded pension liabilities for state-administered plans were thus $170 billion.

---

*Accounting for public pensions is discussed later in this chapter and in chapter 9.

Pension debt should be seen against the backdrop of explicitly recognized state debts. Long-term state debt in 1978 amounted to $72 billion. Thus, the debts implicit in the liabilities of unfunded state-administered pension plans exceeded explicit state indebtedness by nearly two and a half times. State pension debt represented a net liability of over $1,000 for every adult resident in eleven states; the average for all states was $756.[11]

A recent study of teachers' pensions suggests that Arnold's figures may be substantially too optimistic. Using data on selected teachers' pension systems for which comprehensive figures were available, Robert Inman estimated nationwide underfunding of teachers' pensions each year from 1971 to 1980.[12] His findings indicate that the unfunded liabilities of state and local teachers' pensions alone were about $400 billion in 1980. From 1979 to 1980, estimated unfunded liabilities to teachers rose by $40 billion. Thus, teachers' pensions in 1980 cost $40 billion in quiet spending *in addition* to the payments made directly. Inman also observes that while the inflation-adjusted national debt grew by only about 10 percent during the 1970s, the inflation-adjusted unfunded liabilities of teachers' pension plans grew by over 250 percent.[13]

While no comprehensive results are available, large-city pension funds appear on the whole to be more fully funded than state-administered plans.* Police and fire fighter pension systems tend to be more fully funded than general and teacher systems. In the twenty largest cities examined by Arnold, unfunded pension debts were about 60 percent as large as explicit indebtedness.

In several large cities, however, the situation is gloomy. Boston's pension indebtedness of about $1.2 billion (about $1,700 per person) is more than twice its bonded indebtedness of $550 million. In New York and Philadelphia, unfunded pension liabilities also exceed explicit debt. But these cities are the extreme cases; in most other large cities, explicit debts substantially exceed net pension obligations. The local plans of smaller jurisdictions also have pension debts typically on the order of one-half of their explicitly authorized bonded indebtedness.

This brief overview gives a glimpse of substantial public liabilities to current and former state and local government employees. Particularly with respect to state-administered plans, but also in some local plans, taxpayers face pension debt burdens considerably in excess of the explicit debt levels they have authorized. Since unfunded liabilities are not always understood to be debts, most taxpayers considerably underestimate their actual com-

---

*This might be because public employees seek state administration for unsound local pension funds, believing that it results in a higher likelihood that benefit payments will be made as promised.

mitments. While the great variety of reporting practices makes it difficult to assess financial soundness consistently and comprehensively, the financial integrity of pension funds depends crucially on the tolerance of taxpayers who are at present largely unaware of the magnitude of the pension burdens they face.

Are Public Pensions Too Generous?

Public pensions represent a sizable fraction of taxpayer debt at all levels of government. They are part of an agreement—among government workers, legislators, and, perhaps, the public—about how much, when, and in what form government employees should be paid. If total compensation is fixed (perhaps by competition for public jobs in open labor markets), then the pension part of the agreement can properly be regarded as a choice about the composition of compensation. Income is split between wages received during the working career and pension payments reserved for retirement. This choice should not necessarily be of concern to taxpayers, except as it may change the identity of taxpayers who actually pay, by changing the timing of payment. But if the amount paid through pension compensation does not reduce the level of salary compensation—if the level of salaries rather than the total compensation is fixed exogenously—then taxpayers have a deep interest in the split between salary and pension compensation. The choice then affects the level of total compensation. Spending on pensions is less visible than direct salary payments: taxpayers pay more than they think. The fact that the public at large seems less than fully informed about the magnitude of public pension liabilities makes it at least an interesting question whether public pensions are fully accountable arrangements.

The agency approach to accountability suggests that we scrutinize the incentives facing each of the main participants. Workers presumably want to receive the highest possible compensation. They are interested in maximizing the after-tax value of the payments made to them. If they perceive a need for income in retirement, then they might like a pension plan that reduces their current income (and the taxes they pay on it) in return for payments received when they are in a lower tax bracket later. In general, however, for a variety of reasons, people want benefits sooner rather than later. Except for those (relatively rare) workers who are deeply concerned bout their future income, then, the pension arrangement has potentially ttractive tax benefits but unattractive timing. Workers might be willing to ccept some reductions in current salaries to obtain pension benefits but vould probably require some inducement in the form of higher total compensation.

What incentives face government officials in setting the level and composition of compensation for public employees? First, they are under pressure to keep costs down. But the degree of pressure tends to vary with the isibility of the cost in question. Direct wage payments are highly visible; hey are prominent in budget documents and a focus of attention for the media and taxpayers. Deferred wages—increases in the next contract cycle, or in the later years of the current contract cycle—are only a bit less visible. But long-deferred compensation, like pension payments, is a good deal less isible. Usually, future pension payments are not prominently displayed in budgets or fully understood by either the media or taxpayers.

Consider, for example, how difficult it is to assess a labor contract that ncludes overtime in the final years of work as part of the salary base from vhich pension benefits are determined. More senior workers often have a ight of first refusal when overtime work is available. If wages for overtime re included in the salary base when pension benefits are computed, then vorkers in their last few years of employment will have a double incentive to accumulate overtime. First, it raises their current income. Second, it aises their retirement income for the rest of their lives. For a worker about to retire with a pension of 60 percent of salary in the final year, every dollar of overtime earnings in the last year of employment raises the pension he or she will receive by sixty cents *in every year.* The pension payments associated with a dollar of overtime earnings can be more than ten times the value of the direct wages paid. Given the magnitude of this incentive, employees near retirement in such systems work substantial amounts of overtime. Including overtime earnings in the salary base for pensions purposes can thus be a large cost item. The obscurity of the mechanism through which it works, however, virtually guarantees that it will be almost unnoticed by taxpayers.

The long deferment of pension payments, together with their innate complexity, makes them a lower-profile form of compensation than direct wages. Thus, the pressure on public officials to reduce visible costs makes pension settlements an attractive avenue for providing compensation.

In addition, public officials feel pressure to produce visible benefits. This balances the demand that costs be held down. Closing government offices s not the usual solution. The need to produce implies that officials must strike a bargain with public employees.

These twin pressures make relatively obscure forms of compensation such as pensions, quite attractive. Pensions may even be more attractive to public officials than to workers: workers who prefer current payments may have to be offered a larger total sum in order to accept deferred payments. (Individuals tend to apply rather high discounts when valuing payments they will receive long in the future.) The pensions contract, splitting compensation between wage and pension payments, may thus increase total compensation. Workers like it because they wind up getting more (and because it helps prepare for their retirement). Government officials like it because it appears to be less—public benefits are produced, and at least a part of the cost is obscured.

If this line of reasoning is right, then public pensions are not an accountable agreement negotiated by carefully scrutinized agents overseen by financially informed principals. Rather, they are an unaccountable bargain among agents left to their own devices by principals either not sufficiently interested, or too baffled by the complexity of the devices, to scrutinize them meaningfully.

This implies that taxpayers, confused by the system, wind up paying too much for public-employee compensation. From the perspective of the broad interests of the public, this outcome is undesirable. Accountability requires that public officials secure the services of public employees at the lowest total cost. The system should not permit the agents (public officials and public employees) to gain at the expense of the principals (taxpayers) by making it difficult for the principals to understand what is happening.

Are current taxpayers really injured by these arrangements? Pension liabilities may not have the kind of immediacy that would galvanize public reaction, and they may also suffer as a political issue from having their costs diffused among many taxpayers and over time. Yet considerable commentary on public pensions is already available to the public. In a situation with stakes as high as those in setting public pensions, where trades of billions of dollars are taking place, it would be surprising if agreements that clearly waste a great deal of taxpayers' money were routine. If the public is so badly served, why is there not more of a movement toward improvements?

This question highlights a crucial element of the pension arrangement. *The taxpayers who permit the bargain to be struck are not necessarily the taxpayers who will pay for its deferred costs.* When public financial accountability involves trade-offs—and scrutiny—over time, current taxpayers become agents for the broader set of current and future taxpayers affected by bargains entered today. Pension arrangements are thus agreements *just among agents;* only some of the principals are even on the scene as the bargain is reached. It should perhaps be no surprise—and it is surely not an accident—when the interests of the principals on the scene today triumph over the interests of principals who have yet to make their appearance. It is difficult to ensure accountability between principals and agents at a moment in time; the problem of accountability over time is daunting indeed.

These intertemporal bargains reinforce the old adage that there is no such thing as the public interest, at least not as an operational political force. Many taxpayers who favor (or permit) increases in public employment costs to gain a deferral will not be among the taxpayers who eventually pay off the debt. And even some of those who *will* may be myopic in viewing the future, preferring to believe that a deferred cost is a successfully avoided cost. When they act on their own account, taxpayers may not always make rational decisions about the future. When they act as agents for others—future taxpayers other than themselves—only the force of conscience prevents their deferring the costs of current service.

The agency theory provides, then, two alternative interpretations of public pension agreements. First, the taxpayers as principals may lack either the interest or the ability to scrutinize the activities of their appointed agents. These agents carve out bargains that serve their own interests, keeping government employees happy while hiding true costs that taxpayers will bear. Second, the taxpayers may be viewed as agents for future taxpayers. Under this interpretation, pension arrangements are unaccountable because they are negotiated largely among agents with little scrutiny from real principals. Taxpayers are regarded as bad agents for themselves because they do not treat the future rationally, or as bad agents for others because, given the choice, they are likely to impose costs on their principals instead of on themselves.

Agency theory constructs a plausible story about how and why public pensions might be unaccountable. A central accountability question is whether the total compensation of public workers is higher as a result of the pension mechanism than it would be if compensation were kept fully visible through exclusive reliance on direct salaries. On this question, the data are predictably and sadly mixed.

Many investigators addressing this issue were interested primarily in learning whether *underfunding* of pensions has an impact on wages. Workers may value wages, funded benefits, and unfunded but promised benefits differently. As a result of speculation that Congress would require funding of local pension plans, a number of researchers undertook to discover whether governments might be able to decrease their wages if they funded their pensions more fully. If they could, then the true cost of funding would be reduced. In the process, several studies examined how workers trade off wages against pension benefits.

The empirical results are mixed.[14] Robert Smith, in a 1981 study based on retirement systems in Pennsylvania, finds that increases in funded benefits reduce wages essentially dollar for dollar, while unfunded benefits have no impact on wages.[15] This would argue that workers value pension promises—but only when they are backed by hard cash. In a later study of police and fire fighters, Smith finds that funding reduces wages, but less than dollar for dollar.[16] Robert Inman, in a study of aggregated data on public safety workers from sixty large cities, also finds that underfunding of pensions increases wages, but only for police officers, and not on a dollar-for-dollar basis. Inman's work and several other studies *assume* that workers trade pension benefits dollar for dollar against wages; the only issue is how benefits are discounted when the pension till is underfunded.[17] The argument is that underfunding is an indication that promised pension benefits may not be paid; it increases risk. Workers put less stock in promises that aren't backed by hard cash, and accordingly demand higher wages.

These results suggest an incomplete trade-off between pensions and wages. This is exactly the worst case for taxpayers. If there were a full offset —as many researchers have assumed, but for which there is little evidence —then as pension benefits rose wages would be reduced, and the taxpayer would be made no worse off. Part of the cost would still be obscured, leading perhaps to erroneous decisions about whether some services were desirable, but at least the taxpayer would be paying no more in total than was necessary to attract public workers. If, on the other hand, public employees were unwilling to accept lower wages in exchange for unfunded pension promises, then public officials would have no incentive to offer higher pensions. (They might, of course, not be aware of this, so pensions might still continue.) But it is implausible that we would have arrived at current arrangements representing billions of dollars of future commitments without their having some value to public employees. Indications are that unfunded pension promises are neither valueless nor fully tradable for wages. This partial trade-off is an incentive for public officials to offer unfunded pension benefits in exchange for (or instead of increases in) current wages. Public officials' immediate political interests (reducing the apparent cost of government) will be served, and the total cost of government services borne by taxpayers will be increased.

Do taxpayers directly recognize unfunded pension debts? Inman estimates the effect of underfunding on local property values.[18] He argues that taxpayers aware of unfunded pension liabilities recognize them as a debt that will eventually be paid through property tax levies. Future homeowners, who will face these obligations, will consequently reduce their bids for homes in jurisdictions with large unfunded pension liabilities. Inman finds that there is some, though incomplete, capitalization of unfunded liabilities into property values. This indicates that taxpayers are at best only partially aware of pension liabilities (or at least do not respond to them rationally). Current generations can therefore obscure some of the liabilities they will hand on to future taxpayers. Inman's findings are hardly conclusive, but they certainly do *not* demonstrate that taxpayers are fully aware of public pension arrangements.[19]

Agency theory suggests a plausible explanation of why pensions arise, and grow, as a form of public compensation. Government officials are anxious to provide public services and to avoid confronting their full cost. They offer wage agreements in which higher total compensation is partly obscured to taxpayers by being wrapped in a package with deferred and poorly visible compensation. Workers accept these arrangements because they receive higher total compensation. Taxpayers either (1) miss their implications because it is difficult to assess the current value of payments to be made in the future; or (2) acting as agents for themselves, they impose costs upon themselves later because they undervalue the future; or (3) acting as agents for other future taxpayers, they choose to impose costs on them. The empirical issue of whether the use of the pension mechanism actually raises total compensation is unresolved, but both theory and the evidence to date suggest that it does.

Public Pensions and Accounting

What level of accountability does public spending through pensions attain? Except in the relatively rare cases in which an estimate of full normal cost is appropriated to a fund each year, only a portion of pension spending— the pay-as-you-go amount—undergoes budget scrutiny. The rest—the difference between the amount appropriated to pay this year's bills and the full normal cost—is spending of a quieter form. Whether this part of the spending can be considered accountable depends on how effectively we account for and report about the scale of pension debt and the rate of its growth.

What role has the public accounting profession played in scrutinizing public compensation contracts? By and large, it has accommodated quiet pension spending without much protest. The accounting profession regards its function as the development and presentation of reasonable, consistent, and reliable measures of the financial condition of the entities its members examine. Accountants do not judge the wisdom or virtue of the activities they monitor; they merely try to report about them "fairly." Naturally, however, a pure separation of judgment from reporting is sustainable in principle only. Public pension fund accounting grapples with difficult decisions about what constitutes reasonable and proper disclosure.

For example, in many jurisdictions the law says that pension benefits will be funded on a pay-as-you-go basis. Should there be any required disclosure of the financial standing of these pension systems? In such jurisdictions, there may be no pension fund as such; retirement benefits are paid out of the treasury as required. How should we account for a nonexistent pension fund?

Governmental accounting standards issued by the National Council on Governmental Accounting (NCGA) call for reporting about public-employee retirement systems, regardless of their funding method. But governmental accounting standards are not systematically enforced (though Congress has periodically considered asserting some enforcement authority). Little or no information is available on the financial status of many public retirement systems. A report prepared in 1978 by the House Committee on Education and Labor found that more than a quarter of all local pension plans had not reported actuarial valuations in the last ten years. Barely more than one-half reported every three years.[20]

What standards of reporting can be set for public pension systems? In particular, what methods of valuation should be required? The argument advanced above suggests characterizing defined-benefit pension plans—the great majority of public plans—in terms of their full-funding rate and actuarial unfunded liability, both assessed on an entry age normal funding basis. Current practice is a long way from this. After tortuous deliberation, the NCGA released its Statement 6 to provide guidance for reporting about state and local retirement systems.* Before the appearance of Statement 6, public plans could use the wide variety of valuation methods available to private sector plans under the standards articulated by the private sector's Financial Accounting Standards Board (FASB) in its Statement of Finan-

---

*This deliberation was complicated because it became embroiled in attempts to establish a new standard-setting agency for public sector accounting, the Government Accounting Standards Board (GASB). The conflicts with the private sector organization, the Financial Accounting Standards Board (FASB), which declared itself the sole appropriate umbrella for the development of all accounting standards, public or private, were of legendary proportions. Release of the NCGA's Statement 6 was long delayed because it conflicted with the FASB's prescribed treatment, already binding for private plans. This is discussed further in chapter 9.

ial Accounting Standards No. 35 (SFAS 35).* The new statement requires
a different treatment, opposed to the private sector standard prescribed by
SFAS 35. Statement 6 requires projecting benefit increases that will come
from future salary increases when computing current liabilities.

These standards could have a salutary impact on retirement system
reporting, *if* they are widely accepted and applied—but there is no guarantee they will be. Indeed, the conflict over the NCGA's Statement 6 and its
divergence from the private sector standard led almost immediately to a
postponement of the date when it takes effect. There is continuing confusion
about what valuation methods may be required for public-employee pension
systems.

Even if these standards were widely agreed upon and promulgated by an
authoritative organization—or if Congress stepped in and articulated standards or explicitly delegated authority to a standard-setting agency—we
would still not be very far down the road to good and consistent accounting
for public pension systems. There would still be ambiguity about what
actuarial assumptions to use, what economic forecasts to adopt, and so on.
Assumptions about the prevailing rates of inflation, salary increases, disability, retirement, and death have a tremendous impact on estimates of
funding rates and unfunded liabilities. Different jurisdictions would in all
likelihood remain free to present valuations based on substantially dissimi-
lar and largely incomparable assumptions. Developing and enforcing standard assumptions for the relevant variables would almost surely require
agreement between actuaries and accountants, two professions that are
pleased to work side by side so long as neither is required to agree about
anything the other does.

A definitive, comprehensive, and consistent set of valuation methods,
standards, and actuarial and economic assumptions for public-employee
retirement systems will be a long time in coming.† The accounting and
actuarial professions have not developed a sufficiently strong consensus to
allow the articulation of a unified doctrine. The current accounting system is
not adequate to the task of providing a clear, understandable, and consistent
picture of the financial condition of public pension funds and their liabilities.

*The FASB standards were not preferred, but in the absence of an officially mandated
alternative, they were implicitly, if not explicitly, tolerated.
†The new Governmental Accounting Standards Board is making some progress in this
direction. It has released an "exposure draft" of a new proposed statement on pension accounting standards. It would require more uniformity of reporting—but not of exactly the right
estimate of pension liabilities. It would still permit different systems to use different actuarial
assumptions, provided that they were clearly disclosed in notes attached to the financial
statements. It would also continue to permit the valuing of assets at historical cost, though
t would require disclosure of asset market value in the notes. This proposal is not perfect, but
the movement is clearly in the right direction.

If public pension arrangements are unaccountable, it is in part because the fundamental prerequisite to accountability—information intellectually and physically accessible to the principals who need it—is not available.

But neither is information about public pensions entirely lacking. Tax payers seem more aware of pensions than of many other quiet spending programs. Although the information is not complete, there are some reasonably accurate characterizations of the scale of pension debts. Municipal credit analysts are universally aware of the pensions issue and go to some trouble to develop consistent measures of unfunded pension liabilities and their future tax impacts.

It is not obvious that public pension systems would operate significantly differently if accountants and actuaries could provide a better foundation for public education and scrutiny. There are other prerequisites to account ability—such as interest on the part of the principals—and these may not be met either. Nonetheless, accounting practices are part of the problem. While better accounting may not provide a complete solution, it should be able to make some contribution.

Accountants and actuaries are agents, too. Although their professional codes of ethics call for serving the client—the user of the information they produce—they also work for the governments whose activities they disclose and they work with public officials. They have no independent legal author ity to articulate standards that serve only the public; they must develop standards that governments will choose to apply. Together with bond ana lysts, researchers, and commentators, they can cajole and embarrass govern ments into complying with their proposals. But just as governments are not entirely free to accept or reject standards, so the professions are not com pletely free to choose standards they prefer. The outcome is determined by a complicated, and in some cases ritualized, game. Neither party holds all the cards, and neither can act without the other's acquiescence or cooperation. It is small wonder, therefore, that the standards we have serve some of the interests of the agents and not those of more-distant principals.

Improving Public Pension Accountability

We can improve pension accountability by improving our accounting and reporting and its visibility and by bringing more of pension spending out of the quiet shadows and into the light of the appropriations process. This involves enforcing the recognition of pension costs by appropriating funds for them on a current basis.

IMPROVE REPORTING

A crucial problem impairing pension accountability is that a very wide range of economic and actuarial assumptions can plausibly be used to estimate the current value of pension liabilities. Until this ambiguity is either legally or professionally resolved—through the articulation of consistent, comprehensive, and universal standards—public pension systems will report on whatever basis makes them look best. While this range has been narrowed by recent standards issued by the NCGA, the issue is by no means resolved. Furthermore, standards for methods of valuation are not enough; standards for assumptions are also required.

One approach is to have a national standard-setting organization—the obvious choice is the new Governmental Accounting Standards Board—issue a set of actuarial and economic assumptions for all pension funds. Individual funds could use their own sets of assumptions so long as they also reported according to the universally accepted set. While the standardized set of assumptions would fit most jurisdictions imperfectly, the value of consistency in reporting across jurisdictions should compensate for minor distortions.

FUND PENSIONS ON A CURRENT BASIS

All public pensions should annually set aside enough funds to pay for the benefits earned in that year, not simply the amounts that actually have to be paid in that year. This suggestion reflects the principle that taxpayers should pay on a current basis for services they receive. Major investment projects can, of course, properly be financed through borrowing (and this includes borrowing both the wages and the funds for retirement benefits for workers involved in the investment). But accountability demands that this borrowing be explicitly authorized; it should not proceed through the quiet avenue of underfunding pension benefits for all workers.

The systematic underfunding of private pension plans led Congress to require full funding for private pensions in the Employee Retirement Income Security Act (ERISA) of 1974. Periodically since then, Congress has considered legislating similar rules for the funding of public plans, under what has variously been called PERISA, to emphasize its relation to the private sector regulations, and PEPPRA (the Public Employee Pension Plan Regulation Act), to avoid the private sector comparison. There has been some progress with the federal pension systems. Congress recently passed legislation putting the MRS on an accrual basis, and the general trend over the past decade has been to move the CSRS slowly toward more complete funding. However, there does not appear to be any immediate prospect of legislation that would force full funding on public plans. In the absence of legal action, the many state and local plans that are still on a pay-as-you-go basis are unlikely voluntarily to adopt practices that will raise them to higher levels of accountability.

The purpose of funding pensions on a current basis is both to provide accurate information about the cost of public services and to confront current taxpayers with the need to pay for them. Both purposes call for a definition of full funding that recognizes (a) the value of pension rights transferred in a given year, (b) the fact that the value of these rights will be increased by future salary increases, and (c) the liability for pension rights of public employees even when the rights are not fully vested. Public workers cannot readily be dismissed, and many choose to stay precisely to receive pension benefits that become vested after twenty years or more. Ignoring the public's liability for these rights until they are legally vested substantially distorts our view of the taxpayers' true debt. The appropriate basis for evaluating public pension liabilities and full-funding rates, therefore, is some form of projected-benefits method. The entry age normal method spreads the accrual of benefits smoothly over the employee's career as a level fraction of salary paid, and it is as good a choice as any.

KEEP UNFUNDED LIABILITIES FROM GROWING FURTHER

The unfunded liabilities of pension systems change when unanticipated salary or benefit increases raise liabilities, when coverage is extended to new groups, when retirement or disability or death rates change, when poor or unexpectedly good portfolio management changes asset balances, when other assumptions on which the calculations were based turn out to be invalid—and when contributions to the fund are not at the full-funding level. Current taxpayers should make up for these changes in the unfunded liability, keeping it at a constant level.

The law governing the CSRS says that federal taxpayers will do *exactly* that. Since 1969, any statute that boosts the unfunded liability has been "deemed to authorize appropriations to the fund to finance the unfunded liability created."[21] The Treasury will make extra payments. The law states that it will all be handled properly.

Another part of the law tells the Treasury how to implement it. Congress directs the actuaries to assume no future inflation or salary increases when they estimate pension liabilities. This guarantees that the unfunded-liability measure used to determine the Treasury's supplemental payment will be systematically underestimated. Currently, it is low by a factor of about three. Treasury's payment is a token; it mocks the true amount. This results in a wonderful irony. Congress passed a law one section of which requires it to do the right thing—to be accountable. But it included a second section that quietly pulled out most of the first section's teeth.

Many actuaries and accountants believe that if a fund is currently in deficit—if it has an unfunded liability—the taxpayers responsible for it should implement a plan to pay off the debt. Under ERISA, private plans found to be underfunded are required to adopt payment schedules designed to attain full funding (a reduction of the unfunded liability to zero) over a period of at least ten and no more than forty years. Many observers have advocated a similar treatment for public pensions.

It is not self-evident that the existing debts for public pensions should be paid by current taxpayers. Public pension debts have been growing over a long period. No obvious purpose of public accountability is served by having any particular set of taxpayers pay off a debt accumulated by another (at least partly distinct) group. Accountability *is* served by having taxpayers pay on a current basis for the costs of services they consume, or by having them transfer the costs through explicit borrowing to future generations who will enjoy some of the benefits of current spending. But the past lapses of accountability should not necessarily be redressed by current taxpayers. The real issue of accountability with respect to debt has to do with changes in the level of debt rather than with the absolute level. The focal question is whether taxpayers in a given period balanced their contributions against their withdrawals.

MOVE TOWARD DEFINED-CONTRIBUTION PLANS

Practically all public sector plans are defined-benefit plans: they specify the retirement benefits an employee will receive as a function of years of service, salary level, and so on. Plans of this type are inherently difficult to value. It is hard for employees to understand the value of the pension promises they have received, and harder for taxpayers to understand what they have given. The problem is that employees want defined benefits but defined-benefit plans will always be a bit obscure and partially unaccountable.

There is an alternative. IRA and Keogh individual retirement plans point the way. They are defined-*contribution* plans: the amount contributed, rather than the amount to be withdrawn, is specified. The employee owns the funds in a defined-contribution account managed in his or her name.

Defined-contribution plans make clear how much was given in a particular year. They are fully funded by definition: whatever amount is added to the account in a given year is the whole obligation for that year.* Defined-contribution plans are thus easy to account for. Pensions payments can easily be compared to wage payments, and they can be added together to determine total compensation.† There is no fuzziness about how much different workers have been paid or about who paid for it. Defined-contribution plans are inherently more accountable than defined-benefit plans.

They are also less popular. In surveys, workers strongly prefer defined-benefit plans.[23] One attraction of defined-benefit plans is precisely that their relation to current income is *not* clear. With a defined-contribution plan, workers can see how much they are being paid in the form of pension rights and how much their individual retirement funds are accumulating. But they cannot tell how much income they will be able to draw from them when they retire. They cannot easily project how large their funds will be the day they retire, and they cannot easily convert from a capital amount (the fund) to a lifetime annuity (what they will receive each year as a retirement income). Workers want to know what level of retirement income to expect, and that is exactly what defined-benefit plans specify.

We are stuck with a paradox. Defined-benefit plans are unaccountable because they leap across an obscure link, from current cost to future defined income. Defined-contribution plans are accountable precisely because they stay in terms of the present—what is being put away today. But this obscures exactly what workers want to know—what flow of income they will later receive. Defined-benefit plans were invented in the public sector—in part, perhaps, because they helped to obscure public spending but also

---

*This is strictly true only in defined-contribution plans that set aside the same fraction of salary on behalf of every employee. If older employees receive a larger percentage contribution than younger workers, it could be argued that the funding program should anticipate the higher funding in the later years. But if the contributions vest immediately, they become indistinguishable from wages, and they should be funded as they are paid.

†In a defined-benefit plan, the amount of "pension compensation" the worker received for working an additional year is the increase in the present value of his or her claims to a retirement income in excess of interest that would be earned on the existing balance of pension wealth if it were fully funded. This is a sophisticated concept, and the amount is difficult to compute. By contrast, the pension compensation received in a defined-contribution plan is simply the incremental amount added to the employee's account. Interest earned by the funds already on deposit is credited separately, and it represents earnings on previous compensation, not additional compensation for work this year; it would accrue whether the employee worked or not. The incentive to work provided by the pension—and its cost—is thus quite clear both to taxpayers and to employees under a defined-contribution plan; it is obscure under a defined-benefit plan.[22]

because they answer the question workers most anxiously ask: how much will I have to live on when I retire? Despite this directness of defined-benefit plans, could workers be induced to accept defined-contribution plans?

This is partly a marketing problem. With a bit more understanding of IRA accounts—what real rates of interest to expect, and how much retirement income a dollar invested today will yield—workers may be able to understand the retirement implications of defined-contribution plans. But resistance is strong, and it will take a concerted effort to move away from defined-benefit plans. There are a few widely scattered, small public pension plans that operate on a defined-contribution basis, but there is no clear trend to replace the defined-benefit approach. The most promising development is the current debate in Washington on modifying the CSRS; extensive public hearings have been held on a proposal to include a defined-contribution component in the system.

Defined-contribution plans do have advantages. One is that they are portable. Increasing mobility, particularly among senior public employees, fosters concern that public pensions are typically not rapidly vested nor very portable. Under defined-benefit plans, pensions are frequently specified in terms of salary averages in the last years of work. If one period of public service is followed by a second career in another jurisdiction or in the private sector, there is generally no adjustment for inflation in the interim before retirement. Inflation can significantly erode the pension's value by the time the worker begins to collect it.

By contrast, defined-contribution plans are portable and involve no loss. The departing worker rolls the funds in his or her defined-contribution account into another investment fund. The worker can see each year exactly how much is there and how much interest is being earned on it, and it can be carried to whatever next job he or she takes. This is a particularly important issue for younger workers, and they are correspondingly more supportive of the defined-contribution approach.[24]

Defined-contribution plans have considerable accountability advantages over the defined-benefit plans currently in widespread use in the public sector. Effective marketing of defined-contribution plans could emphasize their relationship to IRAs (and other devices with which employees are already familiar) and their portability. They could be developed as an acceptable alternative to existing plans, but not without considerable effort.*

*There have been some minor moves toward defined-contribution plans for public employees. Nebraska has instituted such plans for some police and fire workers; new Arkansas vocational/technical teachers are also covered by a defined-contribution plan that is also available as an option for existing employees.[25]

CASH OUT DEFINED-BENEFIT PLANS

Setting up defined-contribution plans for future pensions is the first step. The second is to convert current defined-benefit plans. The exchange from defined-benefit to defined-contribution plans could be good for all concerned. The worker would receive title to an explicitly funded pension account, in a known amount, in exchange for rights to a well-defined pension that at least some believe will not be paid as promised. Workers can be sure they will receive the amounts held for them in defined-contribution accounts. The amount of funding required for a defined-contribution account sufficient to induce a worker to switch away from a defined-benefit plan might therefore be less than the present value of the taxpayers' liabilities as we have computed them. Thus, taxpayers might also gain from such an arrangement. Moreover, the work incentives provided by the pension plan—for a defined-contribution plan, simply the amount contributed to the employee's account by the employer—are both clearer and often more dramatic than under defined-benefit plans.[26]

Public pensions are a multiplier in the dark: the cost of every salary adjustment, promotion, wage settlement, or new hiring of a public employee is multiplied by a largely obscured pension rider, commonly as much as an additional one-fifth to one-quarter. Public pensions have grown dramatically in recent years and now constitute sizable debts at all levels of government. They are hardly an accident. They are the current solution to someone's perceived problems. We have tried to sort out which problems they apparently solve and for whom. The suggestions advanced here about how public pension accountability might be improved are relatively straightforward, but they will not be easy to implement. It will be hard to build a constituency behind them. The current level of accountability is the outcome of a protracted and continuing debate among the accounting profession, legislative oversight bodies, politicians, taxpayers, and commentators. No narrow constituency's immediate interests are well served by the higher levels of accountability that could be achieved through the suggestions made here. Accountability mechanisms like these provide muscle for the broad interests of the general public. There are many narrower interests with a large stake in this issue, and they will not be lightly swept aside.

Chapter 2

Social Security

THE FIRST social security check was paid to Ida Fuller of Brattleboro, Vermont, in January of 1940. Ida contributed $22 in payroll taxes between the beginning of 1937, when the system began collecting taxes, and the end of 1939, when she retired. Her first monthly check was for $22.54. She continued to receive checks for thirty-four years, until her death in December 1974, shortly after her one hundredth birthday. Her last monthly check was for $112.60. She collected, in all, $20,944.42.[1] For proponents and critics alike, Ida Fuller's story captures much of the essence of the social security system. Critics can point out that Ida joined late, paid almost nothing, and received benefits nearly a thousand times as large as the taxes she paid in. Proponents can point with pride to a system providing a reliable stream of benefits to someone lucky enough to live as long as Ida did, and to the comfort and peace of mind social security gave her. They can also observe that though she received a high return on her contributions, the system was only a small cushion for her. History does not record Ida's other sources of support, but she could not have lived thirty-four years sustained only by her social security checks.

Social security has grown beyond any of its proponents' dreams. Its inventors forecast a 1980 population of 150 million—low by 80 million—and predicted that the number of social security recipients in that year would be 10 million—low by a factor of more than three.[2] The program has expanded almost continuously in terms of whom it covers, of what misfortunes or conditions it insures against, and of the size of the benefits it provides. The Social Security Administration now issues over 400 million monthly checks per year, and its direct beneficiaries include more than one in every seven Americans. The program has been recurrently debated and frequently adjusted, but it remains the preeminent institutional legacy of the New Deal.

Formulation

In the late nineteenth and early twentieth centuries, the elderly faced a bleak existence after retirement. Life expectancies were beginning to lengthen, but few mechanisms existed for ordinary people to accumulate the savings they would need to sustain them during those longer twilight years. Unable to work and with little acquired wealth to fall back on, many of the elderly were literally destitute.[3] A wealthier society saw the need and had the means to assist various groups of unfortunate people—the poor, the mentally handicapped, the infirm, and, eventually, the elderly. The Great Depression, which wiped out the assets of many, including the elderly, fed the drive to develop a program of aid to the elderly and the unemployed. By 1935, there was pressure from all parts of the political spectrum to address the problem of poverty among the aged.

Well before the drafting of the Social Security Act began, the most crucial policy question for the program was framed. Should a federal program to help the elderly be a welfare program or a pension program—in the terms of the day, should it be a "dole" or "insurance"? The resolution of this question would profoundly and permanently shape the politics of social security. If the program were structured as a dole, the attached stigma would limit it—fewer people would aspire to be on it, fewer would have a stake in it, fewer would want to be politically associated with it. If, by contrast, it were an insurance program, one that just happened to be operated by the federal government, its constituency would be proud and potentially broad-based. This political distinction was critical from the start, and it persists in today's social security debate.

The Social Security Act of 1935 emerged from the Committee on Economic Security, a subcabinet group appointed by President Franklin Delano Roosevelt to develop a sound proposal to "give some protection to the average citizen and to his family against the loss of a job and against poverty-ridden old age."[4] Roosevelt consulted actively with the committee, which was chaired by his Secretary of Labor, Frances Perkins. Roosevelt insisted on a long list of features to be included in the committee's proposed program. Principally, he wanted the system to be clearly differentiated from the "dole." It had to be contributory. Contributions and benefits had to be based on earnings so that ordinary citizens could take pride in collecting benefits they had purchased instead of being embarrassed by accepting handouts.

Roosevelt also insisted that the program be self-financing—that it involve "no money out of the Treasury." But that could be interpreted in two ways, either as "pay-as-you-go" or as "pay-for-yourself." In the pay-as-you-go system, it would mean only that the sources of financing had to be earmarked, that a stream of taxes capable of covering projected benefits be identified and legislated. Current taxpayers would pay for the benefits received by current retirees. No money would come from general revenues, but the system would rely on future taxes to pay benefits to those who had contributed earlier. Under this interpretation, the system would be solvent on an operating basis but not on a "shutdown" basis. Closing it down would deny benefits to some future generation of contributors who would nonetheless be required to fund benefits for the generation before it.

The alternative interpretation of self-financing, the pay-for-yourself method, was more conservative; it insisted that each generation of participants pay for its own benefits. Contributions during a person's working life would go to build up a reserve fund, out of which benefits could be paid after retirement. Such a "fully funded" system would be able to pay benefits even if no new contributors entered the system; it could be closed to new entrants without going bankrupt. It would thus be solvent not only on an operating basis (indeed, it would have a large trust fund balance) but also on a shutdown basis.

In the early social security debates, these two alternatives were seen as parallel to the distinction between dole and insurance. If the system paid out current receipts to current beneficiaries, then it was a dole by another name. To be real insurance, it had to be fully funded. Perkins's committee was divided on this issue, with Treasury Secretary Henry Morgenthau, Jr., siding with full funding. Full funding carried with it the prospect of an immense trust fund, projected to rise by 1980 to over $50 billion. Against the then-current GNP of about $70 billion, this conjured up the vision of a government trust fund that owned a huge portion of the nation's economy. Moreover, a fully funded system could not provide benefits either as early or as impressive as those possible under a pay-as-you-go approach. Perkins carried the day—or, rather, the night—in a late-hours session in which the committee reached compromises trimming the future trust fund, adding earlier benefits, and generally moving toward pay-as-you-go financing. This program was presented to Roosevelt on January 15, 1935. It was scheduled for presentation to Congress two days later.

In the meantime, Roosevelt thought the better of the financing scheme. The change may have resulted from lobbying by a still-discontented Morgenthau, or it may have reflected Roosevelt's own commitment to the substance, and not just the appearance, of a contributory insurance system. On January 16, Roosevelt told Perkins she would have to modify the proposal, because it was "the same old dole under another name." He added, "It is almost dishonest to build up an accumulated deficit for the Congress of the United States to meet in 1980. We can't do that. We can't sell the United States short in 1980 any more than in 1935."[5] The committee's proposal was forwarded to Congress, but in February Morgenthau proposed an amendment to put it on an almost fully funded basis. The amendment provided for higher taxes and lower benefits starting later than those of the Perkins committee proposal. The system's reserve fund was still projected to be close to $50 billion by 1980—not quite enough to be fully funded, but enough to insure permanently against cash bankruptcy. Or so it seemed.

Establishment

The sweeping social program embodied in the Social Security Act was presented to Congress in omnibus form—much to the annoyance of some proponents as well as critics. Its passage was by no means assured. Congress chafed at being forced to take all parts of the legislation as a package, but there was substantial momentum behind the move to provide for the elderly, and other, more-radical plans were lurking in the wings. Congress eventually acceded to strong presidential pressure and the lack of a good alternative.[6] The Social Security Act was passed, with the amended nearly full funding scheme, and signed into law on August 14, 1935.

The next hurdle was popular acceptance. The act, particularly its payroll tax financing, was the subject of heated debate in the 1936 campaign. Roosevelt's opponent, Alfred M. Landon, spoke of the new system as a "fraud." His supporters tried to organize workers against the new taxes they would begin paying in 1937. Landon's resounding defeat in November 1936 signaled social security's wide popularity.[7]

The final hurdle was constitutional. Did the federal government have the authority to establish a mandatory contributory savings program—to create its own insurance company and force a great majority of Americans to use it? The constitutionality of the Social Security Act depended on the Supreme Court's interpretation of the relationship between the taxing part (Title VIII) and the old-age-benefit part (Title II). Title VIII, providing for payroll taxes, could be supported under the taxing power of the federal government. Title II could be sustained under the authority of the federal government to spend money to promote the general welfare. But the federal government had no apparent authority to link the two. To avoid infringing on the state's powers, the taxing part and the old-age-benefit part had to remain entirely separate. They did; the sections had been carefully drafted so as not to refer to each other.

By 1937, the Supreme Court had invalidated seven out of nine major New Deal programs.[8] Roosevelt began his second term with a proposal to reorganize the federal judiciary and, not incidentally, to give himself the power to appoint six additional Supreme Court justices. The court-packing scheme was eventually rejected by Congress, but in the meantime the Court found all of the Social Security Act titles constitutional. The payroll tax was just a tax, paid into an account at the Treasury. No funds were appropriated by the act. And the old-age title, which never mentioned "insurance," clearly supported the general welfare in the way other "gratuitous" transfers might. So the Court found.

The Court's view was fundamentally at odds with every aspect of the program's design as expressed in the Perkins committee report, the legislative history, and popular discussion. The designers of the system clearly intended that its payroll taxes be so synonymous in the minds of the contributors with old-age benefits that no Congress could ever divert them to any other purpose. But that logic was political, not legal, and the Court was bound only by what it found in the law. The constitutionality of the act was upheld on the grounds that, as written, it was not a mandatory public insurance program—which, of course, was exactly what it was and what it absolutely had to be to survive politically. To the Court, it was just a tax program and a welfare program financed out of general tax revenues. To the public, it was a contributory insurance program. If either the Court or the public had been forced to accept the other's position, the program would probably not exist. Fortunately for the program, nothing compelled the public and the Court to reconcile their views.[9]

Structural Shift—and Irresistible Logic

By 1939, the social security system had most of what it needed. Legislation. Constitutionality. A growing, loyal, expectant public. Tax revenues building to a year-end trust fund of $1.7 billion. An activist staff committed to the designers' ideals. The program was developing muscle and was preparing to flex it. Of this program, which was not scheduled to pay benefits for three more years, Roosevelt could say in January of 1939, "We would be derelict of our responsibility if we did not take advantage of the experience we have accumulated to strengthen and extend [the Social Security Act's] provisions."[10] So far, the experience had all been on the revenue side. That was about to change.

The Perkins committee had flirted briefly with pay-as-you-go financing. Morgenthau's amendment, adopted with the original legislation, called for essentially full funding. The Supreme Court ignored the full-funding characteristic and treated the system as if it were financed on a pay-as-you-go basis. Many observers were concerned about the potential accumulation of the vast reserve fund implied by full funding. This issue had been raised in the 1935 debate, and the administration had promised to study the issue of reserves further. Senate conservatives, who might have been expected to insist on full funding, soon became more worried about huge reserves in the hands of federal officials. Would they buy up the private sector? Senator Arthur Vandenberg opined in 1937 that "it is scarcely conceivable that rational men should propose such an unmanageable accumulation of funds in one place in a democracy."[11] The time was opportune for moving back toward pay-as-you-go.

In April 1938, Roosevelt asked the program staff to propose a significant liberalization of the system. He requested larger benefits, benefits for wives, widows, and dependent survivors of participants, and commencement of benefits earlier than the planned January 1942 start-up. This proposal went to Congress early in 1939. It embodied a dramatic shift in the logic underlying the system, away from insurance and full funding and toward redistribution and pay-as-you-go. In addition to the specific changes requested by Roosevelt, the amendments proposed that benefits be calculated on the basis of average monthly earnings rather than actual contributions. The direct link between individual contributions and resulting benefits was being dissolved.

A full-fledged debate on system financing ensued. A wide spectrum of proposals was advanced, from full funding to noncontributory pay-as-you-go financing from general revenues (which is what the Court said it had approved). In the end, the changes were dramatic but looked subtle. Benefits were expanded, and scheduled tax increases were deferred; the system tilted away from full funding. The system set sail on a current that would unerringly erode its fundamental premise of not encumbering future taxpayers. An irresistible pattern of political support, benefit expansion, and periodic readjustment was established. As future would-be reformers learned again and again, it is hard to escape from this current once within its grip. The amendments of 1939 adopted a funding orientation that started an intergenerational transfer on a grand scale and set a precedent that, once established, would become practically inescapable for those who followed. The amendments passed less than a month before World War II engulfed Europe and captured much of America's attention. The amendments quietly transformed the system beyond reversal before they were seriously reexamined.

The transformation also fundamentally altered the system's accountability. An insurance program would be accountable if it were fully funded. Promises to spend would then be backed by existing assets. Alternatively, a welfare program is accountable as a pay-as-you-go system since all spending occurs within the appropriations process. Take a welfare program and add the profound sense of entitlement that flows from the "insurance" character; the hybrid will be nearly impossible to challenge.

The social security system entered 1940, the year of its first benefit payments, sheltered by a political fortress. The cornerstone was the widespread notion that the system was directly contributory—that an individual's payroll taxes flowed into his or her personal account, accumulated interest, and would be paid back. This interpretation was explicitly ruled out by the Court's statement of the constitutional basis of the program. It had been rejected as a funding philosophy by the system's staff and by Congress. Moreover, it was inconsistent with the economics of the system's actual financing. But the notion persisted—indeed, it was explicitly promoted—because it played a crucial role in the long-term political impregnability of the system. Roosevelt emphasized from the outset that the system had to be financed by payroll taxes, referred to as contributions. If it was supported by general revenues, it was a gift that could be cut. Contributions were owned by and owed to the contributor. Roosevelt patiently explained this over and over: "Those taxes were never a problem of economics. They were politics all the way through. We put those payroll contributions there so as to give the contributors a legal, moral, and political right to collect their pensions and their unemployment benefits."[12]

The administrative structure of the program reinforced the idea that social security was contributory insurance and not a handout. Participants had accounts identified by account numbers. They could—and many did—

inquire about how much they "had" in those accounts. The social security program paid staff to keep account records even though actual benefits would be determined by earnings, not by contributions. These visible manifestations were vital, as Roosevelt clearly understood. A management expert named Luther Gulick told Roosevelt in 1939 that the clerks adding up the sums in each participant's account were wasting their time and the government's money, to the tune of $1 million per year. Roosevelt observed, "Luther, your logic is correct, your facts are correct, but your conclusion's wrong. Now, I'll tell you why. That account is not useless. That account is not to determine how much should be paid out. That account is there so those sons of bitches up on the Hill can't ever abandon this system when I'm gone."[13] To this day, those who want to trim social security try to explain that it is not really contributory, that a large fraction of the benefits are redistributive rather than earned, that it is not an insurance program. But to little effect. They are right, but their being right makes little difference. When 35 million recipients feel that their benefits are justly earned, there is little short-run prospect for changing the basic character of the system. And when 100 million taxpayers have made their contributions but not yet received benefits, there is little long-run prospect, either.

The program has to resemble a steamroller. Young workers pay into the system and begin to feel entitled to receive benefits when they retire. Their taxes are used to pay current benefits. When they retire, feeling eminently deserving, there is no money available to pay them—unless the next generation of workers is taxed. Once the system is on the pay-as-you-go basis, politically tenable and economically feasible alterations in its basic structure are very hard to find.

Moreover, the system is more likely to encounter financial rather than political difficulties. Trouble can come in two forms: the trust funds of the system can be either piling up money or running dry. Too much money is easy to handle; this is fortunate, since trust fund coffers overflowed repeatedly between 1939 and 1972, as the economy and population both expanded more rapidly than the inventors of social security had foreseen. Various remedies for this "problem" were embraced, often simultaneously. First, social security was extended to many additional types of workers. Farmers were added, for example, in 1949. Second, benefits were increased. Early retirement was added. Cost-of-living adjustments were granted. Third, participants were insured against more conditions. Disability coverage was added in 1956. Health insurance for the elderly began in 1965.

The second form of trouble—running out of money—is more difficult to cope with. Running low on funds is a consequence of having too many justly entitled recipients. The program will experience financial crises precisely when it is politically strongest, when there is a large group of elderly recipients, all convinced that they deserve a return on the contributions they made for so many years. It is not lost on the keepers of the system that a high proportion of these entitled recipients will turn out to vote in the next election. There can be minor adjustments around the edges, but the basic structure of the system will not be put in jeopardy. Threatening to abandon the system would be political suicide. A way will be found to close any financial gap. The fortress is practically impregnable.

Social Security's Quiet Side

Social security is the subject of one of the longest-running and hottest debates in modern American politics. It has been periodically beset by financial problems either of surplus or (more recently) of deficit. As the centerpiece of the New Deal legislation, and as the prime surviving New Deal enterprise, it has been under nearly constant attack from those for whom the New Deal represents taking the wrong fork in the road to progress. And because of its extraordinary growth and scale—its expenditures now represent about one-fifth of all direct federal spending—few serious debates about the federal budget can ignore it.

The operations of social security are also quite visible. Payroll taxes flow into a trust fund, and benefits payments are appropriated out of it. The balance is visible—and closely watched by the trustees, by Congress, by other observers, and by some recipients. Payroll taxpayers do not seem terribly interested in the trust fund balance, but even they become attentive as they approach retirement. The trust fund is supported by an identified tax stream, its rates (including some increases) established far into the future. The trustees annually report on the status of the funds and estimate future accumulation (or drawdown). Anyone who cares to look can find projections for the next seventy-five years of system inflow and outflow and can assess expectations about future benefit and tax changes consistent with the system's projected economics. Few long-term spending programs can boast anything like these reports on future spending or can point to the tax stream from which their financing will come.

Even so, social security has a quiet side, one that dwarfs most other federal spending. Its quiet side is exactly the part of the program that Roosevelt originally warned against and that was explicitly excluded in the

1935 legislation. It was added, without much debate, by the amendments of 1939. It is about half again as large as the more visible part. It is one of the prime forces in the continuing cycle of accumulation, benefit expansion, drawdown, and revision. The quiet side is an unfunded commitment of future resources—the accrual of liabilities to future recipients in the absence of funds to pay them.

The quiet part of social security is a result of pay-as-you-go financing combined with the ethos of a contributory program. Pay-as-you-go financing, as the inventors of social security clearly understood (and as Morgenthau and Roosevelt originally warned), builds up a liability without a balancing set of assets to pay it with. Like the buildup of pension liabilities discussed in chapter 1, it is a form of implicit borrowing.

Implicit borrowing doesn't necessarily have to be *quiet* borrowing. The buildup of liabilities could be directly acknowledged, for example, by appropriating general revenue funds to the social security trust funds. These additional appropriations, in excess of current benefit payments, would provide a way to acknowledge the future liabilities being accumulated today. *But this would explicitly undermine the politically crucial cornerstone of the program—its contributory basis.* To maintain the program's contributory aura, the accrual of liabilities has to be conducted quietly. The adoption of pay-as-you-go financing cast the quiet spending die for social security.

The liabilities accrued by the social security system are immense. From 1940 to 1983, the federal government's direct outlays amounted to about $19 trillion (in 1983 dollars). Explicit social security spending accounted for $2.7 trillion, or about 14 percent of that total. But this impressive visible outflow is less than half of the social security story. Over the same period, quiet social security spending amounted to another $4 trillion of outflow, an average of roughly $100 billion (in 1983 dollars) each year.* Total social security spending was therefore nearly $7 trillion. Total federal spending over this period (including the accrual of public-employee pension and social security liabilities) was about $24 trillion. Social security has thus accounted for about 30 percent of all federal spending since 1940.

The social security program represents a vast intergenerational transfer. The total national product between 1940 and 1983, very crudely estimated in 1983 dollars, was about $90 trillion. Social security transferred about 7

---

*Like the estimates of the pension liabilities described in the preceding chapter, estimates of social security liabilities depend crucially on assumptions about future rates of return, wage growth, choices about early or deferred retirement, and life expectancy. They are thus subject to considerable variation. Current estimates of the value of the system's net liabilities to current participants (including retirees) range from about $3.5 trillion to $4.5 trillion, about four times the combined liability of the federal pension systems. The Treasury's latest estimate, contained in a footnote of a less-than-widely-read Treasury report, is $4.21 trillion. This uncertain—but certainly large—liability represents social security's quiet spending from its inception to today.

percent of that to the elderly and other recipients. It should be no surprise that the program is a large transfer to the elderly; that is its avowed purpose. But because the explicit spending is so enormous, it has been easy to miss the quiet spending part and thereby to underestimate—by more than a factor of two—the actual size of the program.

The quiet spending of social security is more than just a convenient intellectual abstraction. It is also the engine for much of the program's growth. The program has repeatedly expanded on the hidden account, as new members (e.g., farmers) or coverages (e.g., disability) were added. Expansions in coverage tally up a hidden bill because the new promises commonly entail small amounts of benefit payments in their early years followed by increasing outflows later. Expanding a pay-as-you-go system nearly always creates additional unfunded liabilities—and thus involves hidden spending. Gradually, these liabilities come due, as benefits have to be paid. Taxes must be raised to pay them. It is easy to expand the quiet account; and by the time the direct spending takes place, a new collection of righteous entitlees have paid and now profoundly believe they deserve to receive. By virtue of its relatively advanced age—social security is now over fifty years old—much of the liability that it incurred quietly has become visible. This illustrates an iron law of quiet spending conducted through accrual of liability: spending that is hidden when it is done can no longer hide when the bill comes due.

The latest round of social security debates illustrates this recurring cycle of hidden spending becoming visible spending. Social security expanded greatly between 1965 and 1972, beginning with the addition of health coverage for those over sixty-five, followed by several benefit increases, and winding up with the automatic cost-of-living indexing of benefits. Congress had resisted automatic indexing, retaining for itself the prerogative of voting popular benefit increases at opportune times. However, steep inflation in the late 1960s and early 1970s increased pressure for a mechanism of guaranteed cost adjustment. Congress responded with a flawed procedure that indexed benefits to increase both with wages and with prices. Since wages and prices tend to rise together, this double-counted the effect of inflation. Benefits to new recipients rose dramatically with the rapid price and wage inflation of the mid-1970s. Benefits nearly doubled between 1972 and 1977; on an inflation-adjusted basis, benefits rose by more than one-third.

Meanwhile, for the first time in decades, the economy dragged. Business was battered by two energy crises. Real growth (which had always financed expanding social security benefit payments) stagnated, while benefits for retirement, unemployment, and health surged. The long-term demographics of social security had also begun to shift against the system; a large cohort of postwar babies was working its way through the system, followed by a generation that had considerably fewer children per couple than its predecessors. The number of active taxpaying workers per recipient was projected to fall substantially early in the next century, and many had already observed that the long-run economics of the system were out of balance. By 1977, it was clear that the "long term"—when promises had been predicted to outstrip system revenues—was no longer far away.

The Carter administration suggested sweeping reform. Some suggestions were not terribly controversial; for example, "decoupling" to eliminate the double indexation of benefits was easily accepted. Not so the administration's financing proposal. Rather than increase payroll taxes further—they were already far higher than the inventors of the program had envisaged—Carter proposed to substitute general revenue financing. Social security was a good program. It needed additional money. It already accomplished substantial redistribution. It was unwise to rely indefinitely on a regressive tax base like payrolls. Since much of the program was to help poor people, it was time to have everyone, not just moderate-income workers, pay their share.

Whatever the truth of those claims, they were anathema to social security supporters. It was the old dole/insurance debate, wrapped in modern terminology. The proposals were designed to help the poor—recipients and taxpayers alike. But the magic of social security had always been how much help it could provide to the poor without admitting it was a handout. Ironically, these supposedly progressive proposals threatened to undermine the political foundation of the longest-running, largest, and most successful transfer program ever created.

There is an interesting paradox here. Some argued against general revenue financing because they feared it could too easily expand. Benefits would be demanded by the strong lobby representing elderly voters. There would be no way to resist, because there was no intrinsic limit on the share of general revenues that could be diverted to social security. Others feared exactly the opposite—that the use of general revenues would make the program look more like a welfare program. Benefits would be reduced, tailored to minimal needs. The contributory flavor would be eroded, and with it the pride and support of millions of taxpayers.

Congress responded by raising payroll tax rates enough to generate over $200 billion in additional revenues over the next decade. This hike was larger than any previous peacetime tax increase. Substantial tax increases in troubled economic times are usually out of character for Congress; the amendments of 1977 testify to the special nature of the social security program and its unique niche in the American political system.

Some claimed the adjustment was a permanent solution that would carry social security safely into the next century; in fact, it was a temporary adjustment that would barely carry it into the next decade. Renewed stagflation following the second "oil shock" saw to that. The Carter administration immediately set to work on wider reforms. Continuing declines in fertility rates made the program's future increasingly bleak. Taxpaying participants currently outnumbered beneficiaries by about three to one, but that ratio had fallen substantially from over ten to one in the 1930s, and it was projected to drop to two to one early in the next century. Unlike other projections about the system, this one was reasonably certain. By 1977, nearly all of the relevant future workers had already been born, and there were not enough of them.

Carter administration reformers in 1980 and Reagan administration reformers in 1981 were convinced that the system's long-term economics were out of balance. Changes in the benefit structure would be required to right them. Meanwhile, the cash position of the trust funds was becoming perilous, the more so as recession exacerbated the effects of inflation. The immediate need for additional cash seemed to provide an opportunity to rebalance the long-term position of the program. Both sets of would-be reformers advanced proposals to tax social security benefits received by those with incomes over $20,000 and proposed packages of immediate and long-term benefit reductions. Both patiently explained that social security recipients were receiving much more, on average, than they had "earned" through their contributions. Both insisted that adjusting benefits was the only feasible way to balance claims and receipts. And both substantially underestimated the power of the social security coalition—and were resoundingly defeated.[14]

In 1977, and again in the 1980 and 1981 reform debates, Congress categorically rejected both immediate benefit cuts and any proposal that smacked of making social security a welfare program. By 1981, the cash crisis was real and immediate: cash insolvency of the trust funds was projected by July 1983. For the trust funds to survive 1982, Congress had to allow the old-age-benefits fund to borrow from the relatively better-off disability trust fund.

Wary of the intense politics of social security but conscious of the need for change, the Reagan administration proposed a bipartisan commission, appointed jointly by the President, the majority leader of the Senate, and the Speaker of the House. The commission faced a Scylla of irresistible political forces on one side and a Charybdis of immovable financial problems on the other. The long-term balance of the system was not in doubt; 'n the view of nearly all observers, it was untenable. Short-run cash needs were also visible. Moreover, continued hidden spending could be expected to generate real insolvency—as opposed to merely impossible cash shortages—over the longer term.

Given its constraints, the commission provided a remarkable solution.[15] The commission proposed—and Congress accepted, essentially unaltered—two packages of changes, one for the short run and one for the long run.[16] The commission estimated that to keep the trust funds liquid, additional revenues or cost savings of $150 to $200 billion were needed between 1983 and 1989. The commission sought changes providing an amount close to the midpoint of this range, or $175 billion. The short-run package relied on two traditional approaches to close this gap and on one new one.

First, the commission's proposal extended coverage to include employees of nonprofit institutions and new federal employees. Why does expanding the system help a cash crisis? For the same reason that it is hidden spending: under pay-as-you-go financing, new participants provide tax payments before they receive benefits, so the cash position of the trust funds is temporarily improved by adding new members. This change was estimated to generate $20 billion in net revenues over the 1983–1989 period. Second, the commission proposed to move a payroll tax increase scheduled for 1985 to 1984, to increase taxes for 1988 and 1989 slightly, and to increase payroll taxes on the self-employed. Together, these changes were estimated to generate about $60 billion in additional revenues. Similar cash infusions had been used regularly to replenish the trust funds as they ran low.

The commission also added a new and delicate proposal to adjust benefits. The lessons of the decade of debate since 1972 had been learned; Congress would not approve immediate benefit cuts. Rather than directly reduce benefits, the commission proposed, first, to reduce the *increases* in benefits by changing the cost-of-living adjustments and, second, to tax half of the social security benefits received by those with incomes over $20,000. Both changes reduced benefits. A cut in the form of a lower increase, however, could be presented as preserving part of the increase. The benefits earned through contributions would still be paid. Indeed, they would continue to rise with the cost of living. Retirees were still protected from inflation. This "cut" was a victory for those who sought to preserve the system—or so the commission hoped it would seem. And taxing a fraction of benefits for those with already comfortable incomes would not hurt the neediest recipients.* Even Representative Claude Pepper, an ardent de-

---

*The commission made it clear to those who read the fine print that taxing benefits was a benefit cut by providing that the estimated taxes received by the Treasury should be transferred as a permanent appropriation to the trust funds. The members of the 1937 Supreme Court must have rolled over in their graves.

fender of social security benefits and of the contributory-insurance character of the system, joined eleven other commissioners (against three hold-outs) in endorsing the adjustments. These two noncut cuts were estimated to reduce outlays by $70 billion over the critical period.

This package of adjustments narrowed the 1983–1989 gap by $150 billion, still $25 billion short of the commission's target. Moreover, the package did little to solve the system's most immediate problem. The system's cash bankruptcy—when trust funds would have no authority to mail out the next month's checks—was expected to come in July 1983, and all of these changes together provided only $5 billion in 1983, less than ten days' outflow.

The rest was done with mirrors. Many of those covered by social security are members of the armed forces. Former members of the armed services receive social security benefits based on their salaries and on the nonmonetary benefits (housing, food, medical care) they receive as part of their compensation. The government pays both the employee and the employer payroll tax on the nonmonetary part of compensation. Prior to 1983, the Department of Defense had reimbursed the trust funds for benefits based on these "gratuitous wage credits" as the benefits were paid to retirees. This allowed the Defense Department to pay some of its "payroll taxes" in arrears, thus giving it the benefit of the pay-as-you-go financing. (Other employers—and employees—pay their taxes as wages are earned; on average, this is long before the social security benefit based on them will be paid.) The commission called for a $20 billion Treasury credit to the social security trust funds in 1983 to make up for all of these Defense Department arrearages. Thus, the imminent cash bust in the trust funds that had been the instrument for forcing real long-term adjustments in the social security program was, in the end, quietly averted by a paper transfer between two government agencies.

These short-run adjustments also substantially closed the long-run financial gap of the system. The commission recommended that Congress choose between two additional long-run changes. Either the normal retirement age should be increased or a further increase in payroll taxes should be scheduled. In either case, changes would start after 2000. In 1983, Congress adopted the commission package with only minor alterations, choosing to close the long-term gap by gradually raising the normal retirement age from sixty-five to sixty-seven by 2027. The short-run cuts in benefits were disguised so as not to appear to be cuts; the long-run cuts were scheduled so that participants would know about them long in advance. Even though the benefit changes actually adopted were relatively small and far distant in time, the unconventional idea that the system might have to be balanced through benefit adjustments rather than tax increases had been validated.

The shifting demographics of the U.S. population forced Congress to adjust the social security system so that the value of contributions by each generation will more nearly equal the value of the benefits it receives.[17] These long-run changes, of course, are subject to further debate in the intervening years. A major purpose of the changes of 1983 was to get the system through the next few years. This they appear to have accomplished. The trust funds are no longer in imminent danger of exhaustion. The torrent of literature with titles combining the words "social security" and "crisis" that began in the middle 1970s crested in 1982 and has now nearly disappeared.

But an old problem has been reincarnated. It is the flip side of the problem the 1983 commission resolved. The commission focused on the pending cash crisis and the long-term solvency problem beginning, roughly, in the second decade of the next century. No one said there was any middle-term problem, between 1990 and 2010—because there wasn't. In that period the baby boomers will be in their prime working years, and they will fill the coffers of the social security trust funds to overflowing. Since they will not be followed by a similarly larger cohort, the trust funds will have to build up during this period to sustain the benefit drain from the postwar generation as it moves into retirement. This is the inherent logic of a funded system: it builds up reserve funds as participants work, then draws them down after they retire. The latest adjustment toward full funding means that the reserve funds, once they survive the tight-cash period of 1983–1990, will grow to unprecedented proportions.

The 1984 report of the system's trustee indicates that between 2010 and 2020 the reserves of the system will be about five times the yearly outflow.[18] In 1983, this would have been about $1 trillion—an amount roughly equal to the entire outstanding privately held government debt. The trust funds projected for the early years of the twenty-first century are thus of a magnitude similar to those contemplated, and rejected, by the inventors of the system as posing too grave a problem of investment, too large a concentration of funds.

Whatever management problems such a large fund might present, it may also be a source of temptation. In the past, large fund balances have prompted an expansion of the system. Will future Congresses, pressed on every side to provide new and better benefits, maintain the fiscal discipline embodied in the amendments of 1983? Will they keep strict reins on the rising costs of health care for the elderly when money seems to be available in the trust funds to pay for needed benefits?* Solving the short- and long-run problems of the system may generate problems of the opposite sort in the middle term—a different set of perils in the same political minefield.

Strengthening the Financial Accountability of Social Security

Americans are clearly familiar with the social security system, as taxpayers or as beneficiaries or as both. But few are aware of the magnitude of the quiet side of social security. Direct social security expenditures over the last fifty years have accounted for less than half of the program's total spending. Its accrual of debt is well over twice the accumulation of the closely watched explicit national debt. With some $4 trillion in quiet spending over the past fifty years, social security falls far short of the appropriations standard of accountability. What can be done about this?

The preceding chapter suggested that we would generally enhance the accountability for pension programs by funding them on a current basis—that is, making payments equal to current accruals of obligations, rather than pay-as-you-go disbursements. The amendments of 1983 have put the social security system's financing approximately on a current funding basis. Existing unfunded liabilities will not diminish, but at least they are not growing further. This rough balancing was achieved almost accidentally. It was forced on the system by shifting demographic trends, not adopted as a matter of policy. And it is not built into the system; no mechanism guarantees that the system will stay fully funded on a current basis, no formula will adjust rates or benefits to maintain the coincidental current equilibrium. The current financing discipline should therefore be reinforced.

There are several ways to make the system's workings and liabilities more obvious and thus more accountable. First, spending could be made more

*These questions are what gives substance to the current policy debate in Washington over whether the social security system will remain in the federal budget. If it stays in, the surplus run by the trust funds after 1990 can be used to mask an imbalance in other programs. If it is separate, any operating deficit in other programs will be more obvious, and possibly more likely to generate pressure for spending reductions. Either way, the surplus accumulating in the social security trust funds will provide a captive market for Treasury borrowing—a substantial deficit in other programs can be run without requiring any borrowing from the public. This, too, may reduce the pressure holding spending in check.

visible. The implicit debt accumulation could be made explicit. To achieve this, Congress could adopt a policy of annually appropriating to the social security trust funds an amount equal to the increase in the outstanding liability. This would keep the unfunded liability constant. These funds could come either from taxes or from explicit borrowing; either form would be appropriated. The effects would be visible—higher tax collections or greater issues of Treasury debt.*

Any long-term policy of full social security funding that involves funds other than payroll contributions is fraught with thorny problems. First, if Treasury funds come from general revenues or borrowing, the transfer may undermine—or may be seen as undermining—the contributory basis of the system, transforming it into a welfare program. Undercutting this corner-stone of the system's political foundation could have far-reaching effects. Second, if the funds come from additional taxes (rather than from Treasury debt issues), the social security system could wind up purchasing a large fraction of the outstanding national debt. This would complicate control of the money supply by the Federal Reserve; flexibility in adjusting the volume of currency by buying and selling Treasury securities could be jeopardized. We could alleviate this problem by allowing the social security system to hold mortgages or other private securities, but government ownership of substantial amounts of private assets sounds to many people like sneaking socialism. Precisely this prospect led conservatives in 1939 to be proponents of that year's shift to pay-as-you-go financing. Third, the move toward full funding from a pay-as-you-go regime places a double burden on one genera-tion, which pays both for the preceding generation (through pay-as-you-go) and for itself (through full funding). This may be inequitable, or politically untenable, or both.

Whether social security should be fully funded also raises major policy questions about the impact upon the pattern of real savings in the economy. Martin Feldstein and others have noted that young workers, knowing they will receive retirement benefits, may feel less of a need to provide for themselves. As a result, they may reduce their personal savings. Young workers see social security retirement benefits as "wealth," as an asset guaranteeing them income in their old age. From the perspective of the economy, however, this wealth is illusory, for each person's asset is someone else's liability. No physical, productive assets back social security wealth. If workers reduce their own savings in contemplation of the benefits social

*If the social security system is required to invest all of its funds in Treasury debt, it will eventually buy back any Treasury securities issued to fund it. The net transaction with the public will be zero. But the issued Treasury securities, on deposit in the social security trust funds, will attest to the commitment that future taxpayers will pay. Not incidentally, this process will advertise the magnitudes involved.

security will pay them, a net reduction in investable funds will result, with potential consequences for capital formation, the rate of technical change, productivity improvement, and economic growth.[19] The effect of social security on savings, if it is problematic, could be offset by funding the system fully and investing its reserves in private securities, generating investable funds from tax proceeds. In the early 1970s, Feldstein argued that the social security program should be *over*funded—that is, its funding should be used to increase the rate of capital formation in the American economy.[20]

The policy issues surrounding the full funding of social security thus go far beyond the program's accountability. Accountability does not necessarily call for full funding, particularly given the risk that the full-funding regime might foster ways to use accumulated reserves. Full funding for a period followed by a return to pay-as-you-go would be a windfall for the later generation, not an accountable long-term bargain. The period of full funding does nothing to enhance accountability if it can be followed by a raid on the accumulated reserves. Full funding through noncontributory revenue infusions, whether borrowed or taken from general revenues, may undermine what many see as the essential character of the system. And the effects of the program's funding on capital formation may overwhelm concerns about the program's accountability. Accountability should not be society's exclusive concern as it chooses along the spectrum from pay-as-you-go to full funding.*

Trying to select a funding policy on the basis of accountability, then, may be the wrong approach. If the accountability of social security needs to be enhanced, it may be better to approach it through an information strategy. What should a comprehensive report about social security say? An information approach would present appropriate measures of existing liabilities and their annual changes, indicating the scale of the program's quiet side. On average, quiet expenditures have been of the same order of magnitude as direct social security spending, but with wide variation from year to year. In the past, when new participants were added, when benefits were raised, or when coverage was extended, the unfunded liability of the program surged. As a result of the amendments of 1983, each future participant's ratio of benefits to contributions (including interest) is much closer to one, so adding new participants no longer increases the unfunded liability. Moreover, the projections underlying the amendments of 1983 reflect expected cost-of-living adjustments in benefits, so these routine benefit increases do not increase the unfunded liability, either. Unexpected benefit adjustments,

---

*Pay-as-you-go and full funding are not the polar extremes of this spectrum. Farther in the pay-as-you-go direction, we could borrow to make current payments; at the other extreme, we could overfund, as Feldstein suggested.

however—like double indexing from 1972 to 1977—would still boost unfunded liabilities. Comprehensive reporting about the social security system would disclose such changes prominently.

Some reporting of this kind already exists. The system's actuaries annually estimate its unfunded liabilities in an official Treasury publication. Social security liabilities are not, however, given much attention, and they are not presented in a form most observers would find either very accessible or very meaningful. The Treasury's estimate of unfunded liabilities as defined here is contained in an obscure footnote.[21]

The problem is not a lack of data—the data exist. It is that public debate has managed to keep data from being turned into information. Various observers have misrepresented the implications of the unfunded liability, trying to cast doubt on the nation's ability to carry the social security burden. The specter of bankruptcy is often raised by those who emphasize the "unfunded liability" as a measure of the financial condition of the social security program.[22] By itself, the unfunded liability of the system has little meaning; it needs to be put in context. Understandable reporting about social security must portray the system against a relevant backdrop. The social security system represents a large flow of funds over a long time period. Comparing its accumulated magnitude (the current $4 trillion accrued liability) to annual flows like direct federal government spending (approximately $1 trillion) or current personal income (approximately $3 trillion) gives a striking—but quite misleading—view of the program. Its unfunded liability should be viewed, instead, against magnitudes like total federal spending during the same period (about $20 trillion), against total national income over that period (about $90 trillion), or against the current value of future national income.*

Alternatively, we can examine the annual flows of social security—its visible and quiet components—and compare these to annual federal spending, annual national income, and so on. The annual flow of the quiet part of social security is the *change* in its unfunded liability from year to year. This has averaged roughly $100 billion per year in 1983 dollars since the program began, but it has varied considerably from one year to the next.[23]

To consider how much spending is appropriate, we should view annual spending against annually available resources; we must see spending during an entire generation against resources available to a generation. Seen against

---

*The value of future national income might be estimated as follows. Suppose income is growing at 1 percent in real terms and currently equals $3 trillion, and we apply a real discount rate of 3 percent. Then the current value of future national income is the value of a $3 trillion perpetuity growing at 1 percent and discounted at 3 percent, or $3 trillion / (.03 − .01) = $150 trillion. This figure is very sensitive to the differential between the rate of real growth in income and the discount rate.

the relevant backdrop, social security is a large, but not unimaginably large, transfer over generations. It is larger than most taxpayers or beneficiaries understand. But it is not so large as to present a clear threat to the federal Treasury.

Social security proponents rightly reject the presumption that the program is technically and inevitably bankrupt. It is not. The system is *designed* to be balanced in cash, with current income meeting current expenses. Fully funding the system would create a huge reserve, one that pay-as-you-go advocates say would be difficult to invest. The system's designers chose to accumulate liabilities for future payment; these liabilities by themselves provide no indication of the financial condition of the program.

The system relies on future tax payments and, therefore, on the continued acceptance by younger taxpayers of tax burdens in their early years in return for retirement benefits later; it depends on the maintenance of an intergenerational social compact. The broad structure of that compact is in little danger; indeed, it is practically self-enforcing. Each generation's first encounter with the system is as a payer. Each pays taxes to redeem promises to those who have already "contributed." Having paid, each will demand benefits in turn. A compact of that kind can run short of cash, but it is unlikely to go bankrupt or be dismantled. The question will be not whether to continue it but how to balance spending and income, how to reset the expectations of participants about how much they will receive.

As far as most social security advocates are concerned, that ends the debate about unfunded liabilities. Estimates of accumulated debt are advanced by people who say that the sky is falling. The sky is not falling. End of discussion—and end of any serious consideration of unfunded liabilities. But while accumulated liabilities should not be seen as a grave threat to the financial soundness of the program, they are nonetheless critical to any full consideration of the program. They are not a measure of doom, but they *are* a measure of spending. Unfunded liabilities are not relevant to any concern about bankruptcy, for the system will not go bankrupt. Neither are they *ir*relevant. They are no more and no less relevant than the national debt.

The mismanaged debate about social security liabilities has undercut the information approach to social security accountability. The first step in putting an information approach back on track is to use information appropriately. Building better accountability for social security is a complex problem. None of the standard rules applies perfectly. The straightforward funding approach—backing promises with real financial assets—has problematic side effects. And the development of accurate information does not prevent its misuse. Comprehensibility is a difficult standard for a complex program to meet.

Lessons from Social Security

The social security system reveals the interplay of the hidden and the visible. Because the visible part is so vast, the hidden part may be all the harder to see. The quiet side was easy to expand, as the apparent overflow of the cash reserves seemed to permit generous benefit increases and extensions of coverage to new perils and people. Once expanded, the quiet side could not stay quiet forever; hidden spending in the form of accruing future obligations becomes visible spending when those obligations come due. But by the time the promises come due and the spending shifts to the visible account, a benefit constituency has already been created to defend them. Social security's quiet side has proved hard to contract, even in the face of mounting evidence that the long-term economics of the system were out of balance.

Social security's quiet side is part of a seamless web connecting the mythology of its contributory basis to the substance of its operations. Social security shows the political staying power of the marriage of righteous entitlement with pay-as-you-go funding. Its mixed heritage—part insurance and part welfare—is the root of both the program's political strength and its accountability weakness. As either a contributory insurance program (fully funded through contributions) *or* a recognizable welfare program (with "entitlements" always debatable and funds fully appropriated), it would be more in keeping with the ideals of fully visible government spending. But as a combination, it has the unique force of profound entitlement to benefits the recipients believe they have paid for, without any mechanism to force a balance between inflow and outflow. The combined logic is also self-perpetuating; stopping the system, once under way, denies benefits to some generation of contributors. Each generation in turn literally buys into the system. The rules can be changed, and the ratio of benefits received to contributions made can be altered, but the basic structure of the system has resisted generations of reform efforts even in the face of true and immediate financial crises.

In 1983, however, the hidden side of social security *was* confronted and adjusted. Congress modified the system to reduce at least the growth in the hidden side. What made this possible? The opportunity was provided by a cash crisis; previous hidden spending in the form of promises came due and required benefit payments threatened to bankrupt the trust funds. In the context of that cash crisis, Congress not only could modify the short-run financial flows of the system but also could—and did—address the long-run balance of the system. Interestingly, the 1983 cash crisis that precipitated the long-term realignment was actually solved largely by a paper transfer from one part of the federal government to another, not by any substantive adjustment to either benefits or contributions. But with only a few months to go before the cash in the till was used up, a great deal of long-term business could finally be addressed. At the same time, paradoxically, the most immediate short-run business was ducked.

The amendments of 1983 represent an opportunity, rather than a victory, for accountability. It appears that the unfunded liabilities of the system are currently not growing. Quiet spending, long the hallmark of this program and a primary vehicle for forcing changes in later visible spending, has been reduced. But there is no mechanism in place to pressure the system to stay in balance. No policy or structure militates against future hidden spending; Congress fashioned only a temporary and largely accidental respite from quiet spending. The capacity to conduct quiet spending is still very much a feature of the system.

The social security program is strongly supported by the general public. It is much better known and more visible than most programs with extensive quiet spending. It is regularly and hotly debated. Its finances flow through trust funds, and projections about their current and future status are readily available. Yet the quiet side of social security has been the largest quiet spending program of the federal government.

The conduct of social security might be better if it were less hidden. It would surely be closer to what society has said its established order would be. The interested public is supposed to be able to get an understandable description of government spending. In examining social security, if you haven't looked at the quiet side, you literally haven't looked at half of the story.

But social security cannot be dismissed solely because of its accountability flaws. Whether social security is too large or too small—too generous or too stingy—must remain an issue for political debate. We cannot resolve it, as some critics would prefer, by pointing to allegedly inescapable bankruptcy. We will have to judge it on its merits.

Chapter 3

Federal Credit Activities

IN OUR ECONOMY, the movers and shakers are those who control big money. This makes credit a central component of economic power. Credit —the ability to assemble funds for current use secured by promises of future returns—allows some people to use other people's money for their own purposes. It is a source of economic power, wealth, and control. It serves a vital function in modern economies. The fact that credit is available for some purposes and not for others has a powerful impact on the direction of current activities. Since the availability of credit determines patterns of current investment, it plays a vital role in shaping the future. Its volume, form, and allocation are important concerns of government.

In a republic with deep traditions of free enterprise, the allocation of credit might be expected to be one of the bastions of private economic activity. But the presence of the federal government in today's credit markets is sizable, and the pattern of federal involvement in credit is idiosyncratic. Federal credit programs affect virtually every major facet of economic life—housing, health care, business, trade, education, agriculture, even utilities. They influence the scale of credit supply, the shape of credit demands, and the forms through which credit is available. Federal credit programs have grown geometrically over the last two decades, and their growth continues in spite of the best efforts of the current administration to curb it.

The History of Federal Credit Activities

The federal government has always borrowed through credit markets to provide funds for its own use.[1] Its direct provision of credit to other entities, however, is an innovation of this century. In 1916, the Federal Land Bank System was created, establishing twelve banks to make property loans to farmers and ranchers. In 1923, the Intermediate Credit Banks extended the original system to make short-term loans available to the same groups. These two early credit programs eventually shifted to private ownership as components of the Farm Credit System, a publicly chartered government-sponsored enterprise. The War Finance Corporation, which was developed to help underwrite the wartime expansion effort in World War I, was another early example of an active government credit program.

Use of credit as a program device expanded substantially during the New Deal. A variety of new organizational forms developed; government corporations and independent government agencies became popular mechanisms for handling new government responsibilities. Many of these new devices relied on the use of credit. The Reconstruction Finance Corporation (RFC), originally designed to assist banks during the Great Depression, was established in 1932. A variety of modern credit activities of the federal government have their roots in this period. The Federal National Mortgage Association, the Rural Electrification Administration, the Export-Import Bank (usually called Eximbank), and the Small Business Administration all grew out of the RFC. Housing credit programs also originated in this period; the Federal Housing Administration was created in 1934 to expand opportunities for homeownership, and it continues as the federal government's largest single credit program. Federal involvement in the provision of mortgages through support of the savings-and-loan component of the banking system (the Federal Home Loan Bank Board) also dates from the early part of the New Deal.

Forms of Federal Credit

There are three fundamental forms of direct federal credit activity.[2] Direct loan programs are the easiest to find in federal budget documents. Under these programs—two examples are the Rural Housing Insurance Fund, which offers mortgages for housing purchases, and the Small Business Administration Disaster Relief Program, which makes loans to help property owners recover from the effects of natural disasters—the government acts exactly like a bank. It evaluates the credit of the borrower, obtains funds, provides them to the borrower against a note (which sometimes pledges some collateral), and services the loan until it either is repaid or goes into default. The funds lent under these programs are advanced by the U.S. Treasury; since the government has been running deficits consistently over recent years, we can think of these funds as having been borrowed from the public. Thus, in direct loan programs the government acts as a financial intermediary, just as a commercial bank would.

Loan guarantees are the second major form of federal credit assistance. Under loan guarantee programs (the program for students and the special program for Chrysler are probably the best known of these) the government guarantees funds lent by private parties, rather than borrowing and lending the funds itself. The loan is serviced by the private lender unless there is a default. If there is, the guaranteeing agency buys the loan from the lender, using funds from the Treasury, and then tries to collect from the borrower. Thus, loans guaranteed by the federal government become direct loans if they default. From the perspective of the borrower, loan guarantee programs differ little from direct loan programs. Investors view federally guaranteed loans as quite secure since the federal government guarantees full repayment of principal and interest. Indeed, these loans are practically identical to official Treasury securities, so borrowers have little trouble finding willing investors.* Loan guarantees do, however, require the borrower to establish a relationship with a traditional source of funds—typically, a bank—and many federal credit programs are operated through guarantees precisely for that reason. From the perspective of the federal liability involved, direct loans and federally guaranteed loans are quite similar. Loan guarantee programs do not necessarily involve handling any funds, so they are often simpler to administer. Many agencies offer both direct loans and loan guarantees. The Eximbank, for example, provides direct loans to foreign trading partners purchasing goods from the United States and loan guarantees to banks extending trade credit to purchasers of U.S. exports.

Lending by government-sponsored enterprises (GSEs) is the third form of federal involvement with credit provision. In the last several decades, a series of quasi-public, quasi-private organizations has been established. They are not agencies of the federal government, but they are not wholly

---

*Loans guaranteed by the government can actually be turned into direct loans made by the government through the Federal Financing Bank, as will be discussed later in this chapter.

rivate either. The first example, and archetype, is the Federal National Mortgage Association (FNMA or "Fannie Mae"), which was part of a government agency for thirty years before being separately chartered by Congress in 1968. The FNMA is the nation's largest secondary purchaser of home mortgages (though other GSEs are now closing in); it borrows funds through money markets and uses them to buy mortgages from banks, replenishing funds for additional lending at the local level. Although its obligations are not guaranteed by the federal government, it can borrow from the Treasury (on approval of the secretary) if it runs into credit difficulties. While the FNMA is not a government agency, the implicit public commitment behind it is clear. The FNMA is treated by securities markets as if it were part of the government, and it would almost certainly be assisted by the public if it fell on hard times. Lending by the FNMA and other GSEs does not legally involve public funds, but it is treated as public in virtually every other respect.

The Scope of Federal Credit

In 1982 the General Accounting Office was asked by the Senate's Temporary Subcommittee on Federal Credit to prepare a catalog of federal credit programs. The GAO's report found that "about 424" credit programs were authorized to operate during 1982, including 142 direct loan and 116 loan guarantee programs.[3] There is great diversity. Programs range from small activities, like the General Services Administration's sales of surplus property on credit, to extensive commitments like the Government National Mortgage Association's guarantees of home mortgages. They include programs in defense, health, education, housing, energy, domestic and international commerce, agriculture, transportation, banking, utilities, and employment. Federal loan guarantee programs assist Chrysler, New York City, the Washington, D.C., subway system, bankrupt railroads, synthetic-fuel manufacturers, and shipowners. Direct loan programs assist in the construction of academic facilities, the establishment of small businesses by disabled veterans, the development of facilities for energy recovery from municipal waste, and the compensation of experts in the preparation and trial of Native American claims.

The scale of these activities has increased sharply in recent years. Table 4.1 shows the growth of direct loans, loan guarantees, and lending by GSEs

TABLE 3.1

Federal Participation in Domestic Credit Markets

(dollar amounts in billions)

						Actual							Estimates	
	1974	1975	1976	TQ	1977	1978	1979	1980	1981	1982	1983	1984	1985
Total funds advanced in U.S. credit markets[1]	187.5	178.0	243.3	64.9	309.8	385.7	423.5	356.4	414.3	394.2	497.5	(3)	(3)
Direct loans	4.1	12.8	10.9	3.7	11.6	19.8	19.6	24.2	26.1	23.4	15.3	9.3	8.0
Guaranteed loans	10.3	8.6	11.1	-0.1	13.5	13.4	25.2	31.6	28.0	20.9	34.1	39.4	38.9
Government-sponsored enterprise loans[2]	11.2	5.6	4.9	3.1	11.7	25.2	28.1	24.1	32.4	43.3	37.1	39.8	42.9
Federal and federally assisted lending	25.5	27.0	26.9	6.7	36.7	58.4	72.9	79.9	86.5	87.6	86.5	88.5	94.8
Federal lending participation ratio (percent)	13.6	15.2	11.1	10.3	11.8	15.1	17.2	22.4	20.9	22.2	17.4	(3)	(3)
Total funds raised in U.S. credit markets[1]	187.5	178.0	243.3	64.9	309.8	385.7	423.5	356.4	414.3	394.2	497.5	(3)	(3)
Federal borrowing from public	3.0	50.9	82.9	18.0	53.5	59.1	33.6	70.5	79.3	135.0	212.3	183.0	193.0
Borrowing for guaranteed loans	10.3	8.6	11.1	-0.1	13.5	13.4	25.2	31.6	28.0	20.9	34.1	39.4	38.9
Government-sponsored enterprise borrowing[2]	10.9	5.3	4.1	1.4	12.0	21.4	21.9	21.4	34.8	43.8	34.6	39.8	42.4
Federal and federally assisted borrowing	24.2	64.8	98.1	19.3	79.0	93.9	80.7	123.5	142.1	199.7	281.0	262.2	274.3
Federal borrowing participation ratio (percent)	12.9	36.4	40.3	29.7	25.5	24.4	19.1	34.7	34.3	50.7	56.5	(3)	(3)

[1] Funds advanced to and raised by nonfinancial sectors, excluding equities.

[2] The data in table 3.1 for total funds advanced are defined as excluding financial sectors. Nonetheless, the government-sponsored enterprises, as well as federal assisted lending, are properly compared with total funds advanced. Government-sponsored enterprises lending is a proxy for the lending by nonfinancial sectors that is intermediated by the sponsored enterprises. It assists the ultimate nonfinancial borrowers whose loans are purchased or otherwise financed by the sponsored enterprise.

[3] Not estimated.

NOTE: The insurance coverage offered to financial institutions by the Federal Deposit Insurance Corporation, the Federal Savings and Loan Insurance Corporation, and the National Credit Union Administration has not been included in this table, although direct loans made by these institutions have been included.

over the last decade. Direct loans (net of repayments) have climbed from $4.1 billion in 1974 to $15.3 billion in 1983, or by a factor of almost four. New loan guarantees (net of expirations) rose over the same period from just over $10 billion to $34 billion; borrowing and lending by GSEs rose from $11 billion to $37 billion. The 1970s saw large swings and, overall, dramatic increases in all three components of federal credit activity.[4]

These expanding programs were an important component of the increase in the fraction of U.S. credit being absorbed by the federal government. In 1974, about 13 percent of the funds advanced in U.S. credit markets went to fund the federal deficit and federal credit programs, loan guarantees, or GSE loan activity. By 1983, 57 percent of all credit being advanced flowed to or through the federal government. This reflected the vast increase in the federal deficit—and the growth of federal credit activities. Nearly three-fifths of all funds lent by private citizens and businesses in 1983 were either (1) borrowed by the federal government to spend, (2) borrowed by the federal government to lend to others, (3) borrowed under the auspices of a guarantee issued by the government, or (4) borrowed by a federally chartered GSE to be lent out.

Table 3.2 shows total direct loan, guaranteed loan, and GSE borrowing, with the largest programs in each component, for 1983. It is difficult to tell from these figures where federal credit plays the largest role in the economy. Credit is offered under very different terms in different programs, so costs to the taxpayer and the incentive effects of programs vary widely. Some provide credit at heavily subsidized rates, while others charge essentially the market rate. A heavily subsidized program has more impact upon its recipients, per dollar of credit advanced, than one at market rates. It is difficult to compare these programs directly and easy to overinterpret the figures.* Nevertheless, a few impressions emerge.

Direct loan activities were dominated in 1983 by agricultural programs, which include Commodity Credit Corporation price support loans, loans for farm real estate, and loans for rural electrification and telephone installation. All of these involve a subsidy to credit recipients. Foreign military sales and the Eximbank, both mildly subsidized, also account for considerable credit activity.

It is even more difficult to assess the sectoral impact of guaranteed loans and the borrowing and lending by GSEs. In many cases, the credit advanced through these programs appears to be roughly at market rates—until we adjust for risk. The risk premium associated with lending to higher-than-average risk borrowers is absorbed by the taxpayer. No reliable data exist

---

*We will reexamine the issue of the cost of credit programs when we discuss, below, the problems of formulating credit budgets.

TABLE 3.2

Direct Loans, Guaranteed Loans, and GSE
Borrowing, 1983
(in billions of dollars)

Direct Loans 41.4	
Commodity Credit Corporation	13.9
Farmers Home Administration	6.7
Foreign military sales	5.1
Rural Electrification Administration	4.5
Export-Import Bank	.8
All others	10.4
Guaranteed Loans 97.2	
Federal Housing Administration	44.6
Veterans Administration housing	14.7
Low-rent public housing	14.3
Export-Import Bank	8.5
Guaranteed student loans	7.3
All others	7.8
Government Sponsored Enterprises 34.7	
Federal National Mortgage Association	21.9
Federal Home Loan Mortgage Corporation	21.7

NOTE: Total is less than the two entries under GSEs because one element of the "others" category is negative (the Federal Home Loan Bank Board became smaller during this period). All figures are from *Budget of the United States Government, Fiscal Year 1985,* Special Analysis F, tables F–5 and F–16.

with which to estimate the magnitude of these subsidies. Judging merely from the magnitude of funds flowing through different programs, $110 billion in credit in fiscal year 1985 makes housing a dominant interest of federal credit operating through guarantees and secondary market financing. Student loans and the Eximbank are a distant second and third.

Economic Impacts of Federal Credit Activity

The scope of federal credit activity is substantial. Individual credit programs create an extensive web of government support, both direct and indirect, for the extension of credit to millions of borrowers. In light of the considerable scale of these activities, it might be surprising that we know little about the overall impact of federal credit activities on the economy.

Federal Credit Activities

There are many theoretical discussions of how credit activities of the government are likely to influence the level and distribution of total and privately-supplied credit. Empirical estimates of the actual impacts of federal credit programs remain elusive. This is not for lack of a try, or even of several tries. In 1981, the Congressional Budget Office sponsored a conference on credit activity. Leading scholars were invited to produce papers detailing various features of the impacts of credit programs. Seven scholarly papers were prepared, presented, and published.[5] The papers are diverse and well-documented and cover topics ranging from the macroeconomic effects of credit programs to the effects of individual incentives in specific loan programs. But the results, like those of other studies before and since, are inconclusive. We know little about whether and how the federal government's activities alter the volume and sectoral composition of credit in the economy.

The effects of credit extension are subtle and therefore difficult to discern. Consider what happens when the government extends a loan to a student. The loan can be spent only in an educational program. Thus, we know that the public bought a specified number of years of education. But we cannot tell what would have happened without the government loan. Would the student have been idle (what economists like to call "at leisure")? If so, the loan prompted a reallocation from leisure to education. Would the student have worked? Then the loan reduced employment (assuming the job was unfilled while the student studied), or shifted employment from one sector to another (assuming that the job was filled by a worker from another sector), or reduced unemployment (assuming that the job was filled by someone previously unemployed). Or would the student have gone to school anyway, raising the funds from somewhere else? Funds may have come from other borrowing, savings, a reduction in the student's (or someone else's) consumption, additional earnings by the student, or some combination of these. Each in turn would have different impacts, depending on the responses of still other parties. The ultimate effect depends on how the impacts spread in a widening circle around the original loan.

Impacts have been largest where the subsidies have been greatest. When the government and private credit suppliers provide credit to similar borrowers on similar terms, there is little effect on the volume or allocation of credit.* But when government credit is provided to different borrowers—higher-risk borrowers or borrowers ignored by traditional lenders, for example—then it influences who gets credit and who does not. Moreover,

*Some may still feel there is some impact, simply because the money passes through government hands, so that the borrower deals with a government agent.

whenever the program provides credit on more generous terms than the private market would, it directly transfers money (in the form of reduced interest payments) to the recipients.

Using this standard—that the impacts must be small where no subsidy is involved and larger where subsidies are an important component—provides a way to assess the sectoral impacts of federal credit. The problem is that different forms of credit extension—direct loans as contrasted with loan guarantees, for example—have dramatically different subsidy components, some of them quite difficult to estimate. When the government provides a loan at 6 percent interest to a borrower who would otherwise have to pay 14 percent, the subsidy is the difference in interest rates, or 8 percent of the principal amount each year. We can calculate the subsidy involved in direct loans, but only when we know what interest rate the borrower would otherwise have faced. This interest rate is difficult to pinpoint, particularly since the government often chooses to lend to high-risk clients; we cannot simply use the average market rate on loans for similar purposes issued by private banks.

The problem is even more complex with loan guarantees. Government guarantees make private loans risk free. Since we cannot observe what terms the borrower would have obtained in the private market, we cannot tell how much of a subsidy is involved. (In this respect, loan guarantees are similar to direct loans.) One way to measure the subsidy involved is to evaluate the cost of the contingent obligation the government takes on in the guarantee, net of any insurance premium the government charges for guaranteeing the loan. This would require an assessment of the chance that the loan will default. We must estimate the creditworthiness of the borrower, compute the terms the private market would have dictated, and then compare those hypothetical perfect-market terms with the terms extended by the government. For many guarantee programs, the data to support such estimates—detailed records of the terms of loan guarantees and the characteristics of recipients—do not currently exist.

The government has, however, tried to assess the subsidy component in both direct loans and loan guarantees, and the results are revealing. Table 3.3 shows the programs providing the largest subsidies. Total subsidies through direct loans in 1983 were $8.4 billion. Nearly half were in two programs—Rural Electrification Administration electric and telephone loans (with subsidies amounting to $2.3 billion) and Farmer's Home Administration rural housing loans (with subsidies of $1.7 billion). Farm-oriented loan programs include four of the six largest subsidies and involve $3.6 billion, or 43 percent, of all subsidies. If rural electrification is regarded

TABLE 3.3
Value of Subsidies through Federal Direct Loans,
1983

Rural Electrification Administration rural electric and telephone	$2.3 billion
Farmer's Home Administration rural housing	1.7 billion
Commodity Credit Corporation price support and related programs	.7 billion
Farm export credits	.6 billion
Foreign military sales credit	.6 billion
FmHA agricultural credit	.4 billion
Other	2.1 billion
Total	$8.4 billion

NOTE: The value of the farm subsidies indicated in the CCC subsidy figures presented here understates the total value of these subsidies. They record only the difference in interest payments between the estimated rate farmers would pay on private loans and the rate charged on the federal loans. Additional subsidies, not estimated here, include price deficiency payments and the impact these price support loans have on commodity prices through setting price floors.
SOURCE: *Budget of the United States Government, Fiscal Year 1985,* Special Analysis F, p. F–28, table F–9.

as oriented primarily toward farms, the total rises to $5.9 billion, or 70 percent.*

Direct credit subsidies seem to be tilted toward rural and agricultural concerns. Better data on these programs, more complete data on the creditworthiness of the recipients, or data covering loan guarantee subsidies might shift this picture considerably. For example, better data on the cost of loan and loan guarantee write-offs would indicate that subsidies to small business and to homeowners through FHA and VA housing programs are also substantial. Nonetheless, the record we already have shows that the costs of federal credit activity come mainly from programs in a few favored sectors, notably farming, housing, and small business.

It is difficult to show that federal involvement has had any major impact on the volume and distribution of credit. As a result, most observers believe

*These estimates were prepared by the OMB, which attempted to estimate the difference between the rate charged by the government and the rate that would have been charged to the same borrower by a private lender. An alternative approach measures the difference between Treasury borrowing costs and the rate at which the government lends. This ignores the risk component of public lending; it measures only the direct cost of subsidies to the Treasury. This cost was estimated for 1983 at $3.5 billion. Thus, about $4.9 billion, or 58 percent, of federal direct loan subsidy costs in 1983 were in the intangible form of uncompensated risks imposed on federal taxpayers.

that the impact has not been dramatic.[6] For the federal government to have a material impact on the overall level and composition of credit, it must be the *marginal* lender in the markets where it is expanding credit availability. The great bulk of federally assisted borrowing is in housing. While some of these loans add to available housing capital, much of the federally supported borrowing for housing would take place without federal credit intervention. Only where those receiving federal credit dollars are the least creditworthy borrowers in the market has the federal presence really expanded lending. This is a small target, hard to hit consistently.

Yet some activities have been influenced. Rural electrification, for example, would have gotten a much slower start without the substantial extension of federal credit it has enjoyed. Federal credit is also responsible for the development of the standard housing mortgage loan now used almost universally. Federal credit has been instrumental historically through demonstration effects; both housing loans and long-term business credit would probably not exist in their present form if federal credit had not led the way. In many areas where it has had a demonstration impact, private lenders are now active, and continuing public involvement may not be necessary. If the government were now to reduce its role, most observers think the credit landscape would continue to resemble what exists today. But even—or perhaps especially—when federal credit programs have had an impact, it has been difficult to make them fade away after they have done their job.

Examples of Federal Credit Programs

Illustrations may be more useful than comprehensive figures: comprehensive data are scarce, and the aggregates combine programs with different intent and very different credit terms. There is no way to define either a typical or a representative credit program; the diversity of these programs has frustrated comprehensive analysis ever since credit activities became a major feature of federal policy. Eximbank and the Small Business Administration exemplify some of the more common elements of credit programs.[7]

EXIMBANK

Initiated by executive order in 1934 as a subsidiary of the RFC, Eximbank was to provide trade credits to help rebuild the system of international trade that had collapsed during the Great Depression. It has since become a persistent feature of the federal credit landscape.[8] In 1982, it suffered losses of $160 million on a portfolio of loans and loan guarantees amounting to an overall worldwide exposure slightly over $34 billion.[9] Current outstanding loans and loan commitments amount to $26 billion. Eximbank guarantees another $12 billion of private borrowing. Over the years, it has been involved in export sales of over $100 billion.

Eximbank exists to address three problems. First, few private investors will make loans or provide guarantees for trade credit over terms longer than three to five years, yet many export transactions span longer periods. Second, no private insurance market covers the very real risks of political upheaval faced by U.S. exporters. Third, many other countries provide below-market financing for sales of export products manufactured in favored industries. The Eximbank provides similar arrangements for U.S. companies facing competition from other nations' subsidized products.

Each of these reasons offers plausible support for government intervention. If, for example, the long-term trade credit markets do not work because of poor information (but a fair profit could be made if the service were offered), many would argue that the government should help to perfect the market by demonstrating the viability of longer-term trade credit. This argument for market-perfecting intervention is often made for the development of mortgage insurance by the FHA. If, however, the government enters this market and bears losses in it, it is simply providing subsidies.*

Government insurance against political risk provides an even clearer case. Here the government not only can be expected to be a larger and therefore somewhat more risk neutral insurer but may also be in a position to mitigate some of the potential losses faced by a private insurer. The government may have more ready access to remedies through international diplomacy than would a cartel of private insurance companies. It may also be able to use its domestic police powers to confiscate property at home when losses occur abroad (as, for example, in the Iranian crisis in 1980). Whether it is, on balance, a good thing that the government has an incentive to act through diplomatic channels in order to protect its own financial interests is another matter entirely. The image of the U.S. government, partially blinded by its own financial interests, being led into unwise diplomatic (or, worse, military) conflict is a prospect some find terrifying. Nevertheless, the government does have a special ability to seek redress in ways that would not be available to private insurers.

Finally, if other nations subsidize their export industries by underwriting

---

*It is often hard to distinguish between market perfecting and subsidization, for reasons we will discuss shortly.

some of the financing costs, then the United States has the choice of provid ing some similar form of subsidy or exporting only in industries with substantial production cost advantage. If a cost subsidy is desirable, then the argument for government intervention is compelling; no other mecha nism is likely to be effective. Such actions are, however, quite expensive Unlike the provision of long-term credit (which could be financed by ac tuarially fair interest), or of political risk insurance (which could bea premiums), export subsidies given through low-interest trade credit must b paid for by taxpayers. Many commentators have noted that the magnitud of such a program could more easily be assessed if it were carried ou through a direct grant program, but this would conflict with internationa trade and tariff agreements.

It is difficult to assess the frequently made claim that Eximbank inter venes mainly to perfect the domestic market for international trade credit One positive sign is that Eximbank is the only major provider of trad credits of five years' duration or longer. The 1975 survey of exports by th Census Bureau shows Eximbank supporting 84 percent of all trade credit of five years or over, and over 95 percent of all credits of ten years or over By contrast, it supported only 5 percent of trade credits of less than on year's duration.[10]

Under the Reagan administration's philosophy of "privatization," Exim bank has increasingly relied on joint trade credit ventures with two quasi private organizations. The Foreign Credit Insurance Association (FCIA) a consortium of insurance companies, provides short-term trade credi guarantees in conjunction with Eximbank. Eximbank reinsures catas trophic risks borne by the FCIA, so that the risk exposure of the privat concern is carefully limited. Even so, the degree of private involvemen seems to be waning. The second organization, the Private Export Financ Corporation (PEFCO), is a private firm owned by over fifty commercial an investment banks and seven industrial companies. It exists solely to provid short-term trade credit under full Eximbank guarantees; the PEFCO i simply a mechanism for borrowing funds under government loan guaran tees.

While the insurance arrangements carried out under the FCIA provid some private services for a profitable fee, the activities of the PEFCO ar private in name only. The PEFCO uses the administrative capability o insurance companies but does not involve private risk bearing. Lendin under a government loan guarantee is just another form of borrowing an lending by the public; it involves exactly the same public obligation. If tha makes the financed activity *private,* then *all* federal activities funde through deficit borrowing are private as well.[11] It is not clear whether thes private endeavors are a part of Eximbank's market-perfecting activity. On the one hand, a small part of its former activity has been successfully privatized, implying that Eximbank has led the way to a previously neglected market that is now profitably served by private parties. This view is reinforced by the fact that private insurers are now entering the market for export trade credit guarantees. On the other hand, "cream-skimming" by FCIA and purely private insurers may leave Eximbank with only activities involving some form of subsidy.

It is difficult to tell from the financial results of Eximbank whether it is perfecting markets or providing hidden subsidies. If it is truly working only to improve market function, and if it is charging all it can for its services, then it should be making a small profit. But it need not, for it could be undercharging for its services and still mainly acting as a market-perfecting agent.* Moreover, it is difficult to tell whether Eximbank is making a profit. It lost $160 million in 1982, but some years of losses are to be expected even in a generally profitable business, and it made $12 million in 1981. According to Eximbank figures, the loss rate on its existing loan and guarantee portfolios is very low. In 1982, it took write-downs of only $32 million against an active loan portfolio of over $16 billion; in 1983, its stated loan losses were only $5 million.[12] This loss rate of only .2 percent is significantly lower than typical commercial-bank loan default rates. No loan losses at all were written off in 1981. Moreover, Eximbank has accumulated a reserve of just over $2 billion with which to cover any losses it does incur.

These figures may mask a deeper underlying problem, however. Losses can be obscured by rescheduling problem loans and prolonging the process of writing them down. A recent study conducted at the Brookings Institution concluded that about 7 percent of Eximbank's total exposure (including guarantees) should be regarded as seriously at risk; this amounts to nearly three-quarters of the available reserve.[13]

One reason for Eximbank's lack of loan write-offs is that, as a matter of policy, it refuses to write down any loan made to or guaranteed by a sovereign power.[14] This pretense may be useful diplomacy, but it does not make for very realistic reporting. The comptroller general of the United States, in his comment on the 1983 Eximbank annual report, urged Eximbank to take a write-off of $1.0 to $1.5 billion for loan losses. This would nearly wipe out Eximbank's reserve fund. If it were required to operate as a real bank under U.S. banking-insurance regulations, it would be in viola-

---

*If it undercharges, it will also discourage private investors from entering the market; they will find it impossible to make a profit competing against government subsidies. Thus, if the purpose is to demonstrate that viable private loans can be made, the government should charge the full cost of its services.

tion of capitalization requirements and would have to be recapitalized, shut down, merged, sold, or otherwise reorganized. If its loan losses are as high as this suggests, Eximbank does not earn enough to recover its investments and is systematically providing subsidies even in the programs designed to be conducted at market rates. The costs are high, and it is difficult to tell just how high.

Who benefits from Eximbank credit? Generally, the investors and workers in exporting industries receive the benefits of Eximbank assistance. If Eximbank improves market performance, charging a fair return for its services, these beneficiaries also pay its costs. If, however, the program operates as a material subsidy, then export industries are receiving taxpayer dollars. If too low an interest rate is charged to compensate for the risk of Eximbank loans, and defaults are hidden by deferring recognition, taxpayers accumulate unrecorded liabilities that they will eventually have to redeem. There is nothing to guarantee that subsidies they financed through such a hidden mechanism will serve broad interests of the general public.

The distribution of these benefits is by no means uniform over U.S. export industries. Eximbank activity has been dominated by two industries—aircraft manufacture and power plant construction. Over the last ten years, these have accounted for over half of all Eximbank direct loans.[15] Eximbank financed the bulk of trade credits for foreign sales of domestically produced aircraft; it aided nearly half of all sales of power-generating equipment.[16] The 1982 recession caused a slump in both aircraft and power plant sales, which substantially decreased total Eximbank activity. (Loans for aircraft purchase decreased nearly 90 percent.) The economic recovery caused a rebound in aircraft and utility sales and these industries may soon return to their position of preeminence among those supported by Eximbank.

As might be expected, Eximbank is powerfully supported by the industries whose products it helps to sell. Although it is difficult to assess its impact or its cost, Eximbank has been effectively shielded from fiscal austerity cuts by administrations of all political persuasions.

THE SMALL BUSINESS ADMINISTRATION

A second example of existing credit programs is the set operated by the Small Business Administration (SBA).[17] Established in 1952 to take over the business loan programs of the just-abolished Reconstruction Finance Corporation (RFC), the SBA was founded on the premise that private credit markets would not provide adequate long-term credit to small businesses. When the RFC first came into existence, the banking industry was reluctant to make *any* long-term commercial loans. By the time the RFC passed from the scene in 1952, the rebounding postwar economy had given banks the confidence to extend commercial credit on reasonably long terms—to well-established businesses. The SBA's supporters felt that viable loans, even long-term loans, could be made to small businesses, but that the banking industry simply would not make them. The SBA program was specifically intended for businesses that could not otherwise obtain credit; it requires that its applicants show that they have been rejected for credit elsewhere. This focus on "marginal" borrowers was designed to keep the SBA from competing with the private commercial-banking industry. Nevertheless, the inception of the SBA was opposed by the American Banking Association, apparently because it saw the program as infringing on its members' markets.

The SBA is a sizable influence in the supply of credit to small businesses. Although the SBA is not large by comparison to other federal credit programs, its loans in 1983 exceeded $850 million, and loan guarantees amounted to an additional $2.6 billion. At the close of 1983, the book value of its portfolio of direct loans was $3.3 billion and its outstanding loan guarantees totaled $9.5 billion.[18] Collectively, these programs directly aided over 16,700 businesses. While the SBA provides only a small fraction of all business credit (which totaled over $400 billion in 1983), SBA-sponsored loans are a large fraction of the credit available to small businesses. The SBA concentrates on business loans of more than one year's duration—that is, on *term* loans—and it wields considerable influence within this narrow market. For example, it guarantees about one-fifth of all term lending by banks with assets of less than $100 million.[19]

The SBA's credit activities are not particularly concentrated among any special industrial or commercial class of borrowers. The SBA simply lends across the board to small businesses, seeking assurances of loan viability, but without any particular attention to what sector of the economy the loan serves. The pattern of SBA lending closely approximates the distribution of small-business activity, although it reflects a slightly greater proportion of loans in retail and manufacturing small businesses. To the extent that SBA credit is concentrated, it reflects congressional policy choices about which parts of the small-business community are particularly starved for private credit; the SBA has special loan programs for disadvantaged and minority-owned businesses, and these businesses are overrepresented in SBA loans relative to their proportion among small businesses.[20]

There are two conceptually distinct rationales for the existence of an organization like the SBA. The market may imperfectly provide credit, particularly long-term credit, to some kinds of businesses—small and minority-owned businesses, both aided by the SBA, are frequently cited as examples. To address imperfections, the government could run a profitable demonstration program to show commercial banks that viable loans can be made to these businesses. If, instead, it ran market-perfecting programs at subsidized rates, it would improve market performance but would *not* demonstrate that private banks could profitably take over. Indeed, the provision of subsidized credit in a market-perfecting context will prevent commercial banks from entering, since they will not be able to compete with subsidized terms. If market imperfection is the problem, it can be addressed more successfully without subsidies.

If, however, our society has a long-standing affinity for small businesses —as it appears to have—it might decide to encourage them through subsidies. Many have argued that small businesses are more in keeping with our entrepreneurial spirit, that they are more innovative, that they create more new jobs (and new kinds of jobs) than larger, more established businesses do, that they enhance competition in the marketplace. If this is so—or is perceived to be so—society might support a program explicitly designed to subsidize small businesses.

Both of these rationales have been advanced to justify programs operated by the SBA. The first could—but should not—be used to argue for subsidies; the second demands them. If society decides to subsidize small businesses through credit, it faces two inherent difficulties.

First, it is hard to assess how much of a subsidy is being given. Credit is by its nature risky. Defaults are inevitable, particularly when we target riskier clients than the commercial-banking industry does. Furthermore, some loans not technically in default will in fact not be repaid, and they can be rescheduled so as to avoid technical default. It is difficult to assess the value of a portfolio of loans, and thus it will be difficult to estimate how much of the money we put in will not be returned. If we choose to subsidize through low-interest loans or low-cost credit guarantees, we run the accountability risk of not being able to value the subsidy we have given.

Second, subsidies through credit are difficult to provide efficiently because it is hard to focus their benefits on marginal borrowers. When the SBA extends credit in the form of direct loans and loan guarantees, it must by law find a reasonable prospect of repayment. Borrowers must be reasonably creditworthy—but not so creditworthy that they can obtain credit from traditional sources. The SBA portfolio is supposed to be of higher risk than private commercial loan portfolios, but not of excessively high risk. This target is a narrow window. Winnowing the best risks from among those rejected by traditional credit sources is at best a tricky undertaking.

The difficulty of this task is reflected in the high default rates on SBA loans and loan guarantees. Though the SBA constitutes a small fraction of federal credit activity—2 percent of all direct loans and 2.5 percent of all loan guarantees—it is involved in a much larger proportion of federal loan and loan guarantee write-offs. In 1983, 27 percent of all losses on defaulting direct federal loans were from SBA loans; 17 percent of federal loan guarantee payoffs were for SBA guaranteed loans.[21] The *rate* of default is astronomical by conventional lending standards. About 8.5 percent of both direct loans and loan guarantees outstanding in 1983 defaulted; annual default rates on loans by commercial banks were less than 1 percent. The SBA closed 1982 with more than one-fifth of its existing loans in some stage of delinquency, a rate over twenty times that of standard commercial loan portfolios.[22]

If cost, rather than absolute size, is an indicator of the significance of credit programs, then the SBA is one of the more important federal credit programs. Table 3.4 shows the agencies with highest total defaults in 1983. Only the Federal Housing Administration, with a vastly larger portfolio of outstanding direct and guaranteed loans (the FHA closed 1983 with $165 billion outstanding), had a larger volume of defaulting obligations than the SBA, and it had collateral in the form of housing for some of its uncollectible loans. The Veterans Administration, which had defaults slightly lower than the SBA's, had a portfolio nearly ten times as large. If part of the SBA's mission is to make relatively high-risk loans, then it is succeeding. Whether these loans result in social benefits commensurate with their costs is another matter altogether.

Who does the agency theory of government suggest that the SBA will serve? The direct beneficiaries are the loan recipients and, to some extent, the banks that process the loans and receive interest at about 2.5 percent above the prime rate, all under the protection of federal guarantees. The direct beneficiaries form the benefit constituency, and the banks form the provider constituency. Neither of these two constituencies is a strong lobby for SBA programs, however. Recipients of SBA programs are widely dis-

TABLE 3.4

Loan and Loan Guarantee Defaults for Selected Agencies, 1983
(in billions of dollars)

	FHA	SBA	VA
Loan and loan guarantees outstanding	165	13	121
Defaults	2.1	1.2	1.1

SOURCE: Portfolios: *Budget of the United States Government, Fiscal Year 1985—Appendix.* Defaults: *Budget of the United States Government, Fiscal Year 1985,* Special Analysis F, p. F–34, table F–12.

persed and relatively small in scale. They do not belong to any particular association. Most important, the great majority of SBA loan recipients receive only one loan or guarantee from the SBA. Those who may get an SBA loan do not generally know who they are in advance, and so cannot be expected to organize effectively to support the program. And once they have received a loan, they have no particular continuing interest in the SBA's political fate. (Recipients who are involved in more than one transaction tend to have defaulted on the first. Their original loans are often rescheduled through a rollover into another loan. These beneficiaries may be among the most grateful, and they may receive the greatest benefit, but they hardly constitute an effective political lobby for the program.)

Neither are the banks strong supporters of the SBA's effort. The banking industry no longer opposes the SBA as a competitor; banks discovered that they can profitably push riskier commercial loans than they themselves would make into the pool guaranteed by the SBA, earning high interest and service fees while enjoying the protection of SBA insurance. Although the industry provides congressional testimony favoring the continuation of SBA activities, it does not expend great amounts of energy supporting these programs, nor does it appear to be principally responsible for their continuation. Other legislative priorities command its attention.

What, then, is the political force behind the SBA? Elisabeth Rhyne traces the history of the Reagan administration's largely unsuccessful efforts to trim the SBA's program by imposing mandatory ceilings on loan and loan guarantee activity.[23] She concludes that Congress itself stands behind the SBA. According to Rhyne, the members of congressional committees that authorize and oversee SBA loan activity benefit from the program because of their perceived—and, by all reports, actual—ability to ensure that the constituents in their districts receive their share of SBA loans. Since the loans are supposed to be economically viable, an SBA commitment is not seen as an expenditure of federal funds. Moreover, most observers do not consider it a particularly expensive use of federal authority. Rhyne reviews anecdotal evidence indicating that members of Congress find it useful to have a program that can make loans whenever a viable opportunity arises. Members are secure in the knowledge that constituent proposals will not be turned down as a result of bureaucratic rationing caused by a program ceiling.

This process could be morally and ethically reprehensible, but it need not necessarily be. The program exists to advance credit to reasonably viable small businesses. There is no public evidence that members of Congress pressure the SBA to make loans that appear too risky to fit into the standard SBA portfolio. Some congressmen remind the SBA in program hearings that it is supposed to take on loans that are risky by the lending standards of private commercial banks, but this is general programmatic guidance rather than advice about specific loans. When a small businessman from a congressman's home district presents a viable application, however, the congressman may be able to help by cutting through red tape to get the loan approved faster. This provides a useful demonstration of the member's ability to work the machinery of government for constituents—without any moral or ethical impropriety. But while this process is not necessarily corrupt, it can easily cross the line.

Although the SBA appears to consume only a small amount of public resources, it may actually be quite expensive. The high default rate on SBA loans means that the government does not recover a substantial fraction of the money it lends. This constitutes a hidden subsidy: borrowers try a business venture from which they alone stand to gain; if it fails, however, the government shares their loss. The SBA's programs may be a useful and appropriate subsidy, but they are not free. The fact that the program's support comes from Congress—and is possible partly because it appears inexpensive—frames the central question of whether the program's costs have been appropriately balanced against its benefits and of whose benefits are being balanced against whose costs.

Federal Credit Accounting and the Federal Financing Bank

Credit programs deserve special scrutiny. Even if they do not dominate the overall credit picture, they are the main architects of some important parts of it. As we saw above, the SBA probably increases credit flowing to those small businesses (particularly those owned by disadvantaged groups) whose riskiness is greater than that of businesses served by standard private commercial lenders. Housing credit overall may be little affected, but small corners of housing credit markets have clearly expanded—for example, through special programs for the disadvantaged and handicapped.

Government credit programs have a considerable impact on some credit markets by providing subsidies to some borrowers for some forms of credit. The low level of scrutiny that credit programs generally attract makes them a particularly important exercise of federal authority. Poorly represented in budget documents since their inception in the 1930s, systematically exempted from congressional limitations, these programs have not been very visible or subject to close review. Despite repeated recent attempts to improve accountability, many credit programs remain largely outside the boundaries of budgetary limitation and scrutiny. They have traditionally been thought of and treated as relatively inexpensive government interventions. This misapprehension continues and is permitted (if not validated) by the budgetary reporting of credit programs. Some are excluded entirely from official budget documents. Until very recently, even those included in the federal budget were recorded only in terms of *net* flows—new loans net of those repaid—so that the extension of new credit was not visible.

One measure of the robustness of these programs, or of the effectiveness of their shielding, is the degree to which they survived the Reagan administration's efforts to curtail domestic programs. The level of outstanding obligations in every major category of credit involvement—direct loans, loan guarantees, and credit advanced through government-sponsored enterprises—has grown during the Reagan administration. Opponents of credit programs have been able to give credit activities more prominent recognition in budget documents and budgetary consideration, but the programs themselves survive relatively unscathed. This may be because the payoff from reducing programs that are not fully represented in the budget is relatively low. As long as taxpayers and most other observers focus mainly on the budget deficit, it is not worth expending much political capital to cut programs that are not recorded in the budget or included in deficit calculations.

Credit programs do not fit naturally into a federal accounting system designed to reflect the costs of direct expenditures. The government's accounting system is geared to budgetary appropriations. When the government expends funds (with no anticipated cash return), the direct cost of the program is measured accurately by the resources expended. Taxpayers who want to understand the magnitude of public programs get a reasonably complete picture from a record of the dollars expended and what they bought—provided that the direct expenditures are accounted for comprehensively (for example, that pension promises are funded on a current basis, and so on).

This is decidedly *not* true of credit programs. The amount of credit extended is not necessarily an indication of *cost,* since much of the money will be returned. Moreover, funds flow both in and out; new loans are made while principal and interest payments on old loans are received. Direct expenditure programs have one prime indicator of cost—simple outlays. By contrast, we need at least three separate indicators to get an accurate picture of credit programs. We must know the volume and form of new extensions of credit to assess the magnitude of discretionary commitments of public credit liabilities. We also need to know the *net* expansion of outstanding commitments (new commitments net of repayments of old obligations), in order to observe changes in the current magnitude of accumulated public exposure. Neither of these figures measures the actual cost of credit programs—how much they have used up and will not return. If the $10,000 the government lends a creditworthy borrower in one year is returned with market-rate interest the next, the government has been in the credit business for a year, but no public resources have been expended. If, by contrast, a 5 percent loan is provided to someone for whom the appropriate rate of interest is 15 percent, a public cost of 10 percent of the principal value of the loan has been incurred in the form of forgone interest and risk assumed by the taxpayer. Thus, we need a third measure indicating the value of the subsidy given—its true cost—to complete the picture of the credit program.

Unfortunately, accounting for credit programs is neither integrated nor complete. Credit accounting was originally carried out by extending the existing accounting for direct budgetary expenditures. No distinction was maintained between funds permanently leaving the Treasury to purchase goods and services, on the one hand, and funds temporarily leaving with at least some prospect of returning (with interest), on the other. Agencies were seen as simply disbursing funds for different purposes: some for purchases, others for loans. Loan repayments could be netted against disbursements because the only focus was on the net impact on the Treasury (the amount of net new funds that it had to disburse). This allowed credit programs to develop sizable revolving funds, largely outside the control of the budgetary process. Inflation gradually erodes the economic value of loan funds that are fixed in nominal amount; with continuing inflows of interest and occasional infusions of new funds, however, programs could survive comfortably and quietly for many years. Loan guarantee programs could be authorized without any disbursement whatever. Even when loans threatened to default, some debts could be rescheduled under another loan guarantee, masking the default and preventing an actual disbursement of federal funds.[24] This process led to a practice of debt bulldozing: piling up debts but continually pushing them forward through rescheduling.

Added to the problem of obfuscation were the higher costs incurred as a large number of independent federal agencies issued their own bonds. Before 1974, for example, the Tennessee Valley Authority (TVA) issued its own bonds to finance its construction projects. Though these bonds were full faith and credit obligations of the federal government, essentially identical to official Treasury debt, they were smaller in size and less well known than simple Treasury debt. Therefore, they tended to sell at interest rates slightly above those on Treasury securities of similar duration sold at the same time. This was a waste of federal money; allowing the Treasury to consolidate the smaller issues with its regular borrowing would make the issues more marketable and would consequently reduce the interest rate paid by the government.

The higher cost of these agency bonds was unnecessary; there was a real opportunity to reduce federal costs. In 1974, the Federal Financing Bank (FFB) was established to exploit it by consolidating the debt issues of federal agencies. The FFB and debt consolidation were not silly ideas. The FFB's creation was a straightforward application of sound principles of debt management. The Federal Financing Bank Act of 1974 allows the FFB to purchase bonds, loan assets, or loans guaranteed by other federal agencies. Agencies retain the legal right to issue their own bonds but rarely do so, since borrowing through the FFB is less expensive. Two sources of funds were provided to the FFB. First, it could issue its own bonds, which would be consolidated issues of the separate bonds it purchased. To limit the financing this provided to federal agencies, Congress placed a ceiling of $15 billion on the FFB's total outstanding issues of its own bonds. Second, if the FFB had temporary financing or liquidity problems, it could borrow directly from the Treasury.

In its first issue to the public, in July 1974, the FFB sold $1.5 billion in bonds. Though effectively Treasury bonds, they were priced by the securities market to yield interest one-eighth of a percent higher than that on official Treasury debt issued for the same duration in the same week. The market was not immediately prepared to accept the FFB as the same entity as the Treasury. It continued to distinguish between agency securities (even if consolidated by the FFB) and "real" Treasury debt—even though the FFB was legally, bureaucratically, and physically an arm of the Treasury. (It consisted of a small group of federal employees in an office in the Treasury.)

The response of the board of the FFB was immediate: henceforth the FFB would consolidate agency securities by borrowing the necessary funds directly from the Treasury. At its earliest opportunity, the FFB borrowed from the Treasury to buy back its own issues. Since then it has not issued any of its own bonds; it has financed itself exclusively through short-term borrowing from the Treasury.

Like the idea of the FFB itself, this policy was not intrinsically misguided. The securities market might eventually have accepted the FFB as simply another part of the Treasury, but there was good reason to consolidate the Treasury's debt issues completely, for it further reduced the government's overall cost of debt. The market has only one set of securities—real Treasury bonds—to cope with; there are no more confusing nondistinctions.

The form this consolidation took—the FFB's use of its congressionally authorized short-term borrowing authority—had another, unintended but historic consequence: *it effectively eliminated the borrowing ceiling that Congress had imposed on the FFB's activities.* The limit was on issues of its *own* bonds; no limit had been set on "short-term" FFB borrowing from the Treasury. The FFB's borrowing from the Treasury was unlimited, in order to persuade the market that it was completely creditworthy. The FFB did not need—nor did it seek—any authorization to exceed the $15 billion capitalization limit Congress had imposed, so long as it borrowed from the Treasury and not from the public. Neither did the Treasury need special authorization; some of the funds it borrowed for the FFB were explicitly declared, in the FFB's authorizing legislation, to be off the budget. Since they were not reflected in the account of the official public debt, they did not count against the congressionally imposed statutory limit on the federal debt.

The FFB's debts grew rapidly. By May 1984 the FFB had accumulated outstanding obligations of $139 billion, slightly more than nine times the explicitly authorized capitalization.* The FFB was used as the funnel for 15 percent of the $500 billion increase in public borrowing over the period 1974–1981.[25]

While none of the individual steps taken on the road to creating the FFB was a clear error, the combination significantly weakened the accountability of federal credit activities. The FFB works through three major mechanisms to move commitments of the federal government off the budget. First, it extends loans directly to federal agencies like the TVA, REA, and Eximbank. These funds, borrowed off the budget by the FFB, replenish loan funds of the agencies, thereby moving direct agency loans off the budget. The agencies are solely responsible for repaying these funds (sometimes through additional borrowing). Second, the FFB buys "loan assets" of federal agencies. These consist not of the loans themselves but of "certificates of beneficial ownership" (CBOs)—the right to receive interest and principal repayments from a pool of loans. Until recently, "sales" of CBOs to the FFB (fully guaranteed by the agency, as required by the FFB) were treated like an unguaranteed sale to a private party. The FFB is anything but private; its funds come from the Treasury and are part of public borrowing. If, by contrast, an agency sold a loan it had made to a willing buyer (without a guarantee), then it might properly be viewed as having "unlent" its own funds by substituting money from a private lender. CBO sales to

---

*Obviously, Congress is aware of the activities of the FFB, and could limit it if it chose to. But the device has been found useful and has successfully resisted most attempts to control it more closely.

the FFB are quite different; they involve no change in government obligation—the government is still at risk for the loan repayment. But they were treated as if a private lender had accepted the risk. Loan "sales" were thus a conduit for moving direct agency loans off the budget. This treatment has been discontinued in most cases; sales of CBOs to the FFB, together with the Treasury borrowing to pay for the purchases, are now generally viewed as public borrowing, as they should be.*

The final off-budget mechanism of the FFB is the origination of loans guaranteed by other federal agencies. This is consistent with the FFB's mission of consolidating loans that should be similar to Treasury debt. If a federal agency guarantees a privately issued loan, the borrower has to seek a lender. The lender may not view the loan as entirely riskless and may charge more interest than the Treasury would have to pay on an official debt obligation. Thus, some of the benefit of the guarantee—reducing the interest cost to the borrower—is not received. If the FFB, rather than a private lender, issues these loans, the interest rate can be reduced.† The FFB is therefore authorized to issue funds to individuals and firms who have been granted loan guarantees by other federal agencies. This has the effect of converting loan guarantees (whether on or off the official budget) to direct, off-budget loans.‡

Through these avenues, the FFB's existence has allowed relatively uncontrolled credit activity in some agencies. A startling illustration of the impact of these devices is provided by the pattern of REA direct loans from the 1950s to the present, shown in figure 3.1. In the first twenty-five years of this period, REA direct loans increased slowly and fairly steadily, from about $250 million annually to about $850 million. This growth continued, at approximately the same rate, until 1981, when direct loans processed by REA reached a peak of about $1.1 billion. By contrast, direct loans made by the FFB to REA-guaranteed borrowers—which become, in effect, direct loans from the REA—climbed steeply after the FFB mechanism became available. By 1981, they had reached a level of over $4 billion. Thus, while direct REA loans increased steadily, REA guaranteed loans processed by the FFB soared.

The budgetary treatment of the FFB remains a mystery to some, and a major accounting problem to others. The central problem is that inter-

*This treatment was recommended as early as 1967 by the President's Commission on Budget Concepts. The improper treatment is still explicitly allowed for CBOs of the Farmer's Home Administration and the REA.

†This does, however, eliminate one of the advantages of some loan guarantee programs—forcing the borrower to establish a relationship with a traditional lender (other than the government).

‡A proposal of the Reagan administration would put all new guaranteed loan originations on the budget starting in fiscal year 1985.

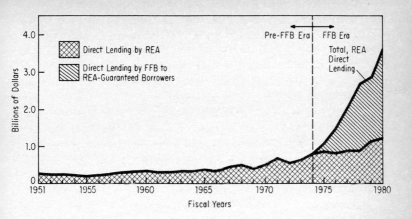

FIGURE 3.1

*New Direct Lending by the Rural Electrification Administration,
Fiscal Years 1951–1980 (end of year)*

SOURCES: *Budget of the United States Government,* Fiscal Years 1952–1982, Special Analyses on Credit;
Congressional Budget Office, *The Federal Financing Bank and the Budgetary Treatment of Federal Credit
Activities,* January 1982, fig. 3, p. 32.

agency transfers, like those between the FFB and other federal agencies,
should be purged from governmental accounts because they do not constitute net flows between the government and other parties. It was to avoid
this double counting that the FFB was initially excluded from government
accounts. The law establishing the FFB provided specifically that its existence would not change the budgetary representation of other programs.
The FFB would merely be an instrument of sensible debt management; it
would not, by itself, cause—nor would it solve—problems of budgetary
representation.

This would be fine if all other government accounting were perfect. Some
agencies, however, are not required to record all of their credit transactions
in budget documents. Excluding their financing transactions with the FFB
means that some credit activities remain outside the "unified" budget—the
most comprehensive record of government activities. The FFB made easier
(and somewhat cheaper) the end run that these credit programs (most
notably the REA and the Farmer's Home Administration) were making
around the budget.

The FFB also exacerbated an existing problem with the representation
of loan guarantees. Since the extension of a guarantee does not immediately

(and may never) involve the disbursement of funds, loan guarantees are not treated as "outlays" in budget documents; they are noted and controlled separately. Direct loans, at least for on-budget agencies, *are* considered part of outlays and are generally counted in budget totals. With the inception of the FFB, however, off-budget loan guarantees can be converted to off-budget direct loans. Thus, direct loans of the federal government are included in budget totals (for most agencies) if they are made directly by the agency, but excluded if they are made by the FFB pursuant to the issue of a loan guarantee by the same agency. From the borrower's—and the taxpayer's—perspective, the financial aspects of the two loans are identical. But they are represented altogether differently in the budget documents considered by Congress. Moreover, through the mechanism of CBO sales to the FFB, even some direct agency loans can be moved off the budget.

The FFB is in most respects an appropriate tool of federal debt management. By consolidating a variety of agency debt issues, it reduces the total cost of federal borrowing. The FFB has also, however, allowed the budgetary representation of credit programs, never exemplary, to be further obscured. It hides the magnitude and cost of important federal credit programs. Some view this as largely accidental; others argue that the FFB's "incidental" benefits are hardly lost on Congress.

The traditional federal accounting treatment for credit—including the initial extension of credit in budget outlays in the year in which the loan is made—considerably overstates the actual budgetary cost for most loan programs, since some of the funds and some interest will be returned.[26] The appearance of high budgetary cost if loans are included in outlays may have spurred the search for mechanisms to lower the profile of loan programs to a level more in line with their actual budgetary cost. The FFB device, although it certainly lowers the profile of loan programs, does not exactly represent them in proportion to their cost; it does not represent them at all.

Reforming the Treatment of Federal Credit

It is intrinsically difficult to measure the costs of credit activities and to present them in a form commensurate with that of direct expenditures. Congress observes that a dollar expended is almost always more costly than a dollar lent, and it seeks a budgetary treatment for credit dollars that lowers their profile accordingly. The extension of credit is not costless, however, as many off-budget accounting devices make it seem. Until recently, many credit programs were not shown at all in the budget documents considered by Congress. Much progress has been made in designing a "credit budget" that records new outlays, net outlays, and loan guarantee extensions. Some of these reforms have been bitterly resisted, and many are still in the works. For example, the Reagan administration proposed to establish a binding appropriations ceiling for SBA lending for the first time in fiscal year 1985 (there is already a binding authorization). On the other hand, some programs of the Rural Electrification and Farmer's Home administrations are still completely off the budget. The general direction—moving toward a more complete budget representation of credit activities —is encouraging.

Credit programs attain an odd mix of accountability levels. Budget disbursements are controlled through the appropriations process. But, until recently, only *net* disbursements were controlled, which gave many programs wide and almost unscrutinized discretion. Even now, the appropriations process controls flows of funds, not flows of *costs,* so credit appropriations are not comparable to funds appropriated for direct disbursements. And some credit programs are still not on the budget. Generally, the subsidy element of credit programs falls short of the constitutional norm of accountability.

Considerable information about credit programs is published annually Most programs are reasonably well described in the budget, and an entire special-analysis section of the budget is devoted to describing both on- and off-budget credit activities. The Congressional Budget Office releases an annual analysis of the "credit budget." The "unified" budget now considered by Congress shows credit flows next to direct outlay requests for most programs.

But the most glaring problem of federal credit accountability remains: the information is about the wrong measures. Nowhere in the current budget documents is there any systematic information about the *cost* of credit extended. Heavily subsidized loans for rural housing and rural electrification issued at rates of 3 to 5 percent are added one for one with virtually unsubsidized 13 percent FHA loans to obtain totals of credit activities. The government currently borrows for the REA and FmHA at rates of 8 to 12 percent and lends at 3 to 5 percent, thus directly losing 5 to 7 percent of the value of principal outstanding *each year.* FHA transactions, by contrast, have little if any direct cost to the government. By adding such figures together (and then adding them to direct expenditure figures), we arrive at a total that is meaningful only as a measure of the total amount of money that flowed through the government; it bears little relation to the cost of government services provided. If costs are to be balanced against perceived benefits, as accountability demands, then we must evaluate the costs of all programs in the same units.

IMPROVE COST INFORMATION

Calculating the costs of credit programs is complicated—but not wholly out of reach. To aggregate the costs of credit properly with the costs of other government activities, the flows of credit must be converted into units of cost rather than outlays. In any credit program, one measure of the cost to the government is the subsidy to the recipient. The subsidy element in credit programs is obscure; it involves some combination of lower interest payments, less stringent collateral requirements, or longer payment terms. The latter two can, in theory, be converted into an equivalent lower interest rate, so that all three can be reduced to one measure of subsidy. The problem is to take the complex terms of the loan agreement, adjust for the creditworthiness of the borrower, and convert them into the equivalent of a direct expenditure payment.

In principle, this is straightforward. The government is extending credit to a borrower, either through a direct loan or through a loan guarantee. It could instead find another credit supplier, perhaps a private bank, and arrange private credit on the same terms. If the terms of the federal loan are subsidized, the private lender will not be willing to make the loan on those terms; it will require an inducement. The smallest amount that the government would have to pay the private lender to make the loan on those terms is an appropriate measure of the size of the subsidy being provided.

In practice, this is not so simple. The subsidy is the difference between the value of payments the recipient will make under the government loan and the value of payments to be made if the loan were obtained in the private market. The private loan rate would depend in turn on the creditworthiness of the borrower, reflecting the risk of default. To assess the public cost of credit requires an estimate of the market interest rate that would prevail for each borrower served in each of the many credit programs. Developing such an estimate is an immense task.

This is not all that is required. It might seem that we can compute the difference in value of the payment streams by taking the difference in the interest rates and multiplying by the amount of principal outstanding in each year of the loan. But the essence of credit programs is that loans are risky. The higher private market rate reflects the fact that some loans will default. Thus, both of the payment streams we are trying to value (in order to be able to find the difference) are uncertain. Moreover, there is probably a better chance that the lower payment stream will be repaid, so the payment streams do not even have the same degree of riskiness. Ignoring the risk in both streams (by simply comparing their interest rates) would overstate the expected difference between them and miscalculate the value of the subsidy.[27]

How should credit subsidies be measured? First, principles developed in theoretical finance could be applied. This method would assess the differing values of payment streams with and without government involvement.[28] Accurate in principle, but conceptually difficult, this method is likely to be politically unconvincing in the short run. It nonetheless deserves continued research and may eventually provide the best answers. Second, we could simply assess the difference in interest rates with and without government credit and multiply it by the principal outstanding in each year. This method, described above, is essentially that used by the OMB to develop its estimates of the subsidy costs of direct loan programs.[29] With improved data on direct loans and substantially more comprehensive information on loan guarantees, this approach would permit a better estimation of the borrowing costs government credit clients would face on the private market. It shows promise of providing a reasonably accurate assessment of credit program costs on a basis comparable to the costs reported for direct expenditure programs.

These methods share an important disadvantage: the costs they estimate are not directly related to appropriated flows of funds. They are estimates, not disbursements. Both methods would indicate program costs and permit more accurate comparisons among credit programs and of credit programs to direct expenditures. But the cost figures would be side calculations, not amounts that would have to be appropriated.

Either method could, however, be the basis for credit limitations. For example, Congress could require a given credit program to make loans with a subsidy cost not exceeding a specified limit, assessed according to a stated method. This would give costs of credit programs both a ceiling and a higher profile. Moreover, this limitation would parallel those used for direct expenditure programs and could be implemented by integrating credit budget accounting with direct expenditures. Once they were represented by cost of subsidy rather than by flows of credit dollars, credit programs could be presented with (and added to) direct expenditures.*

---

*Alternatively, the budgeted costs could be presented separately, since there would be no requirement to appropriate the funds for the subsidy costs. In this respect, this method is similar to that currently used for tax expenditures; estimates of the costs of tax expenditure programs are computed but are presented separately from direct expenditures because they do not require appropriations. Tax expenditures and the tax expenditure budget will be discussed in chapter 4.

REQUIRE APPROPRIATIONS FOR SUBSIDIES

One approach that will reveal the size of the government subsidy—and force Congress to confront it—is simply to pay private suppliers to provide the credit.* For direct loans, this means selling the loan contracts, with no government guarantee. When loans involve a subsidy, they will sell for less than the amount of the funds the government advanced; this loss in value is an assessment of the subsidy provided. For loan guarantees, loan insurance must be purchased from private insurers. The amount of the premium the government has to pay to obtain the guarantees it has issued, net of the premiums the government charged, is a direct measure of the subsidy provided to the recipient.

Accounting for these transactions would fit readily into the existing framework of direct expenditures. The effect of selling the loan assets and netting the proceeds against loan disbursements is precisely to convert the credit flows into current dollar expenditures that represent direct program costs.† These costs are directly comparable to noncredit expenditures. They could be appropriated in the same way. Limits could be set on the maximum subsidy to be provided by a given program, where the subsidy is the amount of direct payments to private credit suppliers providing credit on terms and to borrowers chosen by the programs. This process would integrate credit accounting with the budgetary accounting for direct expenditure programs—a task that has eluded every recent administration.

This market approach will work only if the private market has accurate information about borrowers. If, for example, the purpose of a federal credit program is to compensate for private underestimation of the viability of loans made to a particular class of borrowers (such as small businesses, students, or foreign governments buying military equipment), then the subsidy measure revealed through the market will overstate the actual subsidy provided. Since many government credit programs are portrayed as a response to market failure, the private sale of loans or the purchase of guarantees by the government cannot be universally applied. Where it can be used, however, this measure is probably the most accurate assessment of credit subsidies. Moreover, and perhaps most important, it would promote credit spending to the appropriations level.

---

*This might also improve program performance by getting private lenders to monitor the activities of those who borrow through the government.

†It should be emphasized again that the assets must be sold without any government guarantee that would enhance their value over the pure private market value we are trying to assess.

Whatever method is adopted for heightening credit accountability, credit programs desperately need an appropriate profile of cost information in the budget. A mechanism requiring congressional appropriation of funds equal to the subsidies provided would further boost budgetary discipline. But the prerequisite—recognizing credit program costs in the budget—has eluded two decades of government credit program reformers. Mere budgetary recognition of the programs themselves has been difficult to obtain and is not yet universal. Those closely involved have found it useful to have credit programs be obscure and appear inexpensive. Recipients have no doubts about the benefits they receive through credit programs. Accountability demands balancing these benefits against perceived costs—which are difficult, but not impossible, to assess. The dismal record of credit program accounting and representation in budget documents leaves a gaping hole in the accountability structure.

Prospects for Federal Credit Accountability

Credit programs have long been a thorn in the side of budget and fiscal reformers. The extension of subsidized credit is a particularly popular exercise of federal authority. There are many reasons for this; the main rationale advanced by supporters is that credit assistance is for some purposes the most directly useful and efficient form of help the government can give. If this is true, there is no reason to protect credit programs from scrutiny or to hide them behind the off-budget shield of the Federal Financing Bank. The existence of these shields is partly a response to the awkward mismatch of credit programs with the accounting system designed for direct expenditure programs. That system overstates the apparent cost of credit programs by focusing on their outlays. But treating them in the opposite way—treating only their net outlays or ignoring them entirely—is no solution.

Devices that obscure the volume and cost of credit programs tend to have more to do with the interests of the benefit, provider, and political constituencies than with the interests of the public. Credit is a problematic form of federal largess, because its costs can easily be obscured. Funds need not be appropriated to cover losses when the government borrows at one rate and lends at a lower one. The costs of loans entering delinquency can be masked by rescheduling the debt or issuing new loans to repay the old ones. Guaranteed loan extensions and "loan asset" sales to the FFB can move otherwise controlled loan activities into the netherworld of the off-budget. And the complex role of credit in modern economies—its sources, uses, and impacts —makes assessment of the costs or the effects of government credit programs extremely difficult.

The lack of information about costs or impacts, the incomplete accounting, and the weak budgetary treatment of credit programs combine to make federal loans and guarantees seem virtually costless. Many interests are well served by these arrangements, and those who oppose them find the great scope, variation, volume, and detail of the federal credit machine daunting. The path of serious reform is littered with great obstacles—and the hopes of past reformers.

Chapter 4

Federal Tax Expenditures

AMERICANS have a love-hate relationship with tax breaks. Everyone loves the breaks he can take but always suspects that others—with smarter tax lawyers and more income to hide—are taking more. It is hard to know who is getting them; tax breaks do their best work in the dark. When governments support activities by issuing checks, it is usually easy to identify the activity, the recipient, and the amount of support. All three are in doubt when the support comes through tax breaks.

The tax system is defined in terms of a base (like income, consumption, sales, or wealth) and a set of tax rates. It also incorporates a variety of exemptions, deductions, and other deviations. When the tax system is adjusted to reduce tax payments by people or corporations who engage in a favored activity, the effect (on both those who pay the lower taxes and the public treasury) is very similar to that of an explicit grant. Deviations from the general tax code, then, can be treated in much the same way as public expenditures. For this reason, they are known as tax expenditures. The concept of tax expenditures provides a way of comparing direct public expenditures to tax provisions subsidizing publicly valued actions.[1]

Tax expenditures can offer a number of important advantages over equivalent payments in the form of direct grants. Tax expenditures are decentralized in application; taxpayers decide whether to engage in the subsidized activity, and they claim their subsidies through tax returns. Typically, no applications are required.* Tax-subsidized programs largely administer

---

*Sometimes, however, the activity must be certified as being qualified. For example, nonprofit organizations supported through tax exemptions must file with the Internal Revenue Service to demonstrate that they meet exemption requirements.

themselves. Their authorization is also simple; funds need not be appro
priated, nor do they need to be reviewed from year to year. They can
(sometimes) be targeted easily and precisely to support specific activities

For essentially all of the same reasons, the accountability of tax expendi
tures is particularly suspect. We do not have an accurate picture of who
receives them. Once an activity is made tax exempt, it may not even have
to be reported. We often do not know the scale of the activity we are
supporting, its beneficiaries, or the revenue losses associated with it. Fur
thermore, tax expenditures are shielded from review. The tax code is no
revised every year; once a tax preference has been established, it does no
require reauthorization and new appropriations, as do direct expenditure
programs. Moreover, tax expenditures are entitlement programs; all qua
lified applicants are granted benefits without reference to any ceiling. Like
other entitlement programs, their spending may therefore be hard to con
trol. Tax subsidies are also treated separately from those authorized as
direct grants. They are overseen by the tax committees rather than by the
authorizing committees, and their actions will not necessarily be coor
dinated. They do not directly compete with direct expenditures, and they
may not be held to the same standards of scrutiny. Since no funds need be
appropriated, tax subsidies seem less expensive. The distinction in treatmen
may be the central issue of tax expenditures: they are identical in force and
effect to direct payments without competing against direct expenditures or
being limited by the spending totals set by Congress.

While funds for the federal tax expenditure spending program are no
appropriated, considerable information is made available about the levels of
tax expenditure spending. Are tax expenditures therefore valuable and
accountable uses of public power? One view is that tax expenditures are used
because they can be precisely targeted and administered at low cost—that is
because they are efficient subsidies.* According to the positive view of tax
expenditures, the decentralized, self-electing nature of tax expenditures is a
virtue because it provides a mechanism for fostering publicly desirable
activities without a large and intrusive grant approval bureaucracy.†

The agency theory of government suggests an alternative view. Tax ex
penditures serve the interests of those whose activities are subsidized, and
are often supported by both beneficiary and provider constituencies. The
fact that no large, highly visible federal agency is required to administer

*The "efficiency" of tax subsidies is substantially lessened when the overhead costs—
lawyers' and accountants' fees—are considered, but the advocates of this view suggest that the
savings in reduced bureaucracy easily compensate for these costs.

†Actually, this distinction is less sharp than it appears; with tax expenditures, there is stil
an approval process—the tax return audit—but it is done after the fact, is not universal, and
in most cases, is carried out less visibly.

them makes it harder to mobilize opposition to them. According to this view, tax expenditures provide a fertile setting for unaccountable activity. For example, tax credits for installing energy-saving equipment help homeowners pay for investments that reduce their heating bills, and also benefit equipment manufacturers and installers. The energy investment credit is thus backed by homeowners, manufacturers, and installers. Its benefits are visible; only its costs are obscured.

The Reagan administration recently launched a concerted attack on tax expenditures. Arguing that the tax code is too complex, too riddled with tax breaks—and that as a consequence tax rates are too high—tax reformers have tried to rally bipartisan support for "tax simplification." Reagan has reportedly made revision of the income tax a central initiative of his second-term domestic policy. Tax expenditures have been assailed for forcing poor and middle-class Americans to pay higher taxes to make up for revenues lost to the tax shelters of the rich. Tax breaks have been branded triumphs of "special interest politics."

The administration's proposal takes on all tax expenditures together. Sentiment for tax simplification has been growing for years. It has arisen in part because reformers have found it difficult to win political battles against individual tax expenditures. Each tax break is easier to defend if there are others like it. Each may correspondingly be easier to cut if the reduction is part of a package attacking the generic device. Once a few specially targeted tax breaks are permitted, the cry of "me, too," is hard to ignore. If successful, the administration's strategy would force competition *among* tax expenditures. As proposed, it would significantly alter many long-standing features of the federal income tax. Rates would be lowered, and there would be three tax brackets instead of fourteen. A wide variety of existing deductions and exemptions would be expunged.[2]

The national political debate on tax simplification has barely been joined, but some of its sociology is already clear. The Treasury's proposal is the product of negotiation, not just of principle. The ostensible purpose of treating all tax expenditures together is to avoid having to negotiate them one by one—to be able to appeal to principles of economics and taxation rather than deal with the politics of each deduction separately. But there is no way to exclude them all, and as soon as some are readmitted, there is no longer any generic principle upon which *any* can be automatically excluded. One-by-one negotiation unavoidably reemerges.

The tax expenditures that so far seem to be holding their own in the competition reflect the power of different constituencies that support this form of quiet spending. The homeowners' deduction for mortgage interest and the depletion allowances for oil and gas production both seem to be faring well. The mortgage interest deduction is intensely supported by a broad group of taxpayers, as Jimmy Carter discovered to his cost when he made an offhand remark questioning its value during the 1976 campaign. This deduction may not be as beneficial as many of its supporters believe it benefits mainly middle-class homeowners, and it may spur overinvestment in housing at the expense of investment in other industries. Nevertheless, there was never any question of excluding it from the Reagan tax plan public consent for the mortgage interest deduction may be misinformed, but it is not in doubt.

It would be hard to show anything like the same kind of sentiment supporting the tax breaks for investors in oil and gas tax shelters. Though the Administration's proposal forces competition among tax expenditures, it ultimately recognizes—quite realistically—that some will be retained. Some of those that will survive are supported by overpowering public consent, others by overpowering narrow political interests.

The administration's package represents the most realistic proposal for major overhaul of the income tax code since its inception in 1913. Its form suggests an interesting paradox: tax expenditures may be politically stronger individually than they are as a group. Whatever success the administration's sweeping tax reform effort eventually enjoys, the tax expenditure device will remain part of the fiscal landscape. Indeed, when all the sound and fury of the current tax simplification effort has died down, it appears that Congress will have made only a few minor changes in the broad array of existing tax expenditures. Having failed to increase revenues by closing loopholes, Congress will be forced to raise corporate taxes to finance the widely promised reduction in individual income tax rates. Tax expenditures appear to have largely survived the most concerted modern effort to reduce them. Quiet spending through the tax code has evolved quite naturally, and the struggle to make it accountable illustrates the collision of broad general interests with powerfully concentrated economic forces.

Federal tax expenditures provide a classic example of using information and analysis to try to ensure accountability. Here, then, is a test case for whether information about these activities, by itself, provides a sufficient accountability safeguard. Revenue losses from tax expenditures have been estimated for the last seventeen years. The issues of what constitutes a tax expenditure and what is simply a part of the basic tax system have been debated. Techniques for estimating revenue losses have been developed and refined. The tax expenditure budget (TEB) has figured in congressional debates about tax reform, and it may have helped to limit expansion and reduce the scale of some tax expenditures. But the tax expenditure device has shown itself to be remarkably robust. Most of the tax expenditures listed in the original TEB are still in force. Revenue losses continue to increase. Does this indicate that the tax expenditure device is an effective policy tool —when responsibly employed—that withstands appropriate TEB scrutiny? Or does it simply tell us that information is a poor substitute for the competition over scarce funds forced by the appropriations process?

The Evolution of Tax Expenditures

Subsidies have long been provided through the tax code.[4] The first federal income tax expenditures came in with the first general income tax law. The 1913 income tax law allowed income tax deductions for mortgage interest paid by homeowners, state and local property taxes on owner-occupied homes, and other nonbusiness state and local taxes. These deductions have remained essentially unchanged ever since. None would be permitted under a comprehensive definition of the income tax base.* The revenue losses for these three exceptions amounted to over $50 billion in 1982. The deductibility of charitable contributions, which now costs the federal Treasury over $8 billion annually, dates from the Revenue Act of 1917. Depreciation on business assets—the decrease in the value of machinery and other business property as it is used—is properly deductible from receipts in figuring income subject to tax. But when deductions are allowed in excess of the rate at which the assets are actually used up—that is, faster than "economic depreciation"—then income is sheltered from tax in the early years of ownership. This excess is a tax expenditure. "Accelerated" depreciation schedules became a feature of the federal tax code in 1946 and have been modified many times since; they now cost the Treasury over $10 billion each year.† Special tax allowances that reduce the cost of (and thereby encourage) some activities have been prominent in the federal income tax code from its inception.

Revenue losses associated with tax expenditures have grown steadily in absolute terms and as a percentage of federal revenues, federal outlays, and

*Technically, under the purest definition of the income tax base, homeowners would have to declare "imputed rent" as income but could then deduct mortgage interest and property taxes as "costs" of "earning" it. Unless we seriously contemplate including imputed rent in income, none of these deductions would be allowed.

†Using "cost" in this way may sound odd. It means lost revenue relative to what would be raised in the absence of the "loopholes." How do we lose by not paying taxes? We lose when only some of us are not paying taxes.

the GNP. Table 4.1 shows the progress of tax expenditure revenue losses since the first comprehensive listing was prepared in 1967. Revenue losses in 1967 were $37 billion; by 1984 they had risen to $327 billion, or nearly ninefold. The rise has been particularly steep recently. Tax expenditures are now about half as large as total revenues, and are nearly 10 percent of the GNP. Of each dollar of total federal "spending" (defined to include only the sum of direct outlays and tax expenditures), nearly thirty cents is now distributed indirectly on the tax side of the budget, rather than the direct expenditures side.

Tax expenditures support a myriad of different activities. The distribution across areas, however, is uneven. Table 4.2 shows some of the larger tax expenditures, grouped by the activity they subsidize. Saving for retirement absorbs nearly one-third of all tax expenditures; deductions are permitted for pension contributions, and tax capture of the earned interest is deferred until retirement. Subsidies for investment account for nearly the next fifth of the tax expenditures; these operate through preferential treatment for some kinds of earnings (capital gains), through deferred recognition of current income (accelerated depreciation), and through direct investment tax credits. Homeownership is also strongly encouraged by the tax code; over one-eighth of the tax expenditure budget is spent to reduce the costs of mortgage interest and of property and capital gains taxes faced by homeowners. Three-fifths of all tax expenditures are in these three areas.

Other large tax expenditure subsidies include state and local tax payments and health insurance premiums. The federal government spends more than $20 billion on each of these programs annually.

The distribution of tax expenditures is quite different from that of direct expenditures. Table 4.3 shows the composition of federal outlays and tax expenditures for 1984, classified by the eighteen functional categories traditionally used to report federal spending. Perhaps the most striking difference is in the area of commerce and housing credit, which has an extremely small outlay component (less than $500 million) but contains the second- and third-largest tax expenditures (those subsidizing investment and housing). The tax expenditure share that goes for general fiscal assistance to other levels of government is also substantially higher than the outlay share for this function. This reflects the large subsidy the federal government gives to state and local governments by excluding the interest on their debt from the definition of taxable income and by permitting the deduction of state and local government taxes from income before federal tax is computed. In the other direction, the defense program is a much larger component of direct outlays than of tax expenditures; it is a function carried out by government employees rather than by encouraging private activity.

TABLE 4.1

Tax Expenditure Revenue Losses, 1967–1984
(billions of current dollars)

	1967	1971	1975	1979	1984
Total tax expenditure revenue losses*	37	52	93	150	327
Federal outlays	166	212	326	505	848
Total outlays plus tax expenditures ("spending")	203	264	418	655	1,175
GNP (billions of dollars)	777	1,032	1,480	2,418	3,642
Federal outlays as a percentage of GNP	21	21	22	21	23
Federal "spending" as a percentage of GNP	26	26	28	27	32
Tax expenditures as a percentage of					
Revenues	24	25	33	32	50
Outlays	22	24	29	30	39
Spending	18	20	22	23	28
GNP	5	5	6	6	9

*Revenue loss estimates are not strictly additive, as is explained later in this chapter. Totals are presented here to provide a comparison with other budget aggregates.
SOURCES: Congressional Budget Office, *Tax Expenditures,* November 1982, p. 12, table 3, and October 1983; *Budget of the United States Government, Fiscal Year* 1985.

TABLE 4.2

Tax Expenditure Revenue Losses, 1984

	Subsidized activity:		
Retirement			
Pension contributions	$60.8 billion		
Social security	22.3		
Life insurance	7.4		
Total, retirement		$ 90.5 billion	(28%)
Investment			
Capital gains treatment	$16.3 billion		
Accelerated depreciation	15.9		
Investment tax credit	15.7		
Other	10.9		
Total, investment		58.8	(18%)
Homeownership			
Mortgage interest	$27.9 billion		
Property taxes	9.5		
Capital gains treatment	4.9		
Total, homeownership		42.3	(13%)
State taxes		21.8	(7%)
Health insurance		21.3	(7%)
Municipal bond interest		11.7	(4%)
Charitable contributions		6.8	(2%)
Other		74.3	(23%)
Total*		$327.5 billion	(100%)

*Revenue loss estimates for tax expenditures are not strictly additive, as is explained later in this chapter. The sum is presented here to provide a gross indication of magnitude.
SOURCE: Congressional Budget Office, *Tax Expenditures,* October 1983, table A–1.

TABLE 4.3

Outlay and Tax Expenditure Distributions by Functional Category, 1984

Category	Outlays (percent)	Tax Expenditures (percent)
National defense	28	1
International affairs	2	1
General space, science, technology	1	1
Energy	0	1
Natural resources and environment	1	1
Agriculture	1	1
Commerce and housing credit	0	40
Transportation	3	0
Community and regional development	1	0
Education, training, employment, and social services	3	6
Health	10	8
Income security	32	28
Veterans benefits and services	3	1
Administration of justice	1	0
General government	1	0
General purpose fiscal assistance	1	11
Interest	12	0
Total	100	100

NOTE: Allowances and offsetting receipts are not included in outlays. Detail may not add to totals because of rounding. "0" means less than .5 percent.
SOURCE: Joint Committee on Taxation, *Estimates of Federal Tax Expenditures for Fiscal Years 1983–1988; Budget of the United States Government, Fiscal Year 1985.*

The form and functional distribution of federal tax expenditures tell little about who really receives them. Although it is impossible to identify the income of some recipients of tax benefits, the Treasury prepared a "best" estimate of the distribution of tax expenditure benefits across income categories in 1982. Table 4.4 shows the percentage of tax expenditure benefits for which the distribution could reasonably be estimated in each income category, together with the percentage of income tax liability in that bracket. Tax expenditure benefits are slightly less concentrated than are tax liabilities among taxpayers with incomes between $10,000 and $30,000; they are considerably more heavily concentrated than taxes among low-income taxpayers, and perhaps marginally more among taxpayers with incomes over $50,000. The aggregate impact of tax expenditures, then, is to increase the relative tax burden on middle-income classes, with the benefits flowing mainly to the very poor and (slightly) to the moderately rich.*

At an aggregate level, the distribution of tax expenditures parallels that

*The poor do well primarily because of the heavy subsidies given to retirement savings. The low tax rates faced by the poor generally imply low revenue losses from tax subsidies targeted toward them.

TABLE 4.4

*Distribution of Tax Expenditure Benefits and Income Tax
Liability across Income Categories, 1982*

Income Category (thousands of 1982 dollars)	Tax Expenditure Benefits (percent)	Income Tax Liability (percent)
Less than 10	8	3
10–15	5	6
15–20	6	8
20–30	17	21
30–50	30	30
50–100	20	18
100–200	8	8
200 and over	6	6
Total	100	100

SOURCE: Congressional Budget Office, *Tax Expenditures,* November 1982, tables E-1 and E-2. Figures originally developed by the Treasury, on request of the Joint Economic Committee.

of taxes. Tax expenditures principally affect specific activities like home-ownership, investment in physical assets or municipal bonds, and so on. Some of these activities are heavily concentrated among the rich, others elsewhere in the income distribution—the tax benefits of homeownership, for instance, are concentrated in the middle-income classes. Still others are distributed widely across income classes—the nontaxability of employer-paid medical insurance is an example. All together, the impacts tend to average out. This does not imply that some individual tax expenditures are not heavily concentrated, for many are.*

Mechanisms for Accountability of Tax Expenditures:
The Tax Expenditure Budget

Tax expenditures are a major component of the federal government's activity. One would be considerably misled about the extent, expense, and distribution of federal subsidy programs if only direct expenditure programs were studied and the tax system were thought of as simple and general. The

*For example, the benefits of favorable treatment of retirement saving flow mainly to the poor, mortgage interest subsidies to the middle class, and capital gains treatment to the wealthy.

myriad—and costly—special provisions of the tax code have not gone unnoticed. Since the 1960s, tax reformers have urged closer scrutiny of special-interest provisions of the tax code. Starting in 1968, various executive and congressional offices developed comprehensive lists of tax expenditures and the revenue losses they entail. The first "tax expenditure budget" (TEB) was produced for a 1967 Treasury report. TEBs are now published annually, as the Congressional Budget Act of 1974 requires, by the OMB, by the Congressional Budget Office, and by the Joint Committee on Taxation.[5] Until recently, there has been remarkable consensus on the meaning and method of estimating these budgets, and the three documents have reported essentially identical figures.

The care that has gone into constructing the TEB, and the length of time it has been produced on a consistent basis, makes tax expenditures the quintessential example of a spending program that relies on information rather than appropriations for accountability. Tax expenditures avoid the appropriations process but nevertheless receive devoted attention from observers and substantial circulation of relevant analytic information. The TEB process is an experiment in the "sunshine" approach to accountability: tax-writing committees consider the creation, termination, or modification of tax expenditures, and their decisions are duly recorded, separately but prominently, in documents of the executive and Congress. Starting with the fiscal year 1986 budget, TEB spending is reported in the official budget alongside direct expenditures. True, the TEB need not be voted on. It consists of a set of calculations, carried out on the side, estimating the magnitude of public funds being disbursed through the tax side of the budget. No more comprehensive process of review, publication, and scrutiny is carried on anywhere except within the official budget.

Has this process worked? Has it limited the creation of unwise tax expenditures or the extension of old ones? Has it brought the demise of existing tax preferences? It is very hard to tell. We cannot run experiments on budgetary systems, so we know little about what might have existed in the absence of the TEB system we have. Tax expenditures grew, even under TEBs, steadily and essentially without interruption, at least through 1981. In 1982, facing substantial budgetary pressure, Congress set to work on both sides of the budget. Revenue targets were set, and the tax committees were made painfully aware that reductions in tax expenditures were the preferred way to close fiscal gaps. It looked as though tax expenditures would begin to seem like real money. A strong sentiment to avoid raising taxes led to a tax-side search for "revenue enhancements"—devices for raising revenues without passing new taxes or increasing tax rates. This meant finding loopholes in the existing tax system that could be closed in the interest of fairness, or because they had outlived their usefulness, or because they were unintended, or because they appeared inefficient—or just because they cost money.

This search eventually centered on tax code provisions that had been duly reported for years in both executive and congressional TEBs. Substantial additional revenues were found—or at least projected—from modifications of existing tax expenditures. Limits were placed on the extent to which some existing tax benefits could be used. For example, the investment tax credit was limited so that taxpayers could use it to offset only 85 percent of their tax liabilities; unemployment compensation exemptions were limited for high-income families; the use of tax-exempt state and local bonds to finance private activities was restricted. But when all was said and done, tax reform's bark was much worse than its bite. Estimated tax expenditures were cut by over $100 billion for fiscal years 1983–1987, which still left about $1.5 trillion in tax expenditures over those five years. Only $11 billion of the cuts were scheduled for fiscal year 1984. This represents a reduction of less than 3.5 percent in tax expenditures for 1984. There were no substantial changes in major tax expenditures.

The $11 billion cut was only one component in a deficit reduction package designed to close a substantial gap between revenues and outlays. Given the limited success of the overall effort, it could hardly be said that the failure was largely or even significantly due to any special resistance to tax expenditure reductions. Even if TEBs cannot guarantee accountability, they provide a framework for debate about tax reforms and data on revenue losses from existing tax expenditures that can be used to evaluate proposed modifications. In the absence of this information and structure, the entire process in 1982 would surely have been more cumbersome, less accurate, and less effective. The TEB is a prerequisite to, although not necessarily a guarantee of, accountable use of the tax expenditure device.

Nonetheless, it would be difficult to conclude that the TEB device has been thoroughly effective. Neither in number, nor in the amount of revenue loss, nor in proportion to GNP have tax expenditures decreased substantially in any period since systematic review began in 1968. Fifty tax expenditure items were listed in the first TEB; there are now more than twice that many. The introduction of TEBs does not appear to have altered the historical trajectory of tax expenditure spending. Perhaps this means that most tax expenditures were fully accountable even in the absence of TEB scrutiny and that no changes were needed. Or perhaps pressures for tax expenditure largess increased at about the time the first TEB was developed, and without it we would have seen an even greater increase in tax expenditures. A simpler explanation is that TEBs are not enough, by themselves, to control tax expenditures.

Limitations of the Tax Expenditure Budget

Identifying tax expenditures and estimating the associated revenue losses are complicated tasks, both technically and politically. It is easy to state in very general terms what we mean by tax expenditures. The Congressional Budget Act of 1974, which mandates the compilation of TEBs, defines tax expenditures as "revenue losses attributable to provisions of the Federal tax laws which allow a special exclusion, exemption, or deduction from gross income or which provide a special credit, a preferential rate of tax or a deferral of liability." Stanley Surrey, who did much to popularize the concept of tax expenditures and who was the original architect of the Treasury TEB, argued that the tax code consists of two separable parts. The first gives a general definition of the tax base and rates of taxation. These are the "structural" features of the tax system, which define the baseline "normal" or "reference" tax system. The second part sets forth exclusions, deductions, and other atypical treatments provided for specially identified, narrow portions of the general tax base. These are the tax expenditures.

Once we get beyond these generalities, however, ambiguity takes over. It is hard to tell what provisions actually create tax expenditures. The "married couple" deduction provides a good example. When the two members of a married couple earn similar incomes, they pay more tax under our current tax system (without the two-earner deduction) than if they were single. The system is a disincentive for them to marry (or to stay married) and is generally regarded as an anomaly in a nation that reveres traditional family values. The "marriage penalty" grows out of the system's three mutually exclusive goals: (1) that it be progressive, (2) that two married workers pay no more than the combined taxes they would pay if single, and (3) that households with the same income pay the same tax. These three goals simply cannot all be met, and Congress has resolved the conflict by accepting a marriage penalty.[6] The marriage penalty could be undone by changing the rate structure, but this would sacrifice other valued features of the tax system (notably, progressivity). Instead, the marriage penalty has been (partially) corrected through a special deduction for two-earner families. This is a special provision (since it does not apply to everyone), it subsidizes a particular activity (marriage), and it results in lower revenues. Is it a tax expenditure? According to the congressional definition, it is—and it is so classified in current TEBs. But if the same result had been achieved through a change in the tax rates, it would not be. Whether it is viewed as a tax expenditure depends on our interpretation of what Congress is doing. Is it specifically trying to subsidize marriage, relative to what the general tax code would require? Or is it just using a deduction because it is a simple way to balance conflicting equity principles? And why should the decision about whether a tax expenditure is involved depend on which of two equivalent implementation schemes is chosen?

Similarly, the treatment of capital gains may or may not be viewed as a tax expenditure. Many of these gains accrue over a long period, and a considerable portion of the "gain" simply represents the change in the value of money because of inflation. Under an accurate definition of a comprehensive income base, such holding gains would not be taxed; only the change in value in excess of inflation would be considered actual income. Computing taxes on this basis would be complicated; it would require the use of indices to distinguish inflation from actual gain. Excluding inflation-based gains from income tax would not be a tax expenditure but an adjustment reflecting real conditions. Methods to implement this treatment have been proposed many times to Congress, which has chosen—repeatedly—to use a simpler, considerably less accurate approach: a fixed portion (currently 60 percent) of capital gains is simply excluded from income.[7] Does this constitute a tax expenditure? It is clearly a special adjustment, applied to a narrow portion of the income tax base, to encourage a particular activity. Because of this, the treatment of capital gains is classified as a tax expenditure in both executive and congressional TEBs. If, however, it is merely an administrative device for purging the inflation component from capital gains, then it probably should not be thought of as a tax subsidy. Either way, the real tax expenditure under present treatment is the difference between an accurate inflation adjustment and the 60 percent exclusion currently allowed. Few long-term gains would qualify for a 60 percent exclusion; it is a generous administrative device even if its true purpose is in keeping with the philosophy of comprehensive income taxation.

Even under the best of conditions, developing an accurate TEB would be difficult. "Best" conditions would include a reasonable consensus on what parts of the tax code define the baseline tax system and what parts are special. From 1974 through 1981, there was general agreement among the OMB, the CBO, and the Joint Committee on Taxation. Both executive and congressional tax expenditure budgeters had always used a general (and essentially theoretical) definition of a comprehensive income tax, known as the Haig-Simons tax base.

The consensus dissolved in 1983, when the executive adopted a more restricted definition of tax expenditures for its TEB, arguing that many provisions that had been thought of as special exemptions were in fact general features that should be considered part of the "reference" tax system. The OMB proposed a strict interpretation of Congress's definition of tax expenditures. In 1983 and 1984, the OMB used a revised baseline, which it called the reference tax system, as a point of departure from which to measure tax expenditures. The OMB's argument was that the tax expenditure concept was essentially arbitrary and that classifying some tax code features as tax preferences and others as part of the baseline was both capricious and value laden. Special Analysis G in the fiscal year 1985 budget observes that even the base for taxation is ambiguous—ambiguous because defining income is as hard as defining a tax expenditure.* Rather than relying on theoretical notions, which are clear in general terms but difficult to apply in specific cases, the OMB opted for a more empirical definition of the baseline. The reference tax would be based on the broad rules stated in the income tax law, and tax expenditure items would be identified by the law's special provisions. This was a radical change, because it eliminated an entire class of tax expenditures—differences between the general rules mandated in the law and the provisions that would be consistent with a Haig-Simons income tax would no longer be regarded as tax expenditures.

In practice, the force of this shift was less than some of the rhetoric that surrounded it might have suggested. For 1984, the OMB classified about $34 billion, or about 10 percent, of what had formerly been considered tax expenditures as part of the reference tax system. The most important reclassification was accelerated depreciation. The OMB treated "economic depreciation" (the Haig-Simons baseline concept) as a theoretical construct, arguing that the congressional definition of depreciation embodied in current schedules was as good as any estimate of "appropriate" depreciation, and therefore was not a tax expenditure. This moved a revenue loss of $19.5 billion for 1984 out of the administration's TEB, thereby shielding a favored Reagan administration tax initiative brought in with the Economic Recov-

*The tax base had not previously been an issue; all had agreed that income taxation was the baseline and had accepted some form of the Haig-Simons comprehensive income tax base as the definition of the baseline tax system. The OMB now called that into question. Strong economic arguments can be advanced for consumption-based, rather than income-based, taxation, and some would even argue that Congress is headed toward consumption taxation by providing more and more exclusions for savings (theoretically the difference between income and consumption). These exclusions would not be tax expenditures if the purpose of the tax code were to tax consumption; they would be if the intent were to tax income.

ery Tax Act of 1981. The other sizable reclassification was the two-earner deduction, which was viewed as a correction to an error in the tax rates—in particular, to the lack of distinction in tax rates between one- and two-earner couples. The OMB saw the deduction as an appropriate administrative way to balance the tax rates among one-earner couples, two-earner couples, and singles. Since tax rates have always been considered a part of the tax structure, viewing the two-earner deduction as a component of tax rates removed it from the list of tax subsidies.

The dispute over the right baseline resulted in some confusion because the OMB and congressional TEBs for fiscal years 1983 and 1984 contained different figures. Moreover, the administration's TEB was no longer consistent with its TEBs of previous years. The OMB tried to compensate for these noncomparable TEBs by reporting in its fiscal year 1985 TEB what it referred to as "a number of tax provisions in addition to those that meet the narrower tests for identifying tax expenditures . . . used in 1983 and 1984."[8] This permitted a face-saving retreat to a basis more consistent with that used in the congressional TEB; the OMB's fiscal year 1986 TEB mentions the distinction but reports tax expenditures on a basis fully consistent with the congressional versions.[9]

The OMB's two-year departure from the reservation highlighted the ambiguities inherent in the TEB approach, perhaps undermining its usefulness. So long as the major players agree to the terms of the debate, the device can provide comprehensible information (though parties may differ about how to interpret it). But the ambiguities of its conceptual underpinnings cast doubt on how effective any TEB can be if used more directly as an instrument for limiting spending. For example, what would happen if Congress included TEB spending under the ceilings it sets early in the budget process? A host of definitional and theoretical problems would arise in determining what the new limit meant. No such ambiguity arises in defining direct outlays; a dollar of spending is relatively easy to define. Tax expenditures are not yet subject to such precise definition or estimation. They may not yet be ready to carry a heavier burden in helping to limit spending.[10]

Ambiguous—or at least debatable—conceptual underpinnings are not the only weakness of the TEB device. It is also technically difficult to estimate the required figures and even to determine which figures to estimate. Besides challenging the Haig-Simons baseline, the OMB has argued for a major change in the way the magnitudes of tax expenditures are assessed. If tax subsidies are viewed as public expenditures, the TEB should be directly comparable to the outlay budget. Rather than measuring revenue losses, the OMB has estimated what it calls the "outlay equivalent" in its tax expenditure analyses since 1982. The purpose is to be able to compare the TEB with the outlay budget.*

The subsidy given to a homeowner by the mortgage interest deduction provides a good example. Suppose a household has $10,000 in interest expenses and is in the 40 percent marginal tax bracket. By deducting the $10,000 in interest from income before computing tax, the household saves 40 percent of $10,000, or $4,000, in taxes. The revenue loss from this tax expenditure is thus $4,000. The outlay-equivalent approach measures the grant we would have to give the same family in order for it to be as well off as it is with the tax expenditure. Presuming that the income tax is comprehensive, such a grant would be taxable income; thus, we would have to give the household a grant of $6,667. It would pay taxes of 40 percent, or $2,667 on the grant, leaving it with the same $4,000 net benefit. For this household, the outlay equivalent of the mortgage interest tax expenditure is thus $6,667.

The CBO and the Joint Committee on Taxation have not accepted this alternative form of estimating the cost of tax expenditures, preferring to rely on the traditional device of revenue loss estimation. The outlay-equivalent measure is, however, much more compatible with the tax expenditure view of tax subsidies. It is the preferred measure if we take seriously the idea that tax subsidies are expenditures of public funds. It more accurately assesses the "cost" of tax expenditures to the taxpayer. Revenue loss—the amount of tax forgone—sounds like a perfectly plausible measure of cost. But the purpose of tax expenditure analysis is to put tax subsidies on the same footing as direct outlays, so that we can make direct comparisons and trade-offs between the two. Thus, for example, a direct grant for energy-saving measures like insulation can be compared to the energy tax credit. For purposes of comparison, tax expenditures and outlays must be measured in the same units.

This distinction between tax expenditures as revenue loss or as direct outlay is highlighted if we focus for a moment on the outlay rather than on the tax side. We typically think of outlays as costing a dollar for each dollar distributed. In actuality, however, most outlays result in taxable income to the recipient; the Treasury receives some portion of each government outlay back in the form of taxes. Thus, the net cost of outlay spending is less than it might appear.† A dollar of outlay spending is less costly than a dollar of

---

*This approach is consistent with the argument, advanced in chapter 3, that credit programs should be assessed in terms of the magnitude of equivalent cash grants.

†The chain doesn't necessarily stop here. Macroeconomists observe that the recipients spend much of what they receive, generating additional income to others, who pay taxes as well. This is one form of what is known as the multiplier effect.

revenue loss from which there would be no tax offset. We cannot, therefore, directly compare outlays to revenue losses. To make them commensurate, we must either "gross up" revenue losses to their outlay equivalents or "net out" the taxes that will reduce the cost of outlays. The latter option—trying to predict how much tax will be received against each outlay dollar—is unduly complex. It is simpler, and more appropriate, to think of cost as what we incur when we spend a dollar. This implies that we have to gross up revenue losses to make them commensurate with the figures we examine in the outlay budgets.

Sensible as this concept is, it took fifteen years after the development of the TEB concept for it to make its way into an officially published budget. It has not yet been accepted by congressional tax expenditure analysts, though the latest CBO tax expenditure report contains a sympathetic description of the outlay-equivalent approach and republishes some of the executive TEB outlay-equivalent figures.

The revenue loss approach embodies an inherent contradiction. It asserts that tax expenditures are expenditures but then insists on measuring them in the context of tax revenues—that is, it analyzes them within the framework of the tax side of the budget. By contrast, the outlay-equivalent approach is conceptually consistent; tax expenditures are treated as disbursements of public funds. There are instances, however, when the revenue loss figures are much more useful. When, for example, Congress considers tax reforms designed to meet established revenue targets (as in 1982), revenue loss estimates are considerably more relevant than outlay equivalents.

This presents an interesting quandary. Given current uses of TEBs—to help tax committees modify the tax code in order to "enhance" revenues —revenue loss figures are more useful. But if the TEB device is to play the role its name demands of it—assisting Congress in comparing tax subsidy and direct outlay approaches as alternative means to achieve the same public purpose—then outlay-equivalent measures are preferable. The two approaches are not trivially different; they contain different information. Each is relevant—for a different purpose. This imposes larger informational burdens on the providers, and on the consumers, of these analyses. Understandable confusion results—and has already resulted—from the publication of two sets of numbers, both purporting to represent the cost of tax expenditures. Unfortunately, the definitive use of the TEB device appears to require this level of complexity.

In addition to the need for two related, but distinct, sets of cost figures for tax expenditures, it is technically difficult to develop either set of numbers. Revenue loss estimates for individual tax expenditures are hard to construct. In many cases, activities are subsidized through tax exemptions.

In some of these cases, the activity level need not be reported. For example, municipal bondholders are not required to report interest earnings. In this instance, other sources supply reasonably reliable figures for the amount of tax-exempt interest paid. To form a revenue loss estimate, however, we have to multiply the amount of exempted interest by the marginal tax rate of the bondholder. Since reporting these earnings is not required, we cannot directly observe how tax rates correlate with the use of this exemption, and the revenue loss estimate must be constructed indirectly. Similarly, the value of tax deferral of retirement plan interest earnings depends upon the length of deferment. At the time the initial deduction is taken, we can observe both its amount and the current tax rate of the future retiree. But we do not know how much interest will be earned, how long taxes on it will be deferred, or what tax rate will apply between now and the individual's retirement.

To receive tax benefits for many other subsidized activities, however, the taxpayer must file an explicit description of the activity. For example, we can readily observe deductible charitable contributions, and the amount of mortgage interest deducted by homeowners. Since these amounts are reported, we can directly observe the marginal tax rate to which the taxpayer's additional taxable income would be exposed if these deductions were not allowed. We do not know, however, whether taxpayers would engage in other tax-advantaged activities if some of the existing preferences were eliminated. Thus, the revenue loss estimate calculated for a particular subsidy may not be the revenue gain we should anticipate from its elimination.

What, for example, would be the revenue effect of eliminating or substantially reducing the value of oil and gas tax shelters? These losses were listed at $3.4 billion for fiscal year 1985.[11] The investors are generally high-tax-bracket individuals seeking to shelter current earnings. If this avenue were eliminated, we would expect the level of investment in oil and gas exploration to drop. We might then expect more investment in tax-exempt municipal securities or other tax-advantaged activities. The impacts of a cut in one tax expenditure might well include increases in others, as taxpayers shift among tax-advantaged investment opportunities. Since such responses are difficult to predict, reliable estimates of actual revenue gains from tax code modifications are extremely difficult to construct.

If "revenue loss" means the amount of taxes forgone at current levels of subsidized activities, then they are easy to calculate (at least for reported activities). But revenue loss estimates do not necessarily closely approximate revenue gains if tax expenditures were eliminated. Outlay equivalents allow us to avoid estimating what would happen in the absence of the tax expenditure. The purpose of outlay equivalents is to measure the cost in direct outlays for grant programs supporting the same level of subsidized activity. This is the amount of before-tax income (assuming the grant would be included in income) that would have to be given to the taxpayer to provide an after-tax subsidy equal to the revenue loss. How taxpayers would respond if the subsidy were eliminated is immaterial; the goal is to find the equivalent cost of the program as it is currently operating. For many subsidies, this can be assessed more accurately than the revenue gain associated with a change in the tax expenditure. This illustrates again that outlay equivalents are generally a more useful measure than revenue losses are. Revenue losses at current activity levels do not necessarily correspond to any meaningful assessment of program cost; outlay equivalents convert revenue losses to units commensurate with the outlay budget and thus directly frame relevant policy choices about them.

The difficulty with using revenue loss estimates is compounded when they are totaled, because tax subsidy programs interact. If we eliminate the married couple deduction, additional income of two-earner families will be subject to tax. Because of our progressive tax rate structure, the tax rate applied to this additional income will depend upon the level of other deductions—for example, on whether homeowners are allowed to deduct mortgage interest. If we eliminate both the mortgage interest and married couple deductions, the revenue effects might be greater than the sum of the separate loss estimates because the income subject to tax added by each elimination would be taxed at a higher rate as a result of the elimination of the other.

The fact that revenue loss estimates are not strictly additive is another weakness in the TEB process. *This* conceptual problem of revenue losses is shared by outlay equivalents. Since the amount of the subsidy being received is tied to the tax rate, and thus to the level of other tax expenditures, outlay equivalents depend upon the level of other tax expenditures in the same way that revenue losses do. For this reason, the executive and the congressional TEBs do not usually total tax expenditure estimates.*

TEBs work as an informational device—to a point. They have successfully raised the profile of some tax expenditures. Debate over specific tax provisions can only make tax expenditures feel more like real money; the fights approximate the competition of the normal appropriations process. More information yields more competition.

But the ambiguous conceptual underpinnings and technical inaccuracies of TEBs undermine their usefulness. The information, no matter how as-

*The aggregated figures for tax expenditures presented earlier in this chapter (in tables 4.1 and 4.2) are subject to this criticism. They were given to provide a sense of the overall magnitude and distribution of tax expenditure activity across functional areas of government, not as definitive estimates of revenue losses or of revenue gains that could be anticipated from a elimination of tax subsidies.

siduously developed, is flawed. No enforceable tax expenditure ceiling coul
be imposed, because no agreement could be reached on how to measur
what was being spent. TEBs may help force tax expenditures to compet
more directly with other expenditures, but TEBs cannot match the cer
tainty of direct outlays on the question of how much we are spending.

Prospects for Strengthening the Tax Expenditure Budget

The tax expenditure budget approach rests on an insecure foundation. It
inherently complex and technically and conceptually difficult to implemen
Honest observers can differ over its terms and its message. Yet its greate
limitation as an accountability device lies in its dissociation from the "real
budget and appropriations process. Tax expenditures do not require appro
priations and do not have to fit under expenditure ceilings set early in th
budget process. Whatever the TEB's virtues as an informational device, th
reality virtually guarantees that tax expenditures will not be scrutinized a
meticulously as direct expenditures. Annual authorization and appropria
tion review is a substantial burden carried by direct expenditure program
An expenditure budget not captured within the same "real" process canne
engender the same budgetary discipline.

The difference between the tax expenditure program and an idealize
spending program disbursing appropriated funds can be illustrated with
simple example. Taxpayers currently claim tax expenditures when they fi
their income taxes. Suppose tax expenditures were administered in the for
of grant applications instead of as deductions and exemptions. Each ta
payer would file a simple tax form corresponding to general code principle
Those engaging in tax-subsidized activities would then fill out grant applic
tions, reporting the level of the activity and computing the grant (size
deduction or exemption times marginal tax rate) due from the Treasur
The Treasury would issue checks in the indicated amounts. Cruciall
Congress would have to put appropriated funds into the accounts on whie
these checks were drawn.* Conceptually, this is merely an alternative wa
to administer exactly the tax expenditure system we have now.

*Note how this resembles the outlay-equivalent approach to assessing the scale of t
expenditures. It is because outlay equivalents approximate this way of approaching tax expe
ditures that they are preferable to revenue loss estimates in assessing the magnitude of t
subsidies.

Politically, however, it would be radically different. If tax expenditures were administered as grants out of annually appropriated funds, they would quickly be subject to the same scrutiny as other grant programs. As soon as we started issuing actual checks, we would become more curious about whose names were on them. Disbursing real money has a way of galvanizing public attention.

It is hardly a politically plausible suggestion that we require tax expenditures to operate in this form—though it does illustrate that we could convert tax expenditures to an appropriated spending program with little technical difficulty. But if we did convert tax expenditures to appropriations, the outcome would be materially different. In spite of extraordinary efforts to produce accountability for this program through informational devices like the TEB, tax expenditures fall far short of the appropriation standard.

Short of requiring appropriations, how might we strengthen tax expenditure accountability? The dissociation of the TEB from the appropriations process, which guarantees its sideline status in overall budget review, flows from and accentuates the traditional congressional division between tax and expenditure committees. Expenditures are authorized, and funds appropriated, through a completely different set of congressional committees than those charged with determining tax policies. This forces the TEB device into an anomalous position. It is supported as an appropriate review mechanism on the theory that some tax-side actions are really expenditure actions. *But it is operated solely on the tax side.* This anomaly is at the root of the current debate about whether tax expenditures should be measured by their revenue losses or by their outlay equivalents. If it is to be a real expenditure budget, to encourage balancing of and trade-offs between tax-side and outlay-side expenditures, then outlay equivalents are the sensible answer. If it is really only a device to improve tax-side deliberation, then revenue losses are probably more relevant. Using both sets of figures adds considerable complexity. The debate behind which set of figures to concentrate on frames the central question of how TEBs are to be used.

Restating TEBs in terms of outlay equivalents is only a prerequisite to their use as real expenditure analogues; further structural changes would probably be necessary. Moving the consideration of tax expenditures to the expenditure committees might help, but it would require fundamental changes in the responsibilities of both tax and appropriations committees. If all tax expenditure consideration were moved, finance committees would have little discretion or work left; they would establish the broad tax bases available for taxation and set the tax rates for each. Such a realignment is hardly likely, given the power of both the House Ways and Means Committee and the Senate Finance Committee. The Constitution specifies that revenue matters must originate in the tax committee of the House, which virtually ensures that the House Ways and Means Committee will always be a powerful player in revenue debates.[12]

Even if we could reallocate the responsibilities of congressional committees, there remains a further roadblock to installing the TEB device in the position of arbiter of tax subsidy policy. It is not clear, given the limitations discussed above, that it has sufficient integrity to withstand the strain of that role. The recent dissolution of the long-standing consensus defining the baseline tax system illustrates the difficulty of applying a theoretical concept in a practical setting. The same criticism could be (and has been) leveled against many aspects of government accounting. But in this case the problem goes deeper. When we measure direct expenditures, the baseline—zero —is understandable and unambiguous. When we define tax expenditures, deciding where to start counting—the reference tax system from which deviations constitute tax expenditures—is a major conceptual, theoretical, and, in a political context, *practical* problem. The fact that TEBs require a relativistic perspective (expenditures are "relative to" the reference tax system) gives them an airy character. This, together with technical measurement problems, may prevent the TEB from ever being a fully effective device for enforcing accountability.

Measuring tax expenditure on an outlay-equivalent basis would improve the usefulness of TEBs. This would provide for, or require, some coordination between tax and expenditure committees with respect to the level of tax expenditures. It would permit placing tax expenditures together with direct outlays under the control of binding expenditure targets. These reforms would be difficult to design and would require complex realignments of congressional authority—no mean task. Moreover, there is no guarantee that the more stringent form of budget recognition imposed under these revisions would control tax expenditures any better than they are controlled now. They might still seem a relatively inexpensive means of providing funds for public purposes.[13]

Moreover, the agency theory of government reminds us that the use of tax devices to provide subsidies is no accident. As opponents of many specific tax expenditures have found, and as the venerable character of most major existing tax expenditures testifies, tax expenditures serve interests that are deeply entrenched if not always broadly based. Credits for energy investment, rehabilitation of older properties, and a host of other specific tax incentives are passionately supported—each by a different coalition of taxpayers who will benefit, together with those who provide the subsidized goods or services.

There are some indications, however, that TEBs may be becoming more popular as a result of perceptions that they work. They are used in a number of other countries and in several states.[14] Some state officials involved with the formulation of tax expenditure budgets believe that TEBs accomplish little more than making groups aware that still more tax subsidies might be made available for their favorite activity. But many officials continue to express faith in the value of "sunshine"—in the idea that appropriate and comprehensible information about the activities of government makes its actions more accountable. Better information may be particularly valuable in areas where accountability has not been exemplary in the past.

The tax expenditure program provides an archetypal example of an information-based accountability regime. Great effort and technical expertise have been devoted to making its informational mechanisms as sound and useful as possible. Intense fiscal pressure has made tax committees facing revenue targets aware that money not coming in should be thought of as money going out. But if tax expenditures are any guide, information alone is an inadequate surrogate for the appropriations process. The information is never completely reliable—revenue losses are hard to estimate, not additive, not even the right concept. Because tax expenditure spending is intangible (how much more revenue would we have in the absence of subsidies?), it has an ethereal character. And because it is a theoretical construct, its basis is always subject to debate. You can't see or smell or feel it the way you can real money, and so it remains easier to spend than real money. TEBs, in spite of great effort, are a helpful but imperfect instrument for making tax expenditures accountable.

Chapter 5

State Tax Incentives

and Economic Development

IN THE HALLS of state legislatures, lobbyists and businessmen wait
make their case that the state's business taxes are discouraging new inve
ment by existing firms, the in-migration of outside firms, and the formati
of new firms, while encouraging the out-migration of existing firms, jo
and the state's tax base. This is generally followed by calls for a more leni
tax policy, for tax holidays for new firms, for reduced taxes on busin
activity, for special tax treatment to encourage new hiring and new inve
ment. Legislators are told that firms in their districts, in the absence of
relief, will be forced to move to lower-tax jurisdictions where they can m
the competitive pressure from firms in places that are more business-c
ented. (The Far East and Texas are common choices, though even th
these arguments are commonplace.)

There is a widespread, strongly held conventional wisdom about w
makes firms choose one location over another. It underlies these argume
and gives them superficial plausibility. Its basic tenets are that firms are f
to choose their locations and that taxes are a critical component of the c
of doing business. According to this view, other variables that matter
businesses—the cost and availability of appropriately skilled labor,
acquisition costs, construction costs, and so on—either do not vary m
across jurisdictions or should be compensated for by tax policies. Taxes

make or break the competitive position of firms that might locate, or stay, in a particular jurisdiction.

An assumption is prerequisite to this view, one seldom challenged. It is that the formation of new jobs, new business investment, and the in-migration of new firms and industries is, on balance, "good." Some attempt may be made to distinguish among industries; states and localities would like to attract (or encourage the expansion of) high-paying, environmentally clean, stable firms. Colorado Springs, for example, initiated an active public-private partnership to identify firms that might want to move or expand, that fit into the labor mix the city can provide, and that will not damage the quality of its natural environment. The city actively sold itself as a prime location to carefully selected firms.

Not all areas can offer as many advantages as Colorado Springs, and many cannot afford the luxury of being picky. Obviously, not all new investment or job formation is equally good, but the widespread activity by states under the label of economic development testifies to a general belief that business growth is, for its own sake and for the community, a good thing. This faith may be too strong to overcome, but it is worth noting that business expansion often requires costly services like new or improved schools, transportation, and housing and that it makes increased demands on water, sewage treatment, and other utilities. The impact is by no means always positive. Nonetheless, support for development policies, except in a few jurisdictions, is deeply entrenched.

The conventional wisdom—that firms can and will move in response to favorable tax treatment and that it is desirable to attract them—is politically powerful. Businesspeople, taxpayers, and legislators believe it. It has been presented as fact for so long that this "wisdom" forms part of the unchallenged background in tax policy debates, with the ring of logic and the texture of empirical foundation.

The conventional wisdom is wrong. It is a complex myth about the behavior of firms and the role of state and local taxation. It holds out an elusive carrot and a highly visible stick to a public—and its elected representatives—made anxious by clear international trends that threaten the competitive position of a number of basic industries that once were the bedrock for economic prosperity.

The role of state and local tax policy in encouraging economic development has been assiduously studied by economists and political scientists. No area of vital policy interest—and continuing controversy—has attained as nearly complete a consensus among widely respected authorities. Almost universally, they conclude that the conventional wisdom is not supported

by the evidence: state and local tax incentives have little impact on the ra
of economic development.[1] Few policy issues have remained controversi
in the face of such empirical consensus, but in this case political consens
directly opposes the evidence.

The persistence and political robustness of the conventional wisdo
presents major problems for the reform of state tax systems. States compe
with one another, outbidding each other to attract or retain businesses ar
jobs. Tax changes by any one state could improve its relative attractivene
as compared to other states. But there is ample evidence that tax polici
are a poor instrument for improving competitiveness. And since other stat
will almost certainly respond in kind, all are ultimately dividing what is ve
nearly a fixed pie.* Economists refer to this kind of competition as
"zero-sum" game: the gains of one player are the losses of another. Her
the players also pay to play, so on average they all lose. When all states ha
lowered their tax rates in an attempt to keep existing or attract prospecti
business and industry, they collectively still have the same number of jo
—and less tax revenue to support the public services the jobs require.

States might be better off (collectively) if they could forswear this kir
of competition. But the incentive for each to try to gain at the expense
the others is strong. The idea that firms are mobile (and searching) tant
lizes state legislatures. Given the tenets of the conventional wisdom, ea
state believes that it can attract footloose firms searching for the perfect ta
package. It is difficult to imagine a sustainable bargain among states th
would limit this internecine warfare. Indeed, national meetings of sta
officials frequently bemoan these continuing "beggar thy neighbor" policie
but with little noticeable impact on current practice.†

The diverse collection of state and local economic development progran
raises intriguing problems of public financial accountability. These pr
grams continue to absorb public resources in spite of convincing evidenc
that they are not effective. They also operate across the spectrum of a
countability levels—from appropriated direct grants to tax expenditur
carefully reflected in visible state TEBs to obscure tax breaks unrecorde
in any public record. They thus provide a setting in which differenc
among programs operating at different accountability levels can be e:
plored.

---

*"Supply side" economists would argue that competition among states that results in low
tax levels increases total economic activity. There is little evidence backing this position fro
the experiment tried at the national level, but it persists in some quarters nonetheless.

†The competition among states may have some good effects. For one thing, it may encou
age them to produce desired services efficiently.

Tax Burden Differentials Across Jurisdictions

Interjurisdictional differences in tax rates are used as evidence by firms and their lobbyists to advance "tax incentive" policies. Without question, there are some material variations in the burden of taxes imposed on similar firms operating in different areas. These differences are easy to overstate, however, and they are generally compensated for to some degree by the associated levels of public services.

Wide disparities in the level and composition of taxation across jurisdictions do exist. In 1981, states taxed corporate incomes at rates ranging from zero (Nevada, South Dakota, Texas, Washington, and Wyoming) to over 10 percent (Arizona, Connecticut, Iowa, Minnesota, New York, and Pennsylvania).[2] In 1983 the per capita revenue from corporate income taxes ranged from none to over $100 (Alaska, California, Connecticut, Massachusetts, and Michigan).[3] Business property taxes also vary widely (in 1975, from $31 per capita in Alabama to over $200 per capita in Massachusetts, Montana, and Wyoming).[4] Unemployment compensation, property taxes on inventories, mining severance taxes, and other tax burdens were similarly varied across jurisdictions. In 1978, Missouri commissioned the accounting firm of Price Waterhouse & Company to study the taxes that would be paid by what it characterized as a "typical" manufacturing firm in its first year of operation in various states. The tax bills, computed by using the same income, sales, and other operating data and by applying the state and local tax laws of various jurisdictions, varied from $389,000 (Michigan) to $790,000 (Pennsylvania).[5] A recent study, using a similar approach to assess tax differentials among California cities, concluded that local business taxes levied on a professional firm like a law or accounting firm would range from none (Glendale) to about $30,000 (San Francisco).[6] On the basis of empirical results like these, state and local tax burdens are widely viewed as highly variable.

These kinds of results overstate the impacts of differences in tax policies across jurisdictions. First, while there is considerable variation in the levels of particular taxes, the tax packages differ in composition. Their overall levels are considerably more even than are their individual components. For instance, the per capita burdens of business property taxes differ from one state to the next by a factor of more than six, but overall tax levels examined in the Price Waterhouse comparison differed only by a factor of two. The differentials in taxes as a fraction of profits are also narrow. William Wheaton found that business taxes as a percentage of business income in 1977 ranged from 4.8 percent in Utah to 12.8 percent in Michigan.[7] The effective business tax rate in the forty-fifth-highest state (Georgia) was 5.4 percent; in the fifth highest (Rhode Island), it was 11 percent. While this differential may seem large as a fraction of profits, it translates into only a small variation in profit *rates* across jurisdictions. Assuming the average tax in each state, with all other costs identical, a firm with $100 in business income would be left after state taxes with $94.60 in Georgia and $89.00 in Rhode Island. Such a difference is not trivial, but neither is it enough to compensate for any significant variation in costs or returns to conducting business.*

Several other factors also imply that state and local tax policies have little impact on the location decisions of firms. First, tax subsidies are received by all firms—by those that move or expand anyway as well as by those that would otherwise make a different decision. They are often received by nearly all firms already resident in the state that gives them. Firms whose behavior *is* affected are extremely difficult to distinguish from others. It is therefore nearly impossible to assist only the firms "at the margin," for whom it makes a difference. The others would gladly present a case that the subsidies mattered in their decisions, too, and happily accept assistance. This implies that state tax policies to encourage development reward rather than influence behavior. This dissipates a substantial portion of these subsidies, reducing the impact per dollar expended.

Not surprisingly, states are adept at masking the fact that their programs cannot be targeted to the margin. They take credit for all jobs in firms that move into the state and accept tax assistance. Little or no attempt is made to determine whether a firm was actually influenced by the subsidy. This avoids the painful recognition of how small a fraction of the advertised benefits of these programs are in fact *net* benefits actually derived from program expenditures.

A second factor minimizing the impact of state and local tax policies on location decisions is that firms can deduct state and local taxes before computing federal income taxes. Most corporate income is taxable at the highest marginal rate (46 percent). A state or local tax payment of $1 reduces federal taxes by forty-six cents, so the net payment is only fifty-four cents. This shrinks any differential between the tax policies of different states by nearly one-half.†

---

*This assumes that only state and local taxes have to be paid out of pretax profits. Federal taxes shrink the differential further, as we will discuss shortly.

†Suppose a firm with $100 in pretax profits paid $5 in business taxes in one state and $10 in another. Federal taxes would be 46 percent of profits after state taxes; this would be ($100 − $5) × .46 = $43.70 in the first state and ($100 − $10) × .46 = $41.40 in the second. After-tax profits would then be ($100 − $5 − $43.70) = $51.30 in the first state and ($100 − $10 − $41.40) = $48.60 in the second. The state tax differential is thus reduced from $5 to ($51.30 − $48.60) = $2.70 by the federal income tax.

Third, differentials in state taxation may be captured by landlords rather than by the state. This process, known as tax capitalization, would occur if businesses bid up the price of land (or perhaps wages or other "factor input" prices) by trying to locate in low-tax jurisdictions. If the lower taxes that a firm paid were collected instead in the form of higher rents, there would be no *net* incentive to move from one jurisdiction to another, even if taxes—by themselves—were reduced. In a competitive environment, where landowners are trying to extract all they can, some tax capitalization should be expected, and there is some empirical evidence that it does take place.[8] Tax capitalization undercuts any advantage a state may hope to obtain by offering lower taxes.

Fourth, state and local tax bills are a small fraction of total business costs, rarely in excess of a few percent. By contrast, the cost of labor can amount to three-quarters of total costs. While taxes as a fraction of profits vary across states by only about ten percentage points, wages as a fraction of profits vary from 284 percent (Mississippi) to 557 percent (Michigan)—by over twenty-five times as much as taxes. Of course, the wage bill in Michigan buys a package of services very different from that bought by the wage bill in Mississippi—but so does the tax bill.[9] A very small fluctuation in wage costs between jurisdictions could swamp the tax bill at either site.[10]

Determinants of Firm Location

The overall level of business taxation imposed by different state and local jurisdictions does vary, though it is mitigated by federal tax policies and is small in comparison with other differences among areas in which firms might choose to locate. Even if significant disparities are unequivocally shown to exist, the conventional wisdom also requires that firms be willing and able to move in order to take advantage of them. Are firms really mobile enough for states to reap even the short-run advantages of competitive business tax strategies? Logic and the evidence strongly argue that they generally are not. At any given time, few firms are actively considering moving to or expanding in a new location. Tax subsidies designed to attract these few also subsidize the many—a high price for states to pay.* Since

*Some observers of state policies believe that these tax incentives are not really *designed* to attract new firms or encourage expansion of existing businesses. Rather, according to this view, they are only presented that way to make them politically palatable; their real intent is to reduce taxes for existing businesses.

benefits will be widely diffused, states must keep programs modest to kee| them from being excessively expensive, but modest programs have onl| small incentive effects. Moreover, a great number of factors influence firm| location decisions. Business taxes do not appear to be a very importan| component.

A voluminous literature has developed on the determinants of firm loca| tion. Broadly speaking, two favored approaches to the issue correspon| roughly to two alternative models of how these decisions are made. The firs| focuses on the decision makers rather than on the components of th| decision. Researchers survey firms' executives, inquiring about recent deci| sions and the methods used by the firm to assess alternative locations. Som| studies analyze survey data; others develop detailed case studies of a| individual firm's decisions. The alternative approach examines data of firm| migration and geographic patterns of new investment. It infers from thes| the influences of wage and other cost differentials, tax policies, and so forth| This approach is based on the premise that firm-location decisions ar| driven by economic factors. Firms are expected to optimize their locatio| decisions, taking into account production, distribution, and marketin| costs.

Hundreds of studies over the last two decades have examined thes| questions. Not surprisingly, the results differ widely.[11] Different industrie| are attracted to different features of the economic landscape, and not al| decisions appear to rely solely on economic considerations. Beyond this, few| common generalizations have emerged. Research findings underline th| complexity of location decisions, which balance a wide range of economi| concerns against the wider social and environmental characteristics of pos| sible locations.

Representative of the best of these studies is a recent investigation b| Roger Schmenner.[12] He based his work on an extensive compilation o| existing data as well as on two laborious and expensive surveys he con| ducted (one of 410 of the Fortune 500 companies, the other of all manufac| turing activity in the Cincinnati metropolitan area). Schmenner present| two detailed case studies of several location decisions, summarizes a numbe| of others, and provides survey evidence from still more. He finds that al| of the obvious considerations—labor, transportation, land, and other inpu| costs; the degree and potential for unionization; proximity to the firm'| existing facilities; proximity to raw materials and final-goods markets; "en| vironmental" concerns like local amenities, parks, schools, and climate— are important in differing degrees to different types of firms and for differen| investment decisions. He reaches no general conclusions about what mat|

ers most in firm-location decisions, finding that any of a number of influences can be dominant, depending on circumstances.*

The Role of Business Taxes and Tax Incentives in Firm-Location Decisions

Studies of firm-location decisions suggest that there are many important influences. Are state and local tax policies among them? Can they, with sufficient effort by state and local governments, be made to tip the balance? Although there are no general conclusions on what *does* most strongly affect firm-location decisions, the answer is *not* state and local tax policies.

The effects of tax differentials have been examined by means of four major methodologies. First, many of the studies that interview company executives or survey firms involved in investment decisions inquire about the importance of tax incentives in their decisions. The results can be read as mixed, but many of the more careful and recent studies of this form conclude that state and local business taxes and tax incentives are relatively minor considerations. In spite of a consistent and strongly maintained public position that business taxes are a major impediment to economic development, key decision makers admit privately that other concerns are generally more important. In a 1980 mail survey filled out by executives recently involved in location or expansion decisions, Michael Kieschnick found that business taxes were most often rated either a "moderate" or an "insignificant" influence on location.[13] He found a general lack of awareness of existing business tax incentives, even in firms that had recently made location decisions and among company executives who had been involved in them. Less than half of the firms he surveyed accurately indicated that tax incentives existed in the locations they had chosen.[14]

A 1982 survey by the accounting firm of Coopers & Lybrand, conducted for the state of Illinois, examined detailed data from sixty-one firms, about two-thirds of them large establishments.[15] Here, too, tax factors were found not to be the "primary issue" in either investment or location decisions. The

*A few of Schmenner's firms admit that their location decisions were significantly influenced by personal considerations of a company executive, such as reducing a long commute or accommodating one family member's wishes to be near another. Schmenner argues that these personal influences are likely to be important only when most other relevant features of the decision (like labor costs) are essentially identical across sites in the final runoff.

main determinants identified were traditional economic factors—access
markets and suppliers, labor costs, availability of appropriate skill mix
and geographic convenience to existing company operations.

Schmenner reached similar conclusions. He conducted over eighty inte
views with "key location decision makers," mainly in larger companies.
no instance were state or local tax levels the most important influence c
a location decision. He concludes,

> Almost every company takes a look at taxes; indeed, tax costs are one of the cos
> of a new site which can be quantified and presented in the documentation th
> supports the project's formal capital appropriations request. Nevertheless, tax
> themselves are merely a minor consideration, capable of altering the decision
> favor of a particular site only if almost all other factors are equal.[16]

Schmenner sums up his findings with the statement that his data are n
definitive but "do add weight to the general view that the taxation ar
financing schemes developed by government entities have only a minim
effect on the selection of new plant locations."[17]

In addition to these survey and interview approaches, researchers ha
used three types of statistical techniques to study the influence of state ar
local tax programs on economic development. Some have collected data c
aggregate levels of tax burden within jurisdictions, compared the growt
rates of high- and low-tax jurisdictions, and attributed a cause-and-effe
relationship. Better than most studies of this type is one prepared in 198
by Robert Newman.[18] Newman correlated growth in state employment fc
thirteen industries with changes in the state's relative corporate income ta
rate (as compared to the national average) ten years earlier. He found
statistically discernible relationship in a little less than half of the industri
he examined. This indicates that there has been high growth in som
industries in states whose corporate tax rates have fallen relative to th
national average. This result is not surprising; the areas in the United State
with the most rapidly growing employment over the last several decades ar
largely in the South and the Southwest; these have traditionally had lo
levels of taxation and associated low levels of public services. The centra
question is whether these facts are systematically related—whether th
assumption of cause and effect is legitimate. These areas have other substan
tial advantages: cheap land, low wages, cheap energy. Are they growin
because taxes are low, or for these other reasons? And, perhaps even mor
important, do the firms locating in these areas expect taxes to stay low, c
do they expect them to rise as more public services are demanded by ne
industries? Broad comparisons of aggregate tax burdens shed little light c
these questions.

To be accurate, empirical studies must "control" for other differences among jurisdictions. This is the approach taken by the second set of statistical studies of tax effects. It distinguishes the effects of tax burdens from other influences on firm location. Controlling statistically for all influences is difficult because prior knowledge is required about what form each effect takes. For example, how should the availability of skilled workers be measured? Through the unemployment rate within particular skill categories? Through an index of the "average" skill level of those already employed in the area? Or perhaps through the relative wage rate of each jurisdiction as compared to others (on the theory that higher-paid workers are likely to be more highly skilled)? Note that the last of these would imply that high wages may be a positive influence on firm in-migration, because they indicate the presence of highly skilled workers. Normally, high wage rates (controlling for skill level) are a negative influence, because wages are such a large component of production costs. Each measure has different implications; finding an accurate proxy for each important factor is tricky.

Recent studies have struggled with these empirical problems.[19] Perhaps the strongest studies from a methodological standpoint are a 1979 investigation by Dennis Carlton and a follow-up study he did in 1983.[20] Carlton studied new firms and new branches of existing firms in over one hundred metropolitan areas. He controlled not only for wage, energy, and other input costs, the availability of skilled labor, and the business climate but also for the possible cost-saving effects of locating near other firms in the same business (so-called agglomeration effects). Carlton's econometric results are generally solid. The tax variables perform poorly. He concludes that tax effects are weak, that higher taxes have little impact in discouraging investment, and that lower taxes have little effect in attracting new investment.

In an extensive investigation of the determinants of employment growth and development patterns, David Birch examined the relevance of taxes.[21] He was careful to consider the effects of both taxes and the public services provided with them, on the theory that lower taxes combined with the absence of services might raise costs to businesses by forcing them to develop their own. He finds no evidence that expensive packages of taxes and services deter economic expansion. His central finding is that appropriately skilled labor is critical to the location of business growth.

Two other recent studies are based on more-aggregated data, and for this reason may not be as accurate.* Kieschnick presents econometric estimates

---

*In contrast to studies like Birch's that use data on individual firms, these studies are based on averages within jurisdictions. The process of aggregation—the formation of the averages—may hide some of the effects that could be observed with "micro" data.

of the impacts of tax rates on investment.[22] His tax data are based on a computed average business tax rate for a hypothetical firm in a particular industry, averaged across the jurisdictions in each state. In eleven of the thirteen industries he examines, the impact of taxes on investment is statistically insignificant; in the remaining two, it is weak. He concludes with the traditional caveat that his results are not definitive, but says that

> it is reasonable to interpret them as providing additional support for the hypothesis that for most firms, interstate differences in business taxes play a minor role in investment decisions, and that relatively large changes in relative tax burdens are required to significantly affect investment patterns.[23]

The Advisory Commission on Intergovernmental Relations presented a study in 1981 consisting of compilations of existing data.[24] Part of the analysis was based on overall tax burdens levied by particular jurisdictions rather than on data from individual firms. The report has been criticized because overall averages may not be relevant for any particular firm. In spite of this potential difficulty, the commission felt the evidence was clear. It concluded that interjurisdictional differences in tax policies are of "limited importance" in determining the location of new investment.*

The final statistical methodology used to assess the impact of state and local tax policies on business location decisions—and to assist firms in their location decisions—is to compute tax bills for typical firms in alternative locations. The virtue of this microsimulation approach is that it accurately assesses actual tax burdens, although the representativeness of the hypothetical firms is often in doubt. Nevertheless, this strategy provides a useful assessment of how business tax packages differ at alternative locations.†

The results of these studies are descriptive rather than inferential—that is, they generally do not answer the question of how firms are likely to react to tax differentials; they simply tabulate the differentials that exist. The Price Waterhouse & Company study discussed earlier is of this form. The most detailed recent study of this kind is that by Karl Case, Leslie Papke, and Susan Koenigsberg; it computes tax bills for hypothetical firms in a variety of different industries at seven sites in New York and at seven in other states.[25] This study is particularly interesting because it was commissioned by a state government reviewing its policies regarding business tax

---

*As one of not very many organizations focusing on issues of general interest to all states taken together, the ACIR might be expected to look with disfavor on interstate tax competition. From its perspective, the zero-sum nature of competition among states for existing jobs is painfully apparent.

†It is also useful for firms considering a move, and many large accounting firms routinely prepare hypothetical tax bills for various sites under active consideration by their clients.

incentives.* Because their work was prepared explicitly to be used in the political process reviewing New York State's business tax policies, Case and his associates stop short of conclusions about whether the tax differentials they compute would influence business behavior.

Case, Papke, and Koenigsberg compute after-tax rates of return on new investment at each potential site. To isolate the effects of the business tax system in each area, they assume that the pretax rate of return is the same in every location. They find only slight variations in rates of return attributable to tax differences across the sites. For firms based in New York, the range of possible after-tax rates of return on new investment across the sites is from about 10 percent to about 13 percent. Differences for firms initially located outside of New York are somewhat larger; after-tax rates of return range from about 8 percent to about 13 percent. Tax-induced differences in profit rates of this magnitude are small by comparison to variations caused by other influences, like wage, transportation, and energy cost differentials across sites. To put it another way, the differences in after-tax profit rates caused by tax policies will not go very far to make up for any other production cost disadvantage a location happens to have—and if it has none, then a favorable business tax treatment is unlikely to be necessary.

If business tax incentives *do* manage to attract firms to a given location, they may attract precisely the wrong firms. Which firms are most likely to be influenced by a small cost differential? Presumably, it is firms in highly competitive industries, where a small cost advantage can mean a substantial increment in sales and profits. But, as Bennett Harrison and Sandra Kanter point out in their review of the effectiveness of state tax incentives, jobs in these industries "will in general pay lower wages, offer worse (and less amply capitalized) working conditions, provide less stable employment, and make it more difficult for labor to organize in order to protect its class interests."[26] Given the choice—and they surely have it—states might well decide to save their effort.

The message from these studies is clear: trying to attract firms by giving them tax breaks is not very effective. Favorable tax treatment typically makes only a small difference, and firms tend not to take it very seriously. Tax differentials are mitigated by the federal income tax deductibility of state and local taxes, and they are swamped in importance by much larger differences in other business costs. Even if firms are attracted, the successful jurisdiction may not be better off after it pays for the new services that

---

*That the state commissioned this study reflects the fact that legislatures are constantly being encouraged by business interests to "improve" their tax treatment of business investment —and that they need even-handed analysis with which to resist such pressures.

growth necessitates—and it may be disappointed at the character of jobs it does attract.

What Do State and Local Governments Do?

If state and local governments paid attention to the weight of evidence, they would be rather stingy in granting tax incentives for business investment and in-migration. In fact, many of the studies were a response to the fact that these programs proved remarkably robust politically despite the early empirical findings. In spite of repeated analyses showing little impact on investment levels or location decisions, these programs continue to be widely endorsed by state legislatures.

Information on the extent, form, and magnitude of state programs of tax incentives is sparse. Unlike the federal government, which reports its special tax programs annually, few states estimate the value of special tax reductions they offer.* Sketchy information is available from some states; Massachusetts' new tax expenditure budget, for example, records over $100 million in revenue losses for business tax incentives for 1984.[27] But no comprehensive and reliable estimates have been developed for the revenue losses associated with state business tax programs.

There is, however, evidence of increasing use of tax devices in development policy. Kieschnick compiled data from promotional literature and commercially published information about state tax laws. He reports that in 1980 forty-six states exempted raw materials used in production from their sales taxes and that thirty-one similarly exempted new-equipment purchases. Fifteen had some form of general investment or employment income tax credit; use of these tax credits spread from one state in 1969 to fifteen states in 1980.[28] State tax incentives vary widely in form, scope, and magnitude, and their use is on the increase.

Kieschnick's findings are corroborated by Roger Vaughan's 1979 review of state taxation and its implications for development policy. Vaughan lists thirty-nine different forms of state and local assistance for economic development, including financial, tax, and other special programs. Thirteen of these measures are labeled "tax incentives," including corporate income, personal income, property, inventory, and excise tax exemptions, tax credits for use of specified state products, and so on. More than thirty-five states

*See chapter 4 for a discussion of federal tax expenditures.

offer at least four; no state offers fewer than three. Aside from tax-exempt revenue bond financing (which involves little or no direct cost to the state permitting it), tax incentive programs appear to be the most widespread form of state support for economic development. A 1983 review of state incentives for business investment showed that nineteen states had "job creation" tax incentives, twenty-three had investment tax credits, and thirty-two had some form of business property tax abatement.[29] Vaughan reports that New York City has provided property tax exemptions worth nearly $50 million per year, that St. Louis has exempted half of its property tax base, and that Michigan's state and local tax incentives now cost at least $80 million annually.[30] He concludes,

> A direct result of the belief that business taxes really matter has been the proliferation of special tax incentives designed by states and localities to attract new businesses and to encourage expansion and new investment among existing firms. . . . Smokestack chasing is de rigueur for states that adopt an aggressive development program. . . . [T]he clear conclusion . . . is that, for the most part, *firms are rewarded for doing what they would have done even in the absence of the incentive.* [31]

By contrast with tax-side subsidy programs, direct state aid to businesses appears to be relatively scarce.* Many states have programs of loans and grants for business development, but these are generally small and are usually targeted toward small businesses. A Congressional Budget Office study found that in fiscal year 1983-1984 twenty-one states had direct loan programs to encourage economic development, but they disbursed a total of only $115 million in loans; nine of these and two others had loan guarantee programs, but the total of the loan guarantees issued came to only $23 million.[32] Massachusetts has a $10 million loan fund for community development activities, much of which has been advanced to small businesses. Connecticut has a highly successful venture capital fund for new product development, but this, too, is relatively small. Michigan and Ohio have programs modeled after the Connecticut fund and similar in scale. Initial capitalization for these funds ranges from $5 million to $20 million. Revolving funds are established, designed to run on their initial capital for a long period, with potential for expansion if they are successful. By comparison, state tax credits for business investment and hiring involve tens of millions of dollars of tax revenue annually. Massachusetts, for example, estimates that it sacrificed $40 million in annual tax revenues to encourage business investment through a now expired 3 percent tax credit.[33]

*Once again, no comprehensive data are available. Consistent measures of what constitutes a business assistance program are difficult to find.

When the costs of state economic development programs are visible and appear high, taxpayer resistance emerges. Rhode Island taxpayers recently voted down a $250 million package to provide financing for new job expansion, although virtually every state official and business interest actively supported it. Apparently, they believed that they would bear a significant portion of the costs—and that the costs would be high.[34]

States tend to conduct economic development programs through tax expenditures rather than through direct spending. Direct aid programs are more difficult to defend, particularly in light of the substantial body of evidence that the impacts are slight. Tax expenditures, however, seem a less onerous way of disbursing public funds. This may be particularly true for states, few of which have made serious efforts to measure and report revenue losses from tax expenditures.

Case in Point: Urban Enterprise Zones

An interesting example of states' willingness to enact tax expenditures on behalf of economic expansion is the recent development of urban enterprise zone (UEZ) legislation. The idea behind UEZs is to foster new business investment in designated blighted areas by offering reductions in federal, state, and local taxes. This approach to business development appeals to those who like free enterprise; it argues that *tax*-free enterprise is better still. Britain recently adopted UEZ legislation. Needing an urban policy, but wary about adding new spending programs while trying to reduce old ones, the Reagan administration endorsed the concept of UEZs early and often. Legislation was first introduced in the United States in 1980 in the Kemp-Garcia proposal. The pressing issues of both tax and spending agendas— together with resistance to the UEZ concept by the House Ways and Means Committee—have so far prevented the passage of a federal tax program.

States, however, moved to fill the void caused by the federal government's raising of expectations on the one hand and inaction on the other. By February 1985, twenty-four states had enacted UEZ programs, and more were considering UEZ legislation. Rhode Island adopted a program that requires federal UEZ legislation before it will be implemented, and another three states had policy initiatives under way that required no legislative action.[35]

State UEZ programs vary widely. Most include income tax exemptions or credits for new investment or job formation in a designated UEZ; property and sales tax exemptions or credits; reduction of licensing fees; and targeting of other state aid (small-business loan programs, direct state investment, and so on).[36] These subsidies are often accompanied by some form of deregulation.

The concentration on tax expenditures in these programs is striking. The original UEZ concept intended revitalization through private enterprise, unfettered by the tax burdens and regulations of government. As a result, UEZ programs are, in large measure, tax reduction programs. But the willingness of states to adopt these programs—in advance of the federal government—is remarkable.

State and federal interest led the Small Business Administration to commission a study by Coopers & Lybrand to assess the impacts of proposed federal and existing state UEZ programs on the profitability of subsidized businesses. The study was conducted by simulating the tax bills of hypothetical firms representing several different industries.* The study assessed the impact of UEZ tax reductions on the cash flow of the hypothetical firms. It concluded, first, that cash flow effects on a given firm from the federal program are substantially larger than those from most state programs and second, that federal subsidies are of little value until the third year of operation, after which they remain substantial.† Finally, Coopers & Lybrand found no case where the tax incentives change the cash flow from negative to positive. The impact of the tax incentives is too small in the early years to cancel the substantial negative cash flows associated with start-up or new investment; in the later years they merely accentuate already positive cash flows for businesses that manage to stay afloat.[37]

This last finding is truly telling; it virtually guarantees that the impact of UEZ programs on the investment and location decisions of firms will be small. The author of the SBA study concludes,

> As noted by a number of analysts, EZ incentives are not likely, by themselves, to greatly influence a firm's start-up or location decision. . . . For the most part, the incentives have only a marginal effect on a firm's cash flow during its first years of operation . . . the credits are not available when they are needed most, and, when they are available, they contribute to already positive cash flows. Also, the available credits will be of greater value in initial years to established firms considering expansion than to start-up businesses without an established record of earnings and potentially facing initial cash flow problems.[38]

*This methodology is the same as that described above as the third statistical approach to assessing the impact of business taxes: simulating individual tax bills.

†The proposed federal program is dominated by tax credits, which are useful only to firms that have taxable income. This implies that state programs might be most effective if they provided immediate benefits.

If even the larger federal UEZ tax incentives would have only a small impact on firms' investment or location decisions, then why have states rushed to jump on the UEZ bandwagon?

Conclusions and Prospects for Change

State and local programs of tax incentives for economic development have little impact on firms' investment and location decisions. While there are material differences between the business tax burdens imposed by different states, their influence on investment patterns is not strong, for a host of reasons. Business taxes are a relatively small portion of the overall cost of doing business; variations in other costs across geographic areas have a dramatically greater effect than variations in business taxes. It is hard to target them to ensure that benefits flow only to firms "at the margin"; much forgone tax revenue remains with firms that would have made substantially the same investments without tax reductions. State and local taxes are deductible for federal income tax purposes; this mitigates the value of any competitive tax differential a state offers. It is perhaps more dramatic to view this the other way: nearly one-half of the subsidies provided by state tax incentives flow to the federal treasury, not to the firms for which they were intended. State tax incentive programs are a kind of revenue sharing in reverse.

A substantial body of empirical literature supports these conclusions. The evidence comes in many forms. Surveys of key location-decision makers, inferential studies of what influences their decisions, and descriptive studies computing tax bills for representative firms in alternative jurisdictions all suggest that the impact of these programs is slight. While social science research does not allow ironclad conclusions, if these programs *did* have significant impacts, they would not remain undiscovered in the face of all the careful empirical searches for them. We are as sure as we can reasonably expect to be that tax reduction programs have little impact on firms' investment and location decisions.

Yet these programs persist and appear to be gaining favor. More states now give more generous tax benefits than ever before.* And the recent experience of states leapfrogging the federal government into the business

---

*Comprehensive figures do not exist, but the impressionistic evidence strongly suggests that tax expenditure programs are still on the rise.

of providing tax incentives for urban enterprise zones testifies that states may have less resistance to tax-side spending devices than the federal government does.

The focus of these programs on tax expenditures is troubling. It is possible that direct grant programs would be more difficult to administer without being more effective. But if this is so, there is remarkably little evidence of it. State use of tax expenditures seems part of a general pattern described in the discussion of federal tax expenditures: when governments want to foster a public purpose, but do not want the exposure and scrutiny of the appropriations process, they turn to tax expenditure devices. It is easy to spend in this form since revenues forgone are never counted in quite the same way as revenues collected (which could be disbursed for other purposes). States are in particular danger of sliding into unaccountable tax expenditure activity, since few systematically estimate or review the size of their tax expenditure programs.

It is difficult to characterize the level of accountability these programs attain, because they vary widely. A few state economic development programs are funded through direct appropriations. The majority seem to be conducted through tax expenditures. In states with strong tax expenditure budgets (like Massachusetts, Michigan, and California), the accountability of these programs may be similar to that of federal tax expenditure programs. In many states, though, no reliable estimate can be given of how much revenue is forgone in support of elusive development goals.[39] The accountability of these programs is dubious.

Because they operate across the spectrum of accountability levels, state and local economic development programs give us a rare glimpse of the impacts of differing mechanisms of accountability. Appropriated spending in these programs is relatively restrained; dollars flowing through the appropriations process feel expensive. Programs operating outside the appropriations process seem to be larger and to grow faster. Perhaps these quieter forms of spending are chosen because they are intrinsically efficient, but that argument has resisted attempts to prove it. A less contrived explanation is that quieter spending is easier. State and local economic development programs spend for the same purposes through mechanisms at varying levels of accountability, and the decided preference seems to be for quiet spending.

The impetus behind these programs is simple enough to describe: legislators feel a pressure to act. The evidence says that other influences (labor costs, transportation, and so on) are more important determinants of a firm's location. But these are not under the control of the legislature. Tinkering with tax policies may not work, but at least it is something legislators can do. If opponents of tax breaks are to make real progress, they must provide practical, realistic, *action* alternatives.

How might states replace underscrutinized and generally ineffective tax expenditures for economic development? They can take a variety of steps. Schmenner, in his surveys in Cincinnati, in New England, and nationwide found that while even large corporations use public programs less than is commonly thought, several specific kinds of programs do tend to be used and valued by firms. Some of these are unattractive politically—for example, right-to-work laws, as a salient indicator of "labor climate," appear to be quite effective inducements to the in-migration of firms and jobs.* Other programs, however, advance wider concerns of state governments. For example, Schmenner finds that some training programs—particularly if heavily subsidized—are valued by firms concerned about the skill mix of local labor. Moreover, state investments in the labor force benefit state citizens as well as firm owners (many or most of whom are typically not state residents). Schmenner also notes the apparent effectiveness of inexpensive state and local programs that help firms find and start up on a new site by providing them information and (less often) aid in site development.[4]

Roger Vaughan's review of state taxation and its relation to economic development elucidates other, possibly more efficient state strategies. Vaughan calls for a coordinated development policy providing a general climate conducive to stable business growth. This calls for balancing improvements in what he calls the "residential environment" with development of the business climate. Creating a strong and equitable tax system capable of supporting stable public services is seen as prerequisite to sustained economic expansion. Effective systems of public management, not tax incentives, are the key. Vaughan argues persuasively for programs that will develop the business climate generally, rather than concentrating tax benefits on a small handful of companies.[41] In a later study, Vaughan advocates state actions that help foster a climate of innovation and entrepreneurialism—short of having the state pay entrepreneurs directly.[42]

Studies of the importance of taxes emphasize that *personal* taxes may be as important as or more important than business taxes. Both Vaughan and Schmenner argue that too steeply progressive a tax system may encourage out-migration or discourage in-migration of firms because the executives involved in location decisions are careful of their own financial well-being.

---

*"Right-to-work" laws specify that non-union workers cannot be excluded from a work place. They are viewed as strong anti-union legislation and an attraction to businesses that do not want organized workers at their plants.

†This was an important concern of the New York State Legislative Study Commission recent review of tax policies. New York has been widely cited as having been hurt by heavily taxing upper-income executives.

State Tax Incentives and Economic Development

These alternatives do not appear particularly attractive politically, and it seems unlikely that they will soon sweep aside the long-standing preference for business tax incentives. General business development programs, sensible and effective though they may be, lack the political punch wielded by tax subsidies said to be aimed toward new jobs and investment. The agency theory of government suggests that concentrated programs of tax incentives have considerable political muscle. They are of obvious benefit to the recipients. They do not appear expensive, because they spend funds *before* they are collected and counted. They can be portrayed as serving the broad public interest, because of the widespread and deeply held belief that economic development is a key aspect of prosperity. Simple, though erroneous, measures attest to their effectiveness, counting all investment and new jobs in firms receiving tax benefits as directly flowing from the subsidies. And none of these political advantages depend in the slightest on the actual effectiveness of the programs. State legislatures, eager for the appearance of providing new jobs and business expansion, are likely to remain vulnerable to this politically powerful confluence of forces.

From the perspective of state legislators, the problem may come down to something like this: perhaps tax incentives *don't* work. Perhaps firm location and expansion decisions *are* much more strongly influenced by labor costs, transportation, convenience. *But those are out of my reach.* Taxpayers at least *believe* that tax incentives work. And their costs are obscure.

Given the choice between doing nothing, on the one hand, and doing something that appears inexpensive and that taxpayers think will help them, on the other, doing something wins every time. Whether the program actually works is almost immaterial. One of the main jobs of accountability mechanisms is making program effectiveness matter politically. In this area, at least, much of that job remains to be done.

Chapter 6

Private Use Tax-Exempt

Bond Issues

FEDERAL TAX expenditure spending is less accountable than direct appropriations. State and local business tax incentive programs to foster economic development are politically attractive but largely ineffective. The common thread is that these programs are easier to adopt and maintain because they are financed by tax-side spending. Many states are actively pursuing a variety of strategies to retain, attract, and encourage investment in desirable industries. They are not generous with direct grant programs —at least not with those they pay for themselves—but many want economic development programs so much that they are at least willing to pay for them with uncollected tax revenues.

Imagine what might happen, then, if state and local governments had access to an economic development program that could be financed solely with *federal* funds. Imagine further that the program could be financed at the federal level through tax expenditures that required no annual appropriation, review, or authorization. An agency theory approach would predict rapid growth in such a program and substantial competition among state and local governments to offer it enthusiastically. Additional spending— authorized at one level and paid for out of funds requiring no appropriation and subject to no binding limit at another level—would expand essentially unchecked. This kind of program would be so difficult to check and to hold accountable that it is hard to imagine its explicit authorization. It might, however, arise by accident—the result of actions taken for other reasons, whose joint implications were not obvious.

There would, of course, be some pressures counterbalancing unlimited expansion. Like dinner guests who are still hungry but do not want to overstay their welcome for fear the host will not invite them back, state and local governments might feel some ambivalence about using the program without setting administrative limits of their own. Some states might also want to aim the program at selected areas to influence the pattern of development. But competitive pressures from other, less responsible jurisdictions would keep these from being very effective counterforces.

Eventual overuse of the program might lead to discussions at the federal level about how to limit it. What might be expected then? First, state and local governments—and other direct beneficiaries—would lobby strongly for retention and would advance evidence of how the program's widespread use had helped solve important problems. Second, state and local users, when some form of limitation eventually appeared inevitable, would lobby for directing the program at specific problems and against its elimination or ceilings on its use.

There is a program with this history. Federal tax exemptions for interest paid on state and local bonds issued for private purposes (known as private use tax-exempt bonds) operate precisely in this way. The "program" arose accidentally. Interest paid on bonds of state and local governments has been exempt from federal income taxation since the income tax law was written in 1913.* Since no law or regulation prohibited it, states issued their own bonds to finance purchases of industrial sites, buildings, and equipment, which they could then lease to private firms. Mississippi, not otherwise known as a financial innovator, invented this device in 1936. The state explicitly authorized local governments to issue their own tax-exempt general obligation bonds, backed by their full faith and credit and unlimited taxing powers, to finance purchases of assets to be leased to private firms. Mississippi called the agencies responsible for these bonds "industrial development agencies," and the bonds have come to be known as industrial development bonds (IDBs).[1] The first issue was an $85,000 bond used to persuade a clothing manufacturer to move into the state; the purpose was to diversify Mississippi's economy, then heavily agricultural and suffering terribly from the Depression.

At first, the device was hardly noticed. A few other states followed Mississippi's lead, and the volume of private purpose tax-exempts increased

---

*The exemption for interest on public purpose bonds reflects a long-standing (and arguably incorrect) interpretation of a provision of the Constitution. It is now supported by statute, and despite regular assaults it appears politically sound.

slowly after World War II. But the program was essentially an accident—a creative offshoot of the existing finance mechanism, not the result of explicit authorization. Its legal status was uncertain. The U.S. Supreme Court upheld the Mississippi arrangement in 1938, but unfavorable rulings in other states discouraged investors.[2] The market for IDBs remained thin until additional favorable court rulings and the use of IDBs by larger corporations provided more assurance of their creditworthiness.[3]

The postwar development of revenue-backed IDBs proved an important innovation. These funds were lent to private businesses, but the governments themselves remained responsible for paying investors. Pledges of "full faith and credit" and "unlimited taxing powers" provided strong credit backing, but these issues counted within the state-authorized debt ceilings, which limited the potential for expansion. This constraint led to the development of an alternative credit arrangement—backing the bonds exclusively with revenues from the projects they financed. This avoided debt ceilings and left the state or local government free to use its credit resources for other purposes. So long as the leases financed through the bond issues were firm commitments from reputable businesses, investors accepted revenue bonds at a small premium above the interest rate they would have received on general obligation bonds.

Using project revenues instead of taxing powers to support borrowing severed tax-exempt private financing almost completely from traditional government borrowing. Revenue-backed IDBs (also called industrial revenue bonds, or IRBs) do not rely on government credit and have no impact on the government's own tax-backed general obligation debt. IRB borrowing takes place off to one side and, from the perspective of investors, does not bear on the credit of the government itself. This effectively eliminates the only cost IDB borrowing might impose directly on the governments that permit it. Local taxpayers need not be concerned with the level or character of IRB financing; they are not financially responsible for it, nor does it directly interfere with other borrowing.*

Most IRBs are actually debt obligations of private businesses, not obligations of the development authority. This separates them even further from the government's own credit. In the early years of IDBs, government agencies borrowed funds and then lent them out; the agencies were the link between ultimate private borrowers and investors. Some IRBs followed this pattern. They were backed only by the revenues of the businesses they

---

*In practice, it is not so simple as it is in legal terms; securities markets often impose associations even when there is no legal connection. IRB failures indicate softness in the local economy that might also affect public issues. Thus, a string of IRB defaults in a particular jurisdiction would set off financial alarms if that jurisdiction came to market with a general obligation issue.

supported, but they were issued by a government agency, which lent some additional sense of security to investors—even if it gave them no additional legal claim. Now many tax-exempt IRBs are merely certified by a designated state agency; they are in no sense obligations of any government. They are private loans, typically from a bank to a private firm, except that they avoid federal income taxes on the interest received.

IRBs were also, for most of their history, disconnected from any form of voter approval. Issues of public debt have traditionally been scrutinized very carefully by voters; many jurisdictions require some form of special referendum, or special resolution of the legislature, before public debt can be issued. Voter approval has recently been a considerable damper in many jurisdictions, as taxpayers, given the opportunity, often vote down bond levies they know will raise their tax bills. From 1968 to 1978, voters generally approved between 40 and 60 percent of issues submitted to the electorate; in 1975, only 29 percent of bond issues seeking support in referenda were approved. Faced with this degree of voter resistance, some jurisdictions issue debt in ways that do not require public review. Over the period 1976–1978, for example, only 15 percent of the debt actually issued had to be approved by voters.[4]

IRBs fell neatly into this pattern of bypassing voter approval. Their very existence was an accident of history, so no general issuance procedures—let alone any requirement for public approval—had been specified by Congress. In most jurisdictions, IRBs could be approved solely by an appointed board of a state or local development finance agency. Often there was no public notice requirement. This treatment ended in 1982, when Congress imposed the requirement that private purpose tax-exempt issues had to be approved by at least one elected official, following a public hearing.

Remarkably, this almost complete separation of the IRB from actual public borrowing has not interfered with its tax-exempt status. Funds are lent directly from one private party to another. They are not obligations of any government, legally or otherwise. Until 1982, they required no public approval. Yet the opinions of bond counsels that IRBs were tax-exempt under constitutional provisions have been sustained. Courts, relying on statutory provisions of the federal income tax code, have held that obligations of one level of government cannot be taxed by another.

Once this form of tax-advantaged but nonpublic borrowing was fully developed and legally tested, IRB borrowing began in earnest. The 1960s witnessed a tremendous growth in tax-exempt bond financing of private activities, almost exclusively in the southern states. In the decade following 1958, 87 percent of all IDB issues, accounting for 60 percent of dollar volume, were from six southern states.[5] Congress limited IDBs in 1969 in response to increasing federal revenue losses and perhaps out of a growing conviction that this program was not exactly what the Constitution's framers had in mind when they prohibited the taxation of one level of government by others. The limitation took a convoluted form. State and local government bond issues raising funds to be lent to private parties (through leases or directly) had never been explicitly authorized; now they were declared *un*authorized. Bonds could be issued, but they would not be tax-exempt *unless* one of two exemptions applied. First, a set of "special use" exemptions was granted: bonds issued to finance docks and storage facilities for commerce, certain transportation investments, pollution control facilities, and convention centers, among others, would remain tax-exempt. Second, a general "small issue" exemption was granted: firms were allowed up to $1 million in IDBs in any one jurisdiction at any given time. Almost immediately, the small issue exemption was expanded to $5 million, but the firm had to count capital projects three years back and three years forward against the higher ceiling. The purpose of the small issue exemption was to aim the program at small businesses.

In one swift stroke, Congress clarified the status of IDBs. It explicitly authorized tax-exempt financing for a vast array of private activities—in legislation nominally designed to *de*commission a program that had never been authorized in the first place. The legislation also advertised the availability of IDBs and validated their use in a broad (but technically limited) range of circumstances. This episode remains one of the great ironies of modern legislative history.

The result was general jubilation and explosive growth of IDBs, particularly in the IRB form. Table 6.1 shows long-term tax-exempt borrowing by the purpose for which bonds were issued from 1975 to 1983. From the modest $85,000 beginning in 1936, new issues of private purpose tax-exempt industrial development bonds expanded to over $21 billion in 1983, more than half the volume of *public* purpose tax-exempts issued in that year. Small issue IDBs expanded strikingly, by a factor of over nine between 1975 and 1983, to a volume of over $13 billion.

As table 6.1 indicates, private purpose tax-exempt bonding has expanded outside the domain of its inception. When states discovered they could legally issue revenue bonds to fund economic development, they began issuing bonds to purchase housing mortgages (primarily to assist middle income households), to provide funds for student loans (particularly popular as the Reagan administration tightened the federal student loan program), and for a variety of other purposes. By 1983, the volume of tax-exempt issues for private purposes had grown to 58 percent of total

TABLE 6.1

Long-Term Tax-Exempt Financing, 1975–1983
(billions of current dollars)

	1975	1977	1979	1981	1983
Private purpose tax-exempts					
Industrial development					
Pollution control	2.1	3.0	2.5	4.3	4.5
Small-issue	1.3	2.4	7.5	13.3	12.0
Other	2.3	3.2	2.2	2.7	4.6
Total, IDB	5.7	8.6	12.2	20.3	21.1
Other private purpose					
Housing	1.4	4.4	12.1	4.8	16.9
Exempt entity	1.8	4.3	3.2	4.7	8.9
Student loan	—	.1	.6	1.1	3.2
Total, other private purpose	3.2	8.8	15.9	10.6	29.0
Total, all private purpose	8.9	17.4	28.1	30.9	50.1
Public purpose tax-exempts	21.6	29.5	20.3	24.2	39.4
Total tax-exempts	30.5	46.9	48.4	55.1	89.5

NOTE: "Other" IRBs are mainly special use exception bonds issued to finance sewage disposal, airports, docks, and other specifically exempted activities. Exempt entity bonds are issued to finance loans to tax-exempt organizations (charities, educational institutions, and so on) under Section 501(c)(3) of the Internal Revenue Code.
SOURCE: *Budget of the United States Government, Fiscal Year 1985*, Special Analysis F, table F-13.

tax-exempt borrowing. Issues of private purpose tax-exempt debt first exceeded those for public purposes in 1978—and have never looked back.

IDBs have consistently been used to lower the cost of activities that contribute to economic development by anyone's standards—assisting new businesses in blighted areas, for example, or expanding much needed transport facilities. They have also been put to less worthy uses. The Congressional Budget Office stirred up the controversy over private use tax-exempts in a 1981 report on the uses and abuses of IDB financing.[6] The CBO's examples included financing for commercial real estate development, tourist facilities, private golf courses, and topless nightclubs.[7] Several national retailers used IDB financing to develop their local facilities; K Mart stores and McDonald's restaurants have been frequent beneficiaries. There is nothing inherently irresponsible or surprising about these uses. Even the congressional "reforms" of 1968 only limited particular uses; they set no ceiling on total IDB financing within jurisdictions. Thus, individual uses need not compete against each other for limited credit resources. Borrowers are not competing for a portion of limited debt capacity; each borrower brings its own credit standing to the market. This is a major reason why large, established, creditworthy firms like McDonald's have no difficulty securing IDB financing for their expansions. These uses—with the possible exception of nightclubs and similar aberrations—are components of "economic development." Using IDBs to advance them does not displace other projects that might contribute more to real economic expansion. There is little in the accountability structure of IDB financing to encourage state and local governments to ration its use. The rapid growth and wide application should be no great surprise.

The direct costs of the program—the revenue losses associated with the tax exemptions—are borne by the federal Treasury. Over the period of great IDB expansion, these losses have grown substantially. Table 6.2 shows 1984 revenue losses and outlay equivalents for major categories of private-use tax-exempt financing. The federal government subsidizes state economic development activities by forgiving over $4 billion in taxes on the interest payments for private use IDBs, and another $4 billion in taxes for interest on other private purpose bonds. These subsidies are an entitlement; they are there for the asking, somewhat constrained in form and use, but not limited in total amount.

As the outlay-equivalent figures in table 6.2 indicate, it would cost the

TABLE 6.2
Federal Revenue Losses and Outlay Equivalents for Private
Use Tax-Exempt Financing, 1984
(billions of dollars)

	Revenue Loss	Outlay Equivalent
Industrial development		
Pollution control	1.3	2.2
Small issue	2.0	3.2
Other	.8	1.2
Total, IDBs	4.1	6.6
Other private purpose		
Housing	2.5	4.1
Exempt entity	1.4	2.3
Student loan	.3	.5
Total, other private purpose	4.2	6.9
Total, all private purpose	8.3	13.5

SOURCE: *Budget of the United States Government, Fiscal Year 1985,* Special Analysis G, table G-2, and calculations. Estimates for outlay equivalents are computed using average marginal tax rates of .40 for corporations and of .35 for individuals holding tax-exempt bonds.

federal government over $13 billion in direct outlays to replicate IDBs through a direct subsidy program. Over $6 billion in outlays would be needed to replicate the economic development subsidies alone. This estimate of the program's magnitude can be compared with federal direct expenditure programs. Measured in this form, the $6.6 billion economic development program is about the same size as the entire federal community and regional development program; it is over 40 percent larger than the federal government's general-revenue-sharing program with state and local entities. It is nearly as large as the federal share of the Aid to Families with Dependent Children (AFDC) program. The $13.5 billion federal subsidy for private purpose tax-exempt financing is the same size as the entire federal international affairs budget.[8]

The subsidy provided through tax exemptions on debt is both large and highly inefficient. A direct outlay program designed not to replicate the current tax-side program, but to generate the same effects, could be conducted at considerably lower cost. This inefficiency has long been recognized. The subsidy works by lowering the interest rate that tax-exempt borrowers have to pay in order to attract investors. Lenders will accept lower pretax interest because they do not have to pay taxes on it, and their posttax earnings are thus higher. Naturally, individuals in high tax brackets will be attracted first, since the benefit of tax exclusion makes more difference to them. As state and local governments borrow more, they must attract a wider group of investors, including some who face lower rates of federal taxation and who thus benefit less from the tax exclusion. The interest rate must therefore be higher. Since these higher interest rates apply to all borrowers, borrowers in high tax brackets, attracted first and willing to lend at lower pretax interest rates because of their larger tax benefits, receive a windfall. These excess earnings are unnecessary to keep them interested, but it is impossible to avoid paying them under the current subsidy system. A considerable fraction of the tax benefits provided by the federal government thus serves not to attract the marginal lenders but to provide exceptionally high earnings to individuals in the top tax brackets. This inefficiency hurts both state and local governments (which get less than they might in interest savings) and the federal government (which pays more in subsidies than it needs to).

For example, consider two lenders, one in the 50 percent and one in the 25 percent tax bracket. Both can earn 12 percent interest in the taxable private securities market. After-tax earnings would be 6 percent for the first lender and 9 percent for the second. Suppose a state offers them a tax-exempt bond with an interest rate of 7 percent. Since no taxes will be paid on this income, this is an after-tax rate of return. For the high-income lender, this exceeds the after-tax return available in the private market, so it makes sense to invest in the tax-exempt bond. To attract both lenders, however, the state would have to offer a yield higher than 9 percent.

Let us suppose it offers bonds at 9.1 percent. The marginal investor, in the 25 percent tax bracket, receives about the same after-tax rate of return here as in the private market. The federal government forgoes the income taxes it would previously have collected from this investor—3.0 percentage points, or 25 percent of the 12 percent taxable income he or she would otherwise have earned. Essentially all of this subsidy flows directly to the state; its interest payments to this investor are lower by nearly the amount of tax forgone by the federal government. The subsidy is efficient for this investor.

But consider the high-income investor, who is now receiving an after-tax rate of return 3.1 percentage points higher than before. For this investor, the federal government is foregoing tax payments equal to 6.0 percentage points, or half of the income that would have been earned in the taxable securities market. But the interest rate paid by the state to this investor is only 2.9 percentage points lower than it would be if the state's security were taxable. Thus, the federal government has lost taxes equal to 6.0 percentage points, while the state has reduced its costs by only 2.9 percentage points. The difference is a 3.1 percentage point windfall for the high-income investor. The investor is understandably pleased, but the subsidy is highly inefficient.

A carefully designed direct expenditure program could be much more efficiently targeted than IDB tax exemptions. The outlay-equivalent figures presented in table 6.2 assumed that a direct expenditure program replacing tax exemptions would have the same inefficiencies. The estimates were for a direct outlay program replicating the tax-side payments of the current program with taxable direct subsidies. The OMB has estimated the cost of a well-designed direct expenditure program that would supplement the interest payments made by state and local governments. Each dollar of subsidy would directly offset a dollar of state or local government interest cost. The cost of replacing the current IDB subsidies would be about $4.2 billion; subsidies for other private purposes currently conducted through tax exemptions on bond interest could be replaced for a direct outlay cost of about $4.9 billion.[9] The current subsidy program is both large and wasteful. If it were conducted through a direct grant program rather than through tax expenditures, its cost could be lowered by over $4 billion.

The direct costs of IDB programs fall on the federal government in the obscure form of subsidies paid out of uncollected tax revenues. While state and local governments that administer IDB programs do not feel the direct pinch of the costs imposed, IDBs are by no means costless, even to them. Private purpose tax-exempt bonds seek the same investors as traditional public tax-exempt borrowing. The competitive demand for credit exerted by private users in the tax-exempt markets raises the interest rates state and local governments pay on their own bonds.

This pressure on interest rates is evident in the recent trend in the spread between tax-exempt and taxable debt issues. Table 6.3 shows the average tax-exempt and taxable issue interest rates over the period from 1978 to 1982. Although the absolute spread in interest rates has stayed about the same (roughly three to four percentage points), the relative spread has narrowed considerably. In 1978, the tax-exempt rate was two-thirds that of taxable bonds; by 1982, it had risen to four-fifths of the taxable rate.[10] This trend has two salient implications. First, the wastefulness of the federal tax subsidy is rising. The lower relative spread between the taxable and tax-exempt rates implies that the marginal lenders are now individuals paying lower tax rates. Assuming the last lender would receive the same after-tax rate of return in either market, the spreads indicate that the marginal lender in 1978 was in the 33 percent income tax bracket, while in 1982 the marginal lender's income tax rate was about 20 percent. As the income tax bracket of the marginal lender goes down, the excess subsidy paid to lenders in higher tax brackets increases.

The second implication of these figures is that the advantage of the tax exemption is decreasing for state and local governments. What has caused this? First, the highest marginal rates of federal income tax have been substantially reduced, so investors are generally less interested in tax-

TABLE 6.3
Tax-Exempt and Taxable Bond Yields, 1978–1982

	Interest Rate On		
Year	Tax-Exempt Bonds (Bond Buyer 20 Bond Index)	Taxable Bonds (Moody's All-Industry Corporate Bonds)	Ratio of Tax-Exempt to Taxable Rate (Percent)
1978	6.07 percent	9.07 percent	66 percent
1979	6.53	10.12	65
1980	8.56	12.80	67
1981	9.97	14.09	71
1982	12.96	15.95	81

NOTE: Figures for 1980–1982 are for first quarters.
SOURCE: Condensed from John C. Petersen and Wesley C. Hough, *Creative Capital Financing* (Chicago, Ill.: Municipal Finance Officers Association, 1983), table 3.2.

preferred forms of lending; there are fewer fish in the pond. Second, as result of other changes in tax laws (particularly in 1981), many mor tax-advantaged investments are now available. Tax-exempt issuers n longer have a corner on the supply of tax-preference opportunities; there ar more fishermen working the pond. Finally, private use tax-exempt issue compete directly with traditional public bonding. Over the period covere in table 6.3, total long-term tax-exempt borrowing increased from \$4 billion to \$85 billion, and all but \$6 billion of the increase was in privat use borrowing.

One by-product of state and local use of IDB financing, then, has bee an increase in the pressure on the supply of funds available for tax-exemp lending. This increases the interest rates that state and local governmen have to pay on their own bond issues. This cost of the IDB tax exemptio falls on all state and local governments, so it might seem to be a chec against the indefinite expansion of the IDB device. But the pressure generated by all uses taken together, not by any particular issue. And th burden falls equally on each bond issued—no more (per bond) on heav users than on those who tread lightly. Thus, almost all of the cost impose on any particular jurisdiction comes from IDB activities elsewhere, and th provides no incentive for restraint by any given jurisdiction.*

A confluence of forces—disclosures of occasional abuse of IDBs and their substantial cost, continuing pressures for increases in federal revenu and reduced tax subsidies, a lingering sense that the IDB program was construct of historical accident rather than of policy design—has led on again to moves to eliminate, reduce, or constrain IDB issues. The late round of deliberations was triggered politically by one of the many priva windfalls that have from time to time been features of the IDB system. I 1981, as a rather hasty and perhaps ill-considered addition to a series substantial tax cuts, Congress dramatically liberalized the tax treatment leases, making investment tax benefits easier to transfer between partie Investment in government property was generally excluded, but there we: a few exceptions. No restrictions were placed on combining tax benefits- using the provisions of the new leasing law in tandem with existing pr grams. No one seems to have anticipated the impact this might have conjunction with IDB financing.

---

*Economists refer to situations like this one as "n-person prisoners' dilemmas," after famous example involving prisoners, each of whom was offered the opportunity to turn state witness. If no prisoner confesses, no one is convicted and all win. If a single prisoner confess however, he or she is substantially rewarded. Whether the other prisoners confess or not (this case, whether other jurisdictions are restrained or not), it pays each prisoner to confe (here, each jurisdiction to issue). All therefore confess—all jurisdictions issue—and all be the consequences.

Investors, or their lawyers and investment bankers, were quick to appreciate the potential that Congress had created. Under other provisions of the tax law, substantial tax credits were available for specified activities. For example, investors who rehabilitate historic properties can receive investment tax credits—direct reductions in their tax payments—of 25 percent of their investment. Moreover, IDB financing could be arranged for the rehabilitation, so building owners could borrow the funds on which they could collect these credits at tax-exempt rates. In addition, they could take depreciation deductions according to the new Accelerated Cost Recovery System, a very attractive depreciation schedule.

The result of these unintended "tandems" was a set of complex ("creative financing") transactions in which some investors got back more in tax credits in the first year than they had invested—and continued to receive additional tax benefits in later years. State and local governments sold a number of public buildings to private investors using IDB financing. The investors then used additional IDB financing to rehabilitate the buildings, then leased them back to the government. A syndicate of private investors received substantial tax breaks, and the original owners of the building got rehabilitated space at a very low cost. The balance was paid by the federal Treasury.*

The volume of tax revenue loss was substantial enough to attract almost immediate congressional notice. IDB financing was just one element of these arrangements; many deals relied only on the tax benefits made possible by the leasing law itself. But the role of IDBs was particularly visible, and Congress moved quickly to limit their contribution.

The Tax Equity and Fiscal Responsibility Act of 1982 limited IDB use in tandem arrangements. Accelerated depreciation benefits were denied to any investor whose holdings were financed through a tax-exempt IDB loan. The tax benefits of combining investment tax credits and accelerated depreciation now exceeded those of IDB financing, dramatically decreasing IDB use in tandems. The attention focused on IDBs by their use in leasing deals led eventually to broader IDB limitations. The reforms of 1982 called for approval of each issue by an elected official after a public hearing. This provision was an attempt to raise community consciousness about IDB-financed activities. But there is still virtually no incentive for a community to disapprove IDB financing.

A series of additional reforms proposed in 1983 were finally passed in June 1984. Leasing activity and IDBs were further curtailed. After years of considering some form of volume limitation on IDB financing, Congress

---

*These arrangements are discussed in more detail in chapter 8.

finally established state-by-state caps in the Deficit Reduction Act of 1984. The annual limit for each state is either $150 per capita or $200 million (whichever is greater) in total tax-exempt IDB issues. (This cap is phased in if the current level of IDB activity exceeds it.) Congress also set a $40 million limit on the amount of IDBs that can be outstanding anywhere in the nation for the benefit of one taxpayer. The act also tightens the tax treatment of depreciation on assets financed with tax-exempt debt and specifically excludes "consumer loan" bonds from tax-exempt treatment. Some of the worst consequences of IDBs—in particular, their uncontemplated combination with other tax devices—are now under control. The total volume of annual IDB issues is now limited, and this limit is below the current level of issues in some jurisdictions (though it remains to be seen what impact exceptions will have). Do these provisions signal an end to the era of private purpose borrowing?

Probably not. The Deficit Reduction Act did not limit IDBs across the board. It moved a 1986 sunset for small issue IDBs to 1988. Mortgage subsidy bonds (which amounted in 1983 to about one-third of total private purpose tax-exempt borrowing) had actually been phased out as of January 1, 1984. The Deficit Reduction Act renewed them for four additional years. To paraphrase Mark Twain, reports of the death of private purpose tax-exempt borrowing were greatly exaggerated. The only real threat to the IDB program is the possibility of the kind of wholesale revision of the tax code formerly sought by the Reagan administration. Such a revolution could sweep IDBs away along with a collection of other federal tax expenditures. It currently appears, though, that the biggest change this year will lie in bringing additional types of IDB issues under the volume caps. Congress may also make more IDB interest income subject to the minimum tax. But given the intensity of the reform effort, these are relatively minor changes; IDBs continue to be political survivors.

The IDB program has evolved—originally by accident, later with explicit congressional consideration and redirection, and now with limits—into an almost impregnable political niche. It finances activities that are strongly supported even though they may not have much impact on development. It provides visible, and considerable, benefits to businesses, which can be counted on for grateful and vociferous support. Benefits flow through a politically supportive network of local administrators. State and local government officials can take advantage of IDBs to appear to produce economic development benefits without having to pay for them. Local taxpayers, who face only a small slice of the cost, have little say in IDB decisions. Until recently, IDB issues required no voter approval or attention, and they still require only a minimal review. IDBs qualify for tax benefits as public borrowing, but the borrowing itself is privately conducted, so it does not interfere directly or perceptibly with governmental credit raising. The level at which IDBs are approved—state and local development offices—is decoupled from the level at which the bill is paid. And, when the bill does arrive, it is paid for out of less visible, uncollected federal tax revenues.

It is difficult to conceive of a structure better insulated from the political and fiscal accountability of the annual appropriations process. No part of the private use tax-exempt bond program is subject to appropriations competition. Moreover, whether enough public information is available in the right forms and to the right people to approximate appropriations accountability is highly debatable. The level of government at which this program is generated is completely separate from the level at which the bill is paid; it is unlikely that those who pay are truly informed. It seems reasonable to conclude that this program does not reach beyond minimal accountability. This makes the IDB program an interesting case in point, because it eventually encountered limits in spite of the absence of definitive structural checks and balances in its operation. It became so large and expensive and susceptible to misuse that Congress, under pressure to increase tax revenues, had to impose broad restrictions and eventually a cap on its scale. When these constraints begin to bind over the next few years, they may force some semblance of competition among alternative IDB uses. This will not be the same as appropriations competition, to be sure, but it is competition all the same. Choices about IDBs will be constrained, and constrained choices are more likely to be deliberative. It remains to be seen whether these constraints are the beginnings of more-severe restrictions, whether they improve accountability, or whether they provide only enough control to reduce the program's visibility to a level where it can continue to operate comfortably disconnected from the traditional accountability structure.

Chapter 7

Maintaining Public

Infrastructure

THE 1980s may well be remembered as the decade in which "infrastructure" issues rose suddenly to prominence, only to fade again into what many consider richly deserved obscurity. Never the most exciting of subjects, infrastructure nonetheless claimed top billing in the public finance spotlight as deterioration in basic public service systems—highways, bridges, waterways, ports, mass transit, water, sewers—became increasingly obvious. This intense focus on infrastructure issues collided with tremendous fiscal pressure on federal, state, and local governments as grass roots movements to limit taxes and spending gained hearings at state and federal levels. The result was declining levels of public investment and rising levels of public attention, official oratory, and media comment. The condition of the public infrastructure, and the rather dim prospect for improvement, was referred to as the infrastructure crisis.

The crisis received wide attention in the popular press and through government and academic studies. Some of the discussion was alarmist, but some was truly alarming. The issue was starkly framed in a short but widely distributed and very influential book by Pat Choate and Susan Walter with the jolting title *America in Ruins.*[1] Choate and Walter set the context for much of the debate that followed, and they provided examples that have been cited again and again. *America in Ruins* carefully avoids adding up a bill for infrastructure investment "needs," but it does observe that a substantial increase in spending would be needed to maintain existing (often rather low) levels of service.

What infrastructure "bill" had the nation run up? Choate estimated that between $2.5 and $3.0 trillion would be required in the 1980s to prevent the further deterioration of public services.[2] This is roughly equal to one year's gross national product in the early 1980s; it suggests that annual public investment levels should be between 5 and 10 percent of the GNP. This was far in excess of then-current levels. It rang like an alarm across the public works landscape.

The laundry list approach to "needs" assessment, in which nearly every contemplated improvement was portrayed as part of the rock-bottom minimum required for the survival of the Republic, dominated early discussions of the infrastructure crisis. Popular press reports mixed anecdotal examples and impressive comprehensive price tags. *Business Week, Newsweek,* and *U.S. News and World Report* ran feature articles related to the deterioration of infrastructure systems and the cost of rehabilitation.[3] Commissioned government studies detailed extensive—and expensive—needs for major new construction and reconstruction projects. There was disagreement on the magnitudes involved; none equaled the early estimates of $2 trillion to $3 trillion.[4] Perhaps the most accurate comprehensive national estimates were those prepared by the Congressional Budget Office. They reflected a more conservative definition of what constituted "need" than did earlier figures (used when public works spending was viewed as a potential jobs program). Describing the CBO as "less alarmist" than others commenting on infrastructure requirements, its director, Alice Rivlin, observed, "We think this is a manageable problem, by and large." The CBO estimated that $53 billion (in constant 1982 dollars) annually over the next eight years could provide the necessary infrastructure improvements.[5]

Two major points of agreement emerged from popular, governmental, and academic infrastructure studies. First, the average age of various components of the public services capital stock was rising. Widely cited Bureau of Economic Analysis figures showed, among other trends, that the average age of highways and streets had risen from under twenty years in 1970 to over twenty-two in 1980. The average age of public buildings rose from fifteen years to over sixteen between 1975 and 1980.[6] The little comprehensive evidence available confirmed the widely held perception that our public infrastructure was aging. Moreover, these figures may have understated the

TABLE 7.1

State and Local Capital Investment,
1968–1982 (1972 dollars)

	Capital Spending	
Year	Real Total	Real Per Capita
1968	$35.9 billion	$179
1969	34.0	168
1970	31.9	155
1971	30.9	149
1972	30.5	145
1973	30.8	145
1974	31.8	149
1975	30.1	139
1976	27.9	128
1977	25.7	117
1978	27.6	124
1979	25.3	113
1980	25.3	111
1981	23.3	101
1982	22.3	96

SOURCE: General Accounting Office and Department of Commerce, Bureau of Economic Analysis, cited in Government Finance Research Center, *Building Prosperity: Financing Public Infrastructure for Economic Development* (Chicago, Ill.: Municipal Finance Officers Association, 1983).

trend by not adjusting appropriately for the higher cost of more-recent investments.*

The second point of agreement is that the level of investment in public infrastructure has declined markedly. While government spending on capital investment increased more than 40 percent since 1968, inflation eroded the value of current dollars. In real, inflation-adjusted terms, the level of spending declined by more than a third. Table 7.1 shows the total and per capita capital investment of state and local governments from 1968 to 1982, measured in 1972 dollars to adjust for inflation. Real spending levels declined from nearly $36 billion at the start of the period to just over $22 billion at the end; on a per capita basis the investment level has dropped by nearly one-half.[7]

These aggregate figures are reflected bluntly in everyday experience.

*Treating dollars of investment in different years as having the same value—that is, disregarding the larger purchasing power of dollars spent in the past—understates the relative investment during past years. This overstates the importance of more-recent investments and makes the capital stock appear younger, on average, than it really is.

Maintaining Public Infrastructure

Taxpayers daily confront more bridge and road closures. A pothole in Holyoke, Massachusetts, recently swallowed a 1979 Ford Mustang. The early-morning collapse of a section of the Mianus River bridge on the Connecticut Turnpike killed three people; if it had occurred during rush hour, it could easily have caused scores more deaths. Salient examples like these, captured by the media, have reinforced public awareness of "declining infrastructure."*

Proposed Solutions

Taxpayers were dissatisfied with the condition of roads, bridges, and other visible parts of the nation's infrastructure. Studies pointed to a significant decline in the rate of public investment. Lists of high-priced needs for repairs and rebuilding were widely discussed. The combination led to a profusion of suggested "solutions." There was little discussion of underlying causes; most observers accepted the notion that spending was declining in real terms and took it as both an indication of the problem and an identification of its source. The "crisis" was framed in terms of a reduced flow of funds toward public investment. Proposed solutions were mainly ways to raise it again.

Three major directions were suggested. The first was a search for new revenue sources. Those who pursued this tack noted that the level of public capital spending had declined simultaneously with the rise of tax limitation movements and voter resistance to public spending. Cutting capital expenditures was a natural response because the effects were not immediately noticeable. If existing revenues could not be increased, and were already committed, the solution was to find new sources. "User fees"—charging those who used public facilities for the costs of building and operating them —were widely promoted.[8]

A second approach was actively advocated, often in conjunction with the first, by the financial community.[9] Referred to generally as "creative financing," it consisted of nontraditional forms of borrowing ("leveraging") against public revenues. Historically, bond issues were used to finance most

---

*The Public Works Improvement Act of 1984 established a council to prepare annual reports on the condition of the nation's infrastructure starting in 1986. It also requires separate notation of capital investment projects in the federal budget. The infrastructure issue thus remains politically prominent.

state and local investment not paid for by federal grants.* Until recently, these bonds were normally backed by the full faith and credit of the government issuer (including its powers of taxation), so they were very secure investments. In the 1960s, state and local governments began issuing an increasing volume of "revenue" bonds. Unlike the more traditional "general obligation" bonds, revenue issues were backed by the anticipated income from a designated project.

The "creative financing" approach proposed a variety of ways to expand revenue bonds and other nontraditional borrowing devices by means of new financial instruments, new forms of borrowing, and new revenue streams. Some of the methods involved only a different set of borrowing terms, such as interest rates that were adjusted periodically rather than fixed over the whole term of the issue. Others involved complicated schemes to gain use of assets through leasing rather than purchasing in order to obtain federal tax benefits.†

Creative financial schemes cannot actually manufacture money. They are forms of borrowing; they exchange funds now for funds later. Many of the creative devices advanced to address the infrastructure problem backed loans to the public sector with new and different streams of revenue (rather than taxes). This gave public officials more flexibility as well as greater borrowing capacity. But creative methods, unlike user fees or taxes, are not themselves sources of funds; they always involve some form of future repayment. Creative financing simply moves the payment for current expenditures into the future.

The third proposal was to develop a new institutional device to coordinate, oversee—and pay for—continuing reinvestment. As many saw it, the problem of low investment in infrastructure was not an aberration but a continuing feature of the political landscape. Seeking to capitalize on the political momentum of the infrastructure issue, they made a series of ambitious suggestions calling for the establishment of a national fund for infrastructure investments, often called an infrastructure "bank." It was assumed that the federal government would have to pay for the venture, since the problem being addressed was the inability of state and local governments to afford necessary investments. The federal Treasury would support the new entity by extending low-interest credit. Low-interest loans would

*As was discussed in the preceding chapter, the interest on these bonds is exempt from taxation by the federal government, and they therefore tend to have lower interest rates than corporate or federal bonds. This tax subsidy from the federal government makes bonding an attractive avenue for financing state and local projects. The accountability of this subsidy process was discussed in chapter 4, under federal tax expenditures, and in chapter 6, under state and local bonding.

†Leasing arrangements are discussed in detail in chapter 8.

then be extended on a revolving basis to finance needed state and local projects.

The best-documented proposal of this kind was presented in *Hard Choices,* a report prepared by the National Infrastructure Advisory Committee at the request of the Joint Economic Committee of Congress.[10] Researchers at local universities surveyed infrastructure conditions and needs in twenty-three states. The final report, coordinated by the Graduate School of Public Administration at the University of Colorado, compiled extensive data on existing estimates of investment requirements. The study concluded that $1.2 trillion (in 1982 dollars) in infrastructure investments would be required between 1983 and 2000. Existing flows of resources directed toward meeting these needs were projected to provide about $700 billion. The report argued that a national infrastructure fund should provide the remaining $500 billion. The fund, a new federal financial intermediary, would borrow from the public (supported by the credit of the federal government) and lend to state and local governments on favorable terms. These loans would be used to capitalize state-level infrastructure "banks," which would in turn provide funds for necessary infrastructure projects.

Proposals for infrastructure banks generally agreed on financing but differed on everything else, like the degree of federal control that should be exercised in selecting projects and setting engineering standards. Little interest was shown in specifying the operational details of the banks' functions. The proposals were a reflex response to insufficient infrastructure spending, and they were intended to increase it sharply.

The Role of Maintenance

These three proposed solutions represent the leading thinking about how to address our infrastructure problems. What do they have in common? They all manage to miss the central lesson of two decades of experience with infrastructure—and all would commit us to learning the same lesson again, only on a larger scale and at greater expense. These three solutions look at a set of crumbling infrastructure systems and assume that all we need to do is find enough money to build new ones. But this ignores the key question —why are the current systems crumbling? We would do well to ask before we renew the investment cycle. If what we have falls apart before its time, it was either poorly constructed or poorly maintained (or both). Increased spending on new construction will address neither problem. If our fiscal processes systematically generate inadequate maintenance spending, then a new, larger round of new construction will only condemn us to watch the decay of a more expensive capital investment. The solution lies in finding ways to strengthen maintenance, not in creative ways to raise funds with which to repeat old mistakes.

It is remarkable that the discussions of the infrastructure problem and the proposed solutions give only passing notice to the role of maintenance. The silence of major studies on the trends, levels, role, importance, and prospects for maintenance is deafening. It is also curious, because the link between maintenance policies and a deteriorating infrastructure is no secret.

The studies do not entirely avoid the topic of maintenance. Most note that low levels of maintenance have contributed to, caused, or exacerbated basic structural problems caused by low infrastructure investment levels. *Newsweek*'s reference is representative:

> Although billions of dollars have been spent on public works in recent years, the vast bulk of expenditures has gone not to maintain old facilities but to build ambitious new pork-barrel projects, often determined more by politics than actual need. Says E.S. Savas, Assistant Secretary for Housing and Urban Development, "Have you ever seen a politician presiding over a ribbon-cutting for an old sewer line that was repaired?"[11]

Public officials and other observers report that preventive maintenance was one of the first targets for budget cuts when fiscal stress increased in the late 1970s. Helen Boosalis, the mayor of Lincoln, Nebraska, observed, "In the choice between laying off police and maintaining sewers, the sewers always lose."[12]

While comments about the role of maintenance are commonplace, deeper analysis does not figure in any of these recent studies. Maintenance is not incorporated in any serious way in the proposed solutions. The focus is on investment and major rehabilitation; funding for the future maintenance of what we already have, or of what the proposed "solutions" would have us build, is rarely even mentioned as a problem for serious discussion. Yet if the current deterioration is due to inadequate preventive and supportive maintenance, then starting a new and bigger round of construction without providing the maintenance funding it will require would be unaccountably shortsighted.

The low level of attention paid to maintenance is reflected in—and re-flects—how little we know about it. The figures we have on investment requirements are incomplete, generally unreliable, and are fraught with inconsistencies and vague definitions. Five years ago, no comprehensive figures on investment existed. Many criticize those available today, but current data at least provide a starting point for determining how much reconstruction is needed, in which systems, and by when. By contrast, there are no comprehensive, reliable figures for the trends and levels of public maintenance spending. Governmental accounting standards do not require disclosure of maintenance spending, nor is there any widely accepted definition of what should be included. There is a widespread sense that there has been too little maintenance—particularly recently, in the face of increasing fiscal austerity. But there is no accurate way to evaluate this trend, and no systematic effort is afoot to find one.

Maintenance policies are a vital component of capital investment strategies. Yet they have received next to no attention in the discussions framing the infrastructure crisis and its possible solutions. The low profile of maintenance in the current debate may indicate that it is not an important contributing influence to the infrastructure crisis. Alternatively—and more probably—it may indicate a proclivity to underrate maintenance as an integral part of public investment. This proclivity is deeply rooted in the way assets and maintenance are represented in the financial and budgetary statements of public organizations—and in the thinking and incentives of public officials.

The Budgetary Representation of Public Assets, Investment, and Maintenance

Private companies, recognizing the importance of capital to their prosperity and survival, keep careful records of what they own, its value, and its depreciation. Accounting standards promulgated by the Financial Accounting Standards Board, the official standard-setting body for private accounting, require that such records be maintained. Depreciation—a measure of the amount of a capital asset used up in a given year, based on the expected life of the asset and its original value—is recorded and treated as a cost in computing the income of the firm. Asset depreciation reduces the firm's profit, representing a decline in asset value as the asset ages. This treatment has long been standard practice in accounting for private organizations.

There is no such standard for public organizations.[13] The history of accounting for government entities reveals deep divisions about the purposes accounting should serve. As a result, public sector accounting is not as comprehensive or as logically complete as many would like.* Until recently, government accounting has been oriented more toward preventing explicit fraud than toward tracking the government's financial condition. As a consequence, the accounting profession is not as actively concerned as it might be with assessing the value of public capital and measuring how much it has declined through depreciation.

The current standard-setting organization for public sector accounting, the Government Accounting Standards Board, requires governments to maintain records of "fixed assets"—physical facilities and other capital goods—in a separate "account group," held apart from operating funds. These assets are to be recorded at historical cost. Recording the value of immovable infrastructure fixed assets (such as bridges, roads, and sewers) is explicitly made optional. Recording a depreciation offset to the value of listed assets—that is, recognizing that older assets have partly deteriorated and may need to be replaced—is also optional. Even if the governmental unit does choose to recognize depreciation, it is supposed to show it only as an offset to the value of the assets, not as an indication of costs incurred, as in a private company.[14]

Many state and local governments and their chartered authorities, commissions, and other subsidiary units do not record their asset positions even according to these rather relaxed standards. For those that do comply with the officially promulgated standards, the information available on the level of fixed-asset investment and the cost of using these assets is practically worthless. There is no requirement to keep accounting records of infrastructure assets, so they tend to be incomplete. The prices of assets purchased at very different times (and consequently with dollars of very different purchasing power) are added together as if they were measured in the same units. (This problem plagues private sector accounting as well and casts doubt on the usefulness of private sector fixed-asset records no less than on those of the public sector.) And the values shown are often not adjusted for any measure of accumulated depreciation, so the average age or expected remaining lifetime of the capital in service is unknown.

The budgetary treatment of maintenance further distorts the representation of capital in public sector record keeping. Maintenance is a current payment to offset deterioration in existing capital. The level of current services received is rarely much affected by today's maintenance levels; maintenance, even the routine variety, has its primary impact over the longer run. *Maintenance is a form of investment.* It should be integrated

---

*This history, and its implications for the accountability of public spending, will be reviewed in chapter 9.

with other investment expenditures when we assess the performance of public officials. A sound maintenance policy should be rewarded politically in much the same way as any other policy of investment for the future. And it should be similarly reflected in budget documents.

The representation of maintenance in the budget is almost precisely backward. Maintenance expenditures are treated as current operating costs of government; they are included in operating budgets and are generally funded out of current revenues. No notation is made of their impact on the stored value embodied in the jurisdiction's capital stock. They cannot be "capitalized"—that is, funds cannot be borrowed to pay for them. The current system resolves the difficulty of separating true maintenance from pure operating expenses by treating them as identical. It leaves us, instead, with the problem of separating major rehabilitation and reconstruction projects—recognized as capital items and therefore bondable—from "ordinary" maintenance. When is a maintenance project sufficiently large and long-lived that it should qualify?

This backward record keeping for maintenance also provides bad incentives for public officials. Far from getting any budgetary credit or recognition for using scarce funds to improve the condition of the public's investment holdings, public officials who find room in their budgets for maintenance spending find themselves with fewer remaining operating resources to meet vocal demands for immediate public services. When maintenance is for roads or bridges, or when taxpayers see potholes being filled, officials may get some public credit. (Unfortunately, maintenance crews blocking the road often seem to make a greater impression than the improvements being made.) Maintaining underground water or sewer lines to prevent more costly rebuilding later is even less likely to attract public credit in the political arena. The classification of maintenance as an operating expense thus creates inefficient incentives in addition to being inaccurate.

Why, then, does the current system insist on classifying maintenance as an operating expense? The answer lies in legitimate sensitivity about public borrowing and in the fact that maintenance straddles the boundary between capital expenditures (for which we should permit borrowing) and operating expenses (for which we should not). Operating expenses, maintenance, and capital spending form a spectrum from short-lived to very long-lived services; at the boundaries, each blurs into the next. Distinctions will necessarily be somewhat arbitrary. They are, however, crucial for accountability. The use of borrowing, and the distinction between capital and operating costs, is a fundamental accountability issue; it lies at the heart of the problem of ensuring that those who pay are those who benefit. Future taxpayers should share in the costs of facilities that will last long enough for them to enjoy. This is achieved by spreading the costs over time, through borrowing. But current taxpayers should not hand the bills for the *current* services they use to future taxpayers by borrowing to pay for them. Borrowing should not be used to force later taxpayers to pay for services they will never receive.

Explicit borrowing is therefore more or less strictly limited.* We impose special scrutiny on borrowing. Many jurisdictions require special voter approval or extraordinary legislative action in order to approve bonding. We make a major point of distinguishing capital expenditures—those for which it is legal to borrow—from operating expenditures, for which payment must be made out of current revenues.

Maintenance spending presents a genuine quandary. It is, to be sure, a form of investment. But at what point do routine operations provide improvements long-lived enough to be called investments? Does floor wax last long enough? Paint? Asphalt? If we treat maintenance as a capital item, we would capitalize it in the fixed-asset records of the government unit (if it has any) and allow borrowing to pay for it. There would then be a temptation to classify operating expenses as maintenance in order to bond them and move payment for them off into the future. Indeed, even under current standards, where maintenance spending is not capitalizable, some jurisdictions have nonetheless capitalized some operating expenses. As a protection against having too much of current spending qualify for treatment as capital items, we exclude all of it.

The awkward treatment of maintenance is an uncomfortable compromise between competing logical imperatives. Maintenance occupies the middle of the spectrum between operating and capital spending; it is the part of capital expenditure that looks most like operating spending. There are dangers of misclassifying it in either direction, but the dangers are not equal. If we classify maintenance as an operating expenditure, we lose the ability to bond it as an investment for the future—we have an uneven treatment of different forms of capital spending. If, on the other hand, we classify maintenance as capital spending, we lose the accountability check against allowing current taxpayers to push the costs of current services onto future taxpayers. This is perceived as a greater danger, and we therefore shun treating maintenance as investment. We accept an almost exactly backward budgetary treatment of maintenance—first, because it is difficult to separate maintenance from pure operation, and second, because we do not want to permit bonding for operating costs. Maintenance—current taxpayers' con-

---

*Some forms of implicit borrowing are not easily limited. Pension promises extended to public sector workers are the classic example, treated in chapter 2.

tinuing reinvestment in a valuable public capital stock—should be noted as an investment. Instead it is treated as a cost.

The treatment of depreciation is also backward, but backward in the opposite direction from maintenance. Depreciation should be treated as a current cost. Instead, it is at best noted as a side calculation in a sidelined group of accounts. Usually, it is simply ignored. And often, the basic information needed to compute it—asset records—has not been kept.

Accounting for Capital and the Incentives of Public Officials

It is hard in any consistent conceptual framework of government accounting to justify ignoring depreciation. The misclassification of maintenance can be seen as the outcome of conflicting public interests—the clash of a conceptually appropriate treatment of minor capital expenses with the strong standard that we cannot permit operating expenses to be bonded. But whatever other purposes these budgetary treatments may ultimately serve, both contribute to an incentive structure for public officials that is strongly biased against appropriate levels of maintenance, rehabilitation, and investment spending.

Consider what happens, under current accounting procedures, when funds are short and infrastructure investments are deferred. The accounting system barely notices. Even if the governmental unit kept track of its fixed infrastructure assets, all we would find is that the historical cost of all past investment had not increased. If it chose to do so, a jurisdiction could disclose accumulated depreciation. In this case, we would find a recorded decrease in the net historical cost of fixed assets owned—but only in the separate records of capital assets. Nowhere in the *operating* statement of the entity would we find any recognition of the cost associated with the wear of the assets over the year.

When tight funds result in deferred maintenance, the effect is even more perverse. Operating funds that would have been spent on maintenance are simply freed for other uses. There is no notation, in any capital records, of the decline in value of the capital resulting from the failure to maintain it. The service level will not drop immediately; as with all capital effects, the change will appear in time. No immediate indication will be visible, either on the books of the government or in the service experiences of the taxpayers, when preventive and routine maintenance is curtailed. It makes an attractive target for budget cuts. Nothing forces a recognition that these shortsighted policies ultimately result in greater expense.

Ignoring depreciation and deferring maintenance are both powerful forms of hidden spending. To fail to reinvest in or maintain the existing capital stock to preserve its value as it wears down is to live off an inherited bank account. Current taxpayers, not doing their part to maintain the existing storehouse of value in the form of public service capital, spend assets provided to them by those who came before. They do not pay for services they enjoy; they are drawing against the legacy left to them. This spending is obscured by the lack of records and comprehensive accounting for fixed-asset investments from year to year.

This form of surreptitious spending is encouraged by two persistent features of the capital financing landscape. The first is the federal government's habit of providing capital but not maintenance assistance. On the theory that local taxpayers should assume the burden of operating the facilities presented to them, the federal government generally supplies funds for construction costs only. Thus, localities make capital investments because their share of direct costs of new facilities is kept down. To maintain the facilities, however, they must find funds in their own revenues. As a consequence, maintenance funds often appear to be more constrained than construction funds, and the value of many public investments is reduced by poor maintenance.

The second exacerbating influence is the fact that major rehabilitation and reconstruction costs can be capitalized, and funded through borrowing, but that ordinary maintenance expenditures cannot. Public officials thus face a disturbing choice. They can find room in austere operating budgets for routine maintenance spending for which they cannot borrow, and force other important operating spending aside. Or they can wait, allowing facilities to deteriorate until major rebuilding is needed. The latter strategy is likely to be more expensive in the long run, because the operation of existing facilities is inefficient—we get lower levels of service without correspondingly lower costs. But the rebuilding will often be a capitalizable expense. Spending is therefore deferred at least temporarily—freeing funds for current use in direct service provision—and it may be deferred further through bonding. Moreover, federal assistance may be available for major reconstruction projects. Thus, not only may the cost be deferred—some of it may disappear completely, to land later on taxpayers somewhere else.

Prospects for Change

Using up existing capital assets—permitting a deterioration of infrastructure through deferred maintenance—is a form of public spending that operates at the lowest level of accountability. It requires no appropriation, and there is no obvious way to make it require one. It takes place by default, without explicit authorization. Not only does it *not* need an appropriated spending program to *happen;* it even takes appropriated maintenance or reinvestment expenditures to *keep* it from happening. And, since it is the result of an ongoing physical process rather than of a direct government activity, information about it is rarely collected. The existing system of governmental financial reporting therefore seriously misrepresents maintenance spending. Poor information contributes to the generally low levels of maintenance that have accompanied the fiscal stress of the late 1970s and early 1980s. Inefficiently low maintenance levels, in turn, raise the total cost of services derived from public capital facilities. Without a concerted effort, this form of spending misses all accountability checks.

The generally low profile of maintenance concerns and the weak reporting system through which maintenance is represented also contribute to its not being a central component of major proposals to address the infrastructure problems we face. Although virtually all proposals mention low maintenance as a contributing factor in infrastructure decay, none tackle the structural incentives that keep maintenance spending below appropriate levels. So long as maintenance is politically the least costly portion of a budget to cut, it will continue to be the first target in periods of fiscal stress. Starting a new round of major infrastructure spending without first changing maintenance incentives begins a new cycle of decay rather than a new era of quality public services at the lowest possible cost. That is folly; given the scope of current infrastructure problems, it is folly on a grand scale.

How might we raise the level of accountability for this form of spending? One way to approach the problem is to observe that maintenance spending —what we need to *prevent* quiet spending through deterioration—is itself appropriated. The spending that is needed to ensure accountable stewardship is subject to budget scrutiny while its counterpart on the dark side— what happens if we don't spend maintenance dollars—remains hidden. Improving the way we represent maintenance spending and its value may thus be the most direct attack we can make to enhance the accountability of all capital investment spending.

The profile of maintenance in infrastructure investment policy can be raised. The accountability reasons for treating maintenance as an operating cost for budgetary purposes are sound, and this treatment should probably continue. But we could provide a separate annual accounting of the stewardship of public capital resources, including the level of new investment, the reduction in value due to depreciation, and the reinvestment in the form of maintenance. This might serve to make depreciation and reductions in maintenance more visible, and it might lessen their use as sources of current operating funds for other purposes.

A more dramatic way to raise the profile of maintenance spending would be to establish a schedule of expected reinvestment when an asset is purchased or constructed. The schedule would be treated as a liability to be met in the future. Whether funds were appropriated or not, the force of that liability would be felt, in the form of maintenance expenditures (if funds for maintenance were provided) or in the form of reduced services (if they were not). To the extent that scheduled maintenance was not performed, the amount of underfunding would be added to an "unfunded maintenance liability" recognized in the financial reports of the organization. Like the unfunded pension liability, this would represent a debt of current and past taxpayers to be paid by future taxpayers.[15] In chapter 1, it was argued that reporting unfunded pension liabilities was useful, though not a guarantee of accountability. Introducing the concept of unfunded maintenance liabilities might raise the accountability of maintenance spending to the level of accountability enjoyed by public pensions. This speaks a mouthful about where maintenance accountability is now.

In addition to improving its accounting representation, we could also give maintenance spending greater legal standing. For example, an annual maintenance spending schedule could be created when projects were financed, with the stipulation that the prescribed maintenance spending take place before debt service could be paid on borrowed funds. This would elevate maintenance to a position of real prominence in infrastructure investment and ensure the close attention of bondholders and their trustees (along with other public officials).

It will not be easy to attract for maintenance spending the attention that it deserves. It is not a scintillating subject, and it is caught in a curious paradox. As long as maintenance spending is not permitted as a capitalizable component of infrastructure investment, it is unlikely to be a focus for those who offer new and different proposals for funding infrastructure investment. If it cannot be a part of the borrowing package, the attention of financiers will remain turned away from it. Underwriters' commercial interests are well served by the sale of bonds for new construction; maintenance spending generates no profits on Wall Street. Yet, unless the perverse incentives that public officials face in dealing with maintenance are addressed first, other ways of raising infrastructure spending will merely be ways of throwing good money after bad.

The public does not see maintenance issues clearly. As a result, public officials are naturally tempted to shortchange maintenance spending, drawing down our existing public service capital stock. We will continue to spend in this way unless we act positively, and painfully, by appropriating scarce operating funds for maintenance investments. The current practice of spending our capital assets does not require appropriation; it takes place by default. Spending by default is arguably the most unaccountable spending of all.

Chapter 8

Public Sector Leasing

BY 1982, the fear of an impending infrastructure crisis put enormous pressure on public officials to raise funds for new construction and major rehabilitation of deteriorating facilities. The tax revolts of the late 1970s and widespread grass roots resistance to expanded government spending and taxing constrained the use of traditional sources of public funds.* This led to reduced public investment and also prompted public officials to look for nontraditional funding sources. They searched for untapped reservoirs of money, potentially divertible to public purposes, not yet constrained by tax limitations or by bond referendum refusals.

Taxpayer resistance was only one force chipping away infrastructure funds. Blaming (or crediting) the taxpayer revolt for the pressure on public officials to tap new funding sources misses the deeper and more fundamental evolution of public funding. Traditional sources were becoming exceedingly expensive. At about the time that signs of taxpayer resistance appeared in earnest, the cost of capital to the public sector through traditional sources rose dramatically. Just when voters were growing more sensitive to tax increases, the increases required to maintain traditional levels of public investment (if continued from the same sources) suddenly became larger. The combination of increased resistance and dramatically increased costs prompted a precipitous decline in real public investment.

This was a sharp change from previous decades. For most of the 1960s, the rate of interest on tax-exempt bond issues—the traditional source of public investment funds for projects paid for by state and local governments

*The tax and expenditure limitations flowing from the tax revolt will be discussed in chapter 10.

—was low, generally ranging between 3 and 4 percent. Bondholders expected reasonably stable prices and were willing to lend funds for the large public investments of this period over long terms at low interest rates. The outcome was altogether different from what they projected. In the late 1960s and through the 1970s, inflation pushed prices up sharply; the dollars paid to bondholders (both interest and repayment of principal) had a much lower purchasing power than anticipated. The owners of long-term tax-exempt bonds suffered very large holding losses; for example, inflation between 1965 and 1985 reduced the value of payments on a twenty-year bond issued in 1965 at 3 percent interest by more than one-half.

State and local governments, and their taxpayers, reaped the bondfall. They repaid their debts in cheaper dollars and had funds left over for additional investments, or for other public spending, or to lower their tax rates. As the rapid inflation of 1968–1981 eroded the value of payments to bondholders, state and local governments were able to pay off their capital investment debts for about half price. This means that taxpayers made the substantial public investments of this period for about half of their real cost. This was a form of quiet *un*spending—a concealed tax through which bondholders paid for part of the public's investment.

The inflation that caused this huge transfer—a dramatic gift from those who lent money for public improvements—was unanticipated. If bondholders had suspected that prices would rise as they did, they would have lent only at sharply higher interest rates to compensate for inflation's erosion of the value of their repayments. Bondholders are not likely to be fooled again. Having once suffered substantial erosion in the value of promised long-term payment streams, they are now wary of future price increases. Indeed, all bond lenders (not just those who lend to governments) now seem to be in a state of more or less permanent anticipation of additional inflation. The yields required to attract long-term investors have risen to historic levels, remaining high even as current inflation rates abate. Bondholders realize that inflation need not be sustained to be a problem for them; they can be hurt badly by sharp inflation over a short period, which would reduce the value of payments received for the remainder of the bond issue.

The real interest rates now prevailing in the tax-exempt bond market are about 5 to 6 percent, compared with approximately 1.5 to 2.5 percent in the early 1960s.* In part, this higher real rate reflects a fear of future inflation. Other influences, too, have pushed up the interest rates in the tax-exempt bond market. Congress lowered the marginal tax rates of the taxpayers in the highest brackets, which made investors less concerned about finding

---

*The real interest rate is the interest rate after adjustment for inflation. If the interest rate is 9 percent and inflation is 5 percent, the real interest rate is $9 - 5 = 4$ percent.

tax-sheltered investment opportunities. Simultaneously, more investment tax loopholes have been made available, so investors seeking tax shelters now have a variety of alternatives to tax-exempt bonds. Finally, pressure on the tax-exempt bond market has been increased by growth in the issuance of private purpose tax-exempt bonds.*

The cost of public investment has thus exploded. The expected costs taxpayers must pay are now much higher; the value of total payments on a thirty-year bond with a real interest rate of 6 percent is about 60 percent higher than the value of payments on a 3 percent bond. The current actual cost of investment also feels even higher because taxpayers did not pay the full cost before; in some instances they paid no more (in real terms) than about forty cents on the dollar of the initially agreed amounts. *The current total cost of a dollar's worth of public investment may be more than three times what it was between 1968 and 1979.*

This sharp increase in the cost of investment came at a particularly inopportune time for harassed public officials. They had to contend not only with more resistant taxpayers and with new tax limitations but also with public investment borrowing costs three times higher than those of the last round of investment. Together, these forces were a powerful spur for seeking nontraditional funding sources.

The latter part of the 1970s witnessed a substantial increase in the use of funding devices other than traditional tax-exempt borrowing by state and local governments. These devices are known collectively as creative financing. Some were new forms of borrowing, such as bonds guaranteed by a third party or bonds whose interest rates were adjusted periodically. Others involved new payment methods, such as bonds backed by revenues from specific projects, or particular taxes, or user fees. The device with the most far-reaching implications for the relationships between state and local governments, the private sector, and the federal government was the use of leasing and sale-leasebacks.

Public Leasing as a Financing Alternative

Leases are agreements (by a "lessee") to use an asset (belonging to the "lessor") for a specified rental term in return for a series of payments. Both sales and rentals may be structured as leases. Leases may provide for the

---

*These reasons for the increased interest rates of tax-exempt bonds were discussed more extensively in chapter 6.

sale of the asset at the term's end (installment sales) or merely for its *use* for part (or all) of its economic lifetime. Those that do not transfer owner-ship are long-term *rental* agreements. Those that do involve a sale are better viewed as forms of borrowing: the lessee has borrowed the asset while paying for it, much as a consumer might do with a revolving-credit account at a department store. Rental is also a form of borrowing. Instead of owning the asset, the lessee secures its use and services over part or all of its life. As the exclusive user during the period of the lease, the lessee enjoys most of the rights of ownership. Thus, whether in the form of sale or pure rental, leases use the lessor's money to finance the holding and use of an asset by the lessee. This is borrowing by any sensible definition of the term.

It may not, however, be within the legal definition of "borrowing" as it applies, for example, to limitations on public debt. Most state and local jurisdictions limit the amount of debt that can be outstanding at any given time. Leases often do not count against these ceilings. By definition, debt involves a commitment to make payments over a long time period. Stringent accountability requirements are usually imposed when a legislative body wants to force a future legislature to make appropriations. With most debt issues, a special form of resolution is required, or voters must approve the debt issue in a special referendum. These requirements reflect the fact that debt is a means to pass costs on to future generations of taxpayers—and that the natural proclivity to make someone else pay must be limited through more-stringent review to ensure that those future taxpayers to whom the bill is handed will also receive some of the benefits of the project being financed.

If the defining characteristic of debt issues that calls for careful scrutiny is that they pass costs on to future taxpayers, then lease commitments to make a series of future payments should be subject to similar limitations. In general they are not. Most public leases include a clause that makes future payments contingent on legislative appropriation. These funds are almost always appropriated. Moreover, the contracts often have penalty clauses that render it economically unattractive to break them. But since future legislatures are not legally bound to fund them, in most jurisdictions leases are not viewed as long-term commitments subject to debt issue re-quirements and to debt limitations.

Public officials see this freedom from the stringent limitations of debt as a major advantage of leasing. Another key advantage is that leases can generate favorable tax treatment. Among tax lawyers and the IRS, the treatment of leases for tax purposes is a long-standing area of controversy, involving a myriad of complex rules. The owner (for tax purposes) can take depreciation deductions on the asset and may qualify for other tax benefits as well (including investment or rehabilitation tax credits). The issue of who owns the asset for tax purposes is therefore quite important—and extremely complicated. This is particularly true in a lease between a private taxpayer and a tax-exempt public organization. Since these tax benefits reduce the lessor's cost of ownership, the lessee may be able to secure the asset for a lower rental fee. In most cases, getting the benefits of private ownership through leasing requires the public organization to forgo other, even more valuable benefits—in particular, the ability to finance the acquisition with tax-exempt debt. But if the public entity is limited in its use of tax-exempt financing, either through voter resistance or through a debt ceiling, tax benefits through leasing may become attractive.

Complicated leases can obscure the true sources and amounts of resources being expended. Sometimes even the participants are confused about how much they paid or received and for what. Where a private party, using its own money or funds it borrows itself, purchases an asset and leases it to a public organization, the analysis is straightforward. But public sector leases often begin with the sale of a public asset to a private taxpayer, after which the same asset is leased back to the public. These so-called sale-leasebacks often involve a loan from the lessee (or another public organization) to the lessor, so that public money is actually financing the private "owner" whose asset is being used by the public. In some other arrangements, a facility is sold outright to the lessor, but the ground on which it stands is retained by the public. The ground is leased to the new facility owner, who then leases the package back to the public. The public winds up leasing the ground from itself. The attempt to figure out the tax treatment of such leases, and to discern who got what from whom at what price, can be thoroughly baffling.

As with all forms of creative financing, a primary attraction of leasing is that it generates—or, more accurately, *seems* to generate—"new" funds for public investment. This gain is largely an illusion. While funds can be attracted that would otherwise have been used elsewhere, creative methods cannot actually create new money. Like all forms of financing, they simply rearrange the payments that have to be made over time. Borrowing is an exchange of funds today for larger amounts of funds to be paid later. Creative financing approaches can expand the range of rearrangement choices, but they cannot repeal the basic law that borrowing only exchanges current for future funds. Given the complexity of some creative leasing arrangements, however, it is no wonder that it sometimes seems that money is being manufactured.

Public Leasing in Practice

Public organizations have long leased equipment and, occasionally, other assets. But the advantages of tax-exempt borrowing were traditionally so great that foregoing them to obtain the tax advantages of leasing was too high a cost to pay. The rise of tax-exempt interest rates relative to those of private securities, however, together with the liberalized treatment of depreciation allowed by the Economic Recovery Tax Act of 1981 (ERTA), made public leasing more attractive. Moreover, ERTA heightened the interest of investors (and their lawyers and investment bankers) by liberalizing the rules for private leasing. Several specific provisions permit favorable lease treatment for a few special cases of leasing to public organizations.[1] Much of the public sector leasing activity that followed the adoption of ERTA would have been permitted in its absence, but the volume of public leasing nonetheless grew dramatically after 1981.

Just how much it grew, however, or how large it is now, or how much tax revenue the federal government is losing as a consequence, is largely a matter for conjecture. Some of the proposed transactions were widely publicized; the sale-leaseback of dormitories at Bennington College to its alumni was particularly offensive to some observers. Evidence suggested that major growth in leasing by tax-exempt organizations would lead to sizable federal revenue losses. Many in Congress therefore tried to limit the tax benefits of leases between private taxpayers and public organizations. In June of 1983, extensive hearings on public leasing activity were held by the House Ways and Means Committee. A long roster of government witnesses from the Treasury, the IRS, the General Accounting Office, and the Congressional Budget Office, all favorably disposed to some form of limitation, testified in support of limiting public leasing. Their testimony was followed, predictably, by a long parade of witnesses backing specific uses of leasing. Even most of these witnesses agreed that many public leasing transactions were outrageous, and many supported the broad intent of the limitation. They did, though, advocate that limits not be applied to *their* leasing, which they presented as serving a narrow but important and otherwise underserved public interest.

No one would hazard a guess about total federal revenue losses from leasing, what the volume of transactions was, or how much of it was precipitated by ERTA. John Chapoton, the assistant secretary of the Treasury for tax policy, testified as the first witness that "this unanticipated revenue loss could be as high as billions of dollars annually."[2] When one of the sponsors of the bill questioned him on this rather vague estimate, Chapoton replied that he could not be more specific. No other witness was prepared to be more specific, either. Many noted that tax-exempt entities owned large amounts of capital that they could potentially use in sale-leaseback arrangements, and they argued that the practice could be expensive for the federal Treasury. Yet no one was willing to provide an estimate of the volume of existing leasing activity or of its revenue implications.

This uncertainty reflects the decentralized and private nature of lease transactions. Most are so small that investors are found privately, without any advertising. Registration of the offering is generally not required by the Securities and Exchange Commission or by any other regulatory agency. Tax benefits from leasing are usually available only through corporations or partnerships. They will eventually file tax returns, but the data will not distinguish private and public leasing and will in any case not be available immediately. There is thus no comprehensive information on the volume or composition of public leasing. Most important, it is difficult to tell why public officials choose the lease option; the aggregate data are entirely silent on this issue.

Why Do Public Organizations Lease?

Leasing by public organizations is prompted by a variety of forces. Sometimes, whether because of federal tax benefits or because of a new leasing company's desire to break into the business, it is simply cheaper than purchasing. Sometimes it is used to circumvent an existing managerial restriction (as in the case of debt limitations). Sometimes it provides temporary fiscal relief, at the expense of future taxpayers. But often it provides only a temporary respite, and the ultimate price frequently is high.

Since the aggregate data about leasing say little about the motives of those involved, exploring case histories of individual leasing arrangements may provide the greatest insight into the patterns underlying lease financing by public organizations. The examples that follow are not comprehensive, but they illustrate some of the more important and persistent features of creative deals. They show some of the wide range of motives involved, some of the variation in terms these deals involve, and some of the differing outcomes of attempts to be financially innovative.

Public Sector Leasing

Example 1: Leasing to take advantage of federal tax benefits: the rehabilitation of Stewart House. Lease contracts are often used so that federal tax benefits that would otherwise accrue to a tax-exempt entity can instead be taken by a private taxpayer set up as the nominal "owner." One public-spirited example of this form is the rehabilitation of Stewart House, carried out through the Pike Place Preservation and Redevelopment Authority in Seattle. Interested in preserving the historic character of several sections of its waterfront area, the city arranged the sale-leaseback of the historic property. The building was substantially rehabilitated by private investors and then leased back to the public. It is now a mixed-use building, with some retail space in the lower part and low-income-elderly housing and single-occupancy units above. The tax benefits from the arrangement are substantial. Because it is a historic building, the investors qualify for a 25 percent rehabilitation tax credit, reducing the net cost of their investment from $4 million to $3 million. They can also depreciate their investment over a period as short as five years. These tax benefits substantially cut the cost of the building's rehabilitation; the difference was paid by the federal Treasury. The same rehabilitation could have been done with funds raised through tax-exempt bonds by the city, but if the city or the redevelopment authority had been the owner, the 25 percent subsidy in the form of the rehabilitation tax credit would have accrued to a tax-exempt entity and thus been worthless.

Example 2: Leasing to take advantage of specific public leasing provisions: the MTA vehicle sale-leaseback. ERTA contains a specific provision permitting "safe-harbor" treatment for leases of mass-commuting vehicles. Any arrangement will be treated as a lease for tax purposes if the involved parties say it is one. Without the provision, an arrangement that the IRS construed as a sale—so that ownership resided in the public sector—would have been ineligible for depreciation tax benefits. The safe-harbor provision was negotiated by the then-chairman of the New York Metropolitan Transit Authority (MTA), Richard Ravitch, and the MTA was the first to use it. The MTA doubled its tax break, since the interest payments on state or local industrial development bonds issued to finance the acquisition of commuting vehicles were exempt from federal income tax.* Through an ingenious sale-leaseback arrangement, the MTA managed to preserve the tax-exempt status of the bonds used to finance the vehicles and still transfer ownership to the private sector for depreciation purposes.

The transactions were quite complicated.[3] First, industrial development

---

*The tax treatment of industrial development bonds was discussed in chapter 6.

bonds were issued and the proceeds used by the MTA to purchase the vehicles. The vehicles were then sold to Metromedia (a corporation) and to Vista Resources (a group of private investors). About 85 percent of the funds the investors used to purchase the vehicles were lent to them by the MTA—that is, the sale involved "seller financing," so that the investors had to provide only about 15 percent of the purchase price. The vehicles were then leased back to the MTA for fifteen years, at the end of which the MTA can purchase them for $1. The interest rate on the MTA's loan to the investors was set so that the annual debt service on the loan (the payment from investors to the MTA) exactly cancels the agreed lease payment (the payment from the MTA to the investors). Thus, except for the fraction of the purchase paid by investors at the signing of the agreement, no funds change hands over the term of the lease.

What did the investors get? The authority lent them 85 percent of the purchase price, and their lease income covers the debt service on that loan; that part of the bargain has no impact on them. They are, however, the nominal owners of about $100 million in depreciable assets. At the closing of the deal, they received tax reductions of about $40 million, spread over the five-year depreciation period. (Accelerated depreciation is permitted for transit equipment.) For this the investors paid about $15 million of their own funds. The complex contractual arrangements add up to a sale of tax benefits.

What did the MTA get? It arranged—and is paying the interest and principal on—tax-exempt debt for 85 percent of the purchase price. It obtained the other 15 percent from the investors, in exchange for tax benefits (the depreciation deductions) that were of no value to it as a tax-exempt governmental entity. Thus, the net impact of the arrangement on the MTA was a 15 percent purchase price discount.

The arrangement was complicated, but the outcome was simple. The federal government allowed the MTA to separate the tax benefits of ownership from the other benefits and obligations normally associated with owning an asset. The MTA was then able to sell the tax benefits as a marketplace commodity. The complex tangle of reciprocal contractual agreements had no operational substance; it merely surrounded—and perhaps obscured—the sale of tax benefits.

Before ERTA's adoption, this transaction would have been viewed as a transparent veil insufficient to hide illegitimate tax benefits. The IRS would have ruled the arrangement a tax "sham" existing solely to reduce tax payments. It would have disallowed the depreciation deductions of the "owners" on the basis that they were not really the owners. The reciprocal financing alone (the MTA's advancing 85 percent of the purchase funds to the investors) would have disqualified the deal as a lease. Moreover, the low-price repurchase option at the end of the lease term would have been viewed as evidence that the arrangement was really a sale and not a lease. (In that case, tax ownership, if it had ever been transferred to the investors at all, would be transferred back to the MTA.) By explicitly permitting mass-commuting vehicle transactions under safe-harbor treatment, Congress suspended these traditional tests of whether the arrangement was a true lease and opened the door for deals like the MTA's.

The MTA transaction was clearly carried out to appropriate federal tax benefits explicitly made available in ERTA. The MTA reaped $15 million of these benefits in the reduced purchase price. The investors also received a substantial portion. Even if we assume that investors should earn an after-tax return of 19 percent (roughly the interest rate then prevailing, considering the inherent riskiness in being the first to try a new tax device), the tax benefits were sold for about $8 million less than they were worth.[4] Thus, their $15 million investment returned 19 percent after tax *and* an $8 million bonus. The reward for the risk they ran was handsome indeed.

Other groups also fared well. The novelty and complexity of the arrangement, the IRS's inability to produce regulations promptly, and the speed with which the first deal had to be put together forced the MTA to rely on outside legal assistance and financial advice. The legal and underwriting fees for the first transaction were over $1 million. In subsequent deals, the MTA simply relied on the legal work it bought with the first transaction, and its legal and underwriting fees were next to nothing. But the investors and the MTA (and its riders!) were not the only beneficiaries of the first public sector safe-harbor leaseback.

Example 3: Leasebacks for arbitrage: the Oakland Convention Center. Arbitrage is the process of purchasing in one market for the purpose of profitably selling, more or less immediately, in a different market. Because state and local government entities can borrow funds in the tax-exempt bond market at interest rates considerably below those prevailing for taxable securities, they are often in a position to profit from the arbitrage of borrowed funds. They can borrow at low rates and invest at higher rates.

This is not the intent of the federal tax exemption granted state and local governments' debt. These opportunities are therefore circumscribed by a number of IRS restrictions. In general, when borrowed funds are reinvested at a higher interest rate, tax-exempt status is denied on the borrowing. The rules are complex, allowing some exceptions. For example, funds from construction bond issues can be reinvested during construction, subject to restrictions. State and local governments can and do enjoy some minor benefits of arbitrage, but the system of IRS limitations on these devices effectively prevents serious abuses.

Under some circumstances, however, leasing creates very profitable arbitrage opportunities. While a tax-exempt bond issuer cannot borrow funds to reinvest at higher rates, there are few restrictions on what state and local governments can do with assets they already own. Consider what happens when they sell an asset and borrow funds to buy it back. The proceeds of the sale are not borrowed, so they can be invested. The borrowed funds are used for a public purpose—purchasing a facility—so interest payments on them are tax-exempt. The net effect of these transactions, of course, is that funds have been borrowed and then invested. Normally, this borrowing would not be tax-exempt. But because it is intermediated by the sale of an existing asset, the "laundered funds" (proceeds from the sale) can be invested without threatening the tax-exempt status of the bond issue used to repurchase the asset.[5]

Leasing serves as a handy laundry for such transactions, as the Oakland Convention Center arrangement illustrates.[6] In 1981, the city of Oakland faced intense financial pressures, created by, among other things, California's stringent Proposition 13 tax limitation. The state had threatened to condemn Oakland's auditorium for code violations. Oakland sought "alternative" means to finance rehabilitation and conversion of the auditorium and museum into a convention facility. The city devised a package in which it issued "municipal improvement" bonds to pay for rehabilitation of the auditorium, then sold the two buildings to a private syndicate. Oakland maintained ownership of the site, which was leased to the syndicate. Because the project was planned as a convention center, tax-exempt industrial bond financing could be arranged for the investors to purchase the buildings and finance their rehabilitation.

But what was the city to do with the proceeds? Technically, these were city funds, not borrowed funds, for the city had owned the facilities outright before their sale. The proceeds were used in part to pay off the municipal improvement bonds that had supplied funds for the auditorium's reconstruction; the remainder was invested in high-yield securities. The principal and income of this fund are being used for lease payments and will be available to repurchase the facility at the end of the lease term. A report to the city council summarizing the impact on the city's budget concludes:

> The sales proceeds from the Convention Center Extension will be invested in governmental securities or other high yield corporate securities. The interest from these securities will be more than sufficient to pay lease payments for thirty years, with funds remaining to repurchase both facilities. No additional city funds will be required to finance the proposed actions.[7]

These transactions clearly—even gleefully—involve arbitrage. The city could have issued tax-exempt bonds to finance these improvements. Instead, it arranged to issue tax-exempt bonds to finance the purchase and rehabilitation by private buyers eager for the benefits of low interest costs and eligible for depreciation deductions. Some of these benefits were handed back to the city in the form of low lease payments. Rather than absorb the funds generated by the arrangement into its current budget, the city invested in a reserve fund of taxable securities. This reassured investors about future lease payments and reassured taxpayers by providing for facility repurchase at the end of the lease term. Not incidentally, it turned a handsome arbitrage profit, shifting part of the cost of rehabilitation from local to federal taxpayers.

As in the MTA deal, complex arrangements yielded a simple net transaction. Tax-exempt bonds were issued, and funds were invested in the taxable securities market. In most business transactions, a cost that is deductible to one party generates income that must be declared by another. Here, the corporations that borrow money from Oakland's reserve fund can deduct the interest they pay as a cost of business. But there is no offsetting declaration of income: the city is not taxable. And the city's borrowing does not generate taxable income either. The core of this transaction is a sizable loss to the federal Treasury from arbitrage. The rest of the deal is effectively a series of "wash" transactions—in two senses of the word.

While many believe that the tax treatment allowed in the Oakland case will not be permitted again (the arbitrage aspect of the transaction is too straightforward), other, less blatant forms of arbitrage are still possible through lease transactions. The essential trick is to find a legitimate purpose served by having the state or local government body sell an asset and then acquire it again through a lease or a lease-purchase. Arbitrage opportunities exist wherever state and local governments own assets that they could have financed or that they can refinance. Leases are one key that unlocks arbitrage possibilities.

Example 4: Leases to hide asset sales: the proposal to sell the streetlights in Midtown. * Many state and local governments have accumulated large investments over time, sometimes by making an outright purchase from tax revenues, sometimes by issuing bonds for a purchase and paying them off from taxes, and sometimes by making a purchase from gifts or other

---

*This is obviously not its real name. I was asked for private advice about this arrangement, which was eventually not pursued and which is therefore better left as a skeleton in the closet. I like to think I was persuasive, but I suspect other factors weighed against it more heavily than my advice did.

sources. In times of fiscal stress, when operating budgets are under heav
pressure but taxpayer demands for services are still strongly felt by cit
officials, the bank of accumulated assets often seems an attractive source
funds. Taxpayers often react negatively, however, if elected officials liqu
date assets to generate current funds. Leases involving the sale of asset
though, can sometimes be made sufficiently complicated to obscure what
really happening. They can be used as a smoke screen for sales providir
funds for current activities.

In the early 1980s, Midtown faced a series of deep fiscal problems. Tryir
to carry out an ambitious revitalization program and increasingly co
strained in its ability to raise new funds or to cut operating expense
Midtown was in dire need of money for a long list of capital improvement
During the 1970s, it had been effectively shut out of the tax-exempt bor
market; as the 1980s began, its credit was precarious. Raising capital fun
in the bond market was out of the question, and for the most part capit
spending simply came to a halt. Some repairs, however, could not be pos
poned. And so it was that the streetlight rehabilitation project came to
a subject of heated discussion.

No explicit borrowing was in the offing. No funds currently existe
Federal grants were not available. Additional operating funds might hav
been available through transfers from other, lower-priority uses. But capit
funds were not forthcoming from (or for) any avenue.

Creative financing approaches were being discussed in fiscally har
pressed cities across the nation, and gradually an approach for Midtow
took shape. Although the city could not afford the millions of dollars
required reinvestment, it could perhaps afford to pay—mainly out of futur
revenues (indeed, largely out of anticipated increases in aid from the stat
—to rent a rehabilitated system. The current system would be sold
private investors, who would rehabilitate it using funds they raised then
selves. The streetlights would then be leased back to the city, with a contra
for maintenance.

The intriguing element of the proposal was that the payment of futur
rentals was not linked in any way to the proceeds of the sale. No reserv
fund was to be established, nor were the proceeds to be used to pay for th
early years of the rental. They would not even be invested to genera
arbitrage income (as in the Oakland case) to pay the higher rentals on th
rehabilitated system. They were simply to flow into the general fund,
meet other current operating costs of government.

This is most easily understood as "A Tale of Three Taxpayers"—taxpa
ers past, taxpayers present, and taxpayers future. Taxpayers past had bui

up an investment in a physical system—a physical bank account. Taxpayers present would liquidate this account, using the proceeds for other current service needs. Taxpayers future would then have to build the city's investment in the system back up through a leaseback of the rehabilitated system. The tangled lease obligations would make it hard to tell what had happened, but taxpayers past and taxpayers future would have every right to see this as a quiet raid by taxpayers present.

This arrangement would have had two principal parts, each skirting the usual forms of accountability checks. First, a sale would generate funds to be absorbed into the current operating budget. Spendable funds would be increased without voter approval or scrutiny. Second, a new purchase and borrowing arrangement, set up as a lease, would isolate the borrowing from the usually stringent scrutiny applied to transactions that create long-term commitments. Under most state and local accounting systems, including Midtown's, the newly available funds would still have to be appropriated.* And the new lease contract would have to be approved or at least overseen by the city council. Nonetheless, the review process is hardly traditional. The individual parts of the arrangement show what is going on and what is at stake. But when the package is all rolled together, the individual pieces get obscured. The whole is both more and less than the sum of the parts. More spending. Less accountability.

This proposal eventually disappeared, like many other creative financing approaches. It would have threatened the jobs of some public works employees, and the city already faced serious labor problems. The amount of money actually freed, even under favorable assumptions, would not have been very large, and the exercise was rather complex for the promised return. Moreover, putting a thin mask over the sale of public assets for current use was politically risky.

Despite its (timely) demise, this proposal illustrates an opportunity presented by leasing. When a government sells an asset and leases it back, there are three ways to use the proceeds. First, they can be reinvested in the capital budget. This is what the MTA did when it sold the tax benefits through its sale-leaseback. Second, the public entity can invest in income-producing assets to help pay for future costs under the lease. This is what Oakland did with the proceeds of its building sales—in a now-questionable form of arbitrage. Finally, the proceeds can be absorbed in the current operating budget; this is the approach that Midtown flirted with—and rejected.

*Nearly all disbursements of cash require an appropriation. If the department in question is budgeted on a gross-outlays basis, its receipts do not automatically become funds that it can spend.

Example 5: Leasing to avoid capital spending restrictions: ambulances for City Alert. * Commitments to make debt service payments over time are more carefully scrutinized than other public spending decisions because they impose obligations on future taxpayers. This concern is reflected structurally in many state and local governments by the maintenance of separate capital and operating budgets. Most state and local units also operate under explicit ceilings on the amount of debt they can have outstanding.

Leases can provide a way around both of these restrictions. Most jurisdictions consider lease payments to be operating expenditures and scrutinize them within the framework of operating budgets. Virtually all treat them outside the limitations imposed on long-term debt issues. Long-term lease obligations are made into short-term commitments (for legal purposes) through a "nonappropriation" clause: leases can technically be canceled if a future legislature chooses not to appropriate funds. Continuing the lease for its whole term is thus not a legally binding obligation. But any jurisdiction that used this escape hatch would have difficulty finding lessors and bar its own access to a useful instrument. Thus, even leases with nonappropriation clauses are generally regarded by both sides as fully binding. The net effect of this implicit market convention is to create a long-term borrowing instrument disguised as a short-term obligation—and thus to move this form of long-term borrowing out from under debt limitations.

This "advantage" is touted by the advocates of leasing. In a 1978 discussion of municipal leasing, Edward Dyl and Michael Joehnk observe, "Leasing may provide municipalities with a means of avoiding cumbersome and costly voter approval and other legal constraints on the capital raising function of municipalities, such as statutes that limit the levy on property . . ."[8] In a footnote, they add, "Of course, municipal managers may also have ulterior, or at least questionable motives for avoiding citizen scrutiny of capital expenditures."[9] The interpretation that leases are not a part of debt has led to some light moments. When the House Ways and Means Committee was considering limitations on governmental leasing, Jacque Schlenger, an attorney who had constructed many lease deals, gave this colorful history of the lease-versus-debt issue:

> There are all sorts of legal things involved here, one of which [is,] is that a bona fide lease by the municipality or is it a debt?
>
> Our firm took that case to the Maryland Court of Appeals. I think it is the first modern case in the area and the Maryland lower court and the Maryland Court of Appeals by a 5-to-2 decision said that a lease is a lease is a lease, and the

*Not its real name. Again, the advice I gave this organization was private, and I agreed not to disclose details of the arrangement.

dissenting judge in a Rube Goldberg cartoon opinion illustrated with a graph said that a debt is a debt is a debt.[10]

The last word on the question of whether leases are debts has not been spoken.

The ambulance procurement by City Alert illustrates how leases may be used to move capital expenditures and borrowing away from traditional scrutiny. The request for authority to purchase the ambulances was made through the normal capital budget process and rejected—not because ambulances were not needed but because capital funds were exceptionally tight and the city did not want to expand the size of its capital bond issue. The city's budget office felt that this closed the issue, but City Alert was left without enough operational ambulances to get through the year without having its response times get significantly longer. A search for alternative funding sources began.

City Alert's finance office proposed a standard lease-purchase arrangement in which ambulance ownership would be transferred to the city on an installment basis. The IRS would view this as a sale; ownership for tax purposes would reside with the city. Since the city would not immediately pay the full purchase price, some of its payments under the lease would be regarded as interest payments on the unpaid balance. Because City Alert was a municipal organization, these interest payments would be tax-exempt —they would be treated as if a tax-exempt bond had been issued and the funds used to purchase the ambulances. From the perspective of the federal tax code, the transaction was simple—and a sale.

The city's financial office viewed the arrangement quite differently. The lease contract would have a nonappropriation clause: since funds for the lease payments were not absolutely committed, the contract would not be treated as a debt issue. It was a rental agreement to be considered under the operating budget. City Alert was prepared to make room for the lease payments within its operating expenditures, so the contract was approved. From the city's perspective, too, the transaction was simple—but *not* a sale.

Thus, the IRS and the city adopted fundamentally inconsistent treatments of the contract. Both interpretations were precisely what City Alert needed. The IRS, which could deny the tax exemption on debt if the deal was not a sale, said it was a sale. And the city, which would put it under the capital budget and disallow it if it was a sale, said it was a lease. No one required the city and the IRS to agree. City Alert could obtain its ambulances.

This process, though a bit untraditional, was not illegitimate. No one questioned that the ambulances were needed, and no one profited excessively or personally from the transaction. Nonetheless, the arrangemer deliberately circumvented the city's capital budget process, which had bee established to provide comprehensive review and planning of all publ capital investments. The lease also avoided the city's debt limitation. Publ sector leasing does not quite fit into the traditional budget consideratic process. It can push standard spending restraints aside, because it is capit spending dressed in operating spending clothing.

Example 6: Leasing as a source of confusion: leasing tankers for the Nav Lease and sale-leaseback arrangements are often so complex as to be baf ing. As a consequence, they sometimes hide spending rather than sav money. The history of the leasing of ships by the Navy provides an intrigt ing example.[11] The Navy's tanker leasing program has been controversi for years. Serious advocates of the practice have argued that providir federal income tax breaks to private owners of ships used by the Nav lowered the cost of those ships to the investors, which reduced the rent pa by the Navy and thereby saved the federal government money.

The Navy insisted that the federal government could recover more tha a dollar in lowered rents for each dollar of income tax benefits it distribute to investors. This is virtually impossible. The argument persisted becaus those scrutinizing the financial studies—analysts from the Navy, the secr tary of defense's office, the Treasury, and from various congressional con mittee staffs—could not agree on the details of how the analysis should t conducted.[12] Should it be done on a before-tax or an after-tax basis? Ho should tax credits on machinery purchased to build the leased ships t treated—are tax credits costs of the lease, or costs of the ships that woul have been incurred whether the ships had been purchased or leased? An so it goes. The Navy was roundly criticized in congressional hearings i February 1983 for its costly leasing practice. Leasing does cost the gover ment more than purchase, but it cost the current Navy budget less. Exce costs were passed on in two directions: some went to the Treasury (in tl form of tax breaks to be taken by the investors); others will return to hau future Navy budgets.[13] Complicated analyses showed that the Navy's pr gram was more expensive for taxpayers than a straight purchase would ha been. The Navy's own (similarly complicated) analysis showed that it ha saved money. Four independent analyses of the acquisition of a $200 millio ship were presented at the hearing; two showed the Navy's program costin more than $200 million, and two showed it costing less than $200 millio As it turned out, all four were wrong.[14] It is unclear whether the Navy desire to shift some of its costs out of its current budget clouded its abilit to evaluate the arrangement. The fact that intelligent analysts in four ager cies got it wrong—each in a different way—testifies that analyzing leases correctly is very hard.

Accountability Problems in Public Leasing

As these examples illustrate, leasing can be hidden from the usual forms of expenditure scrutiny. It is often used to transfer costs to the federal government by taking advantage of explicitly authorized or unintended features of the tax code or by circumventing the general restrictions on arbitrage. Leasing can also be a way around traditional restrictions on the issuance of debt, a way to avoid the capital budgeting process for capital acquisitions, or a way to avoid taxpayers' resistance to selling assets to gain temporary fiscal relief (in return for greater future fiscal misery).

Leasing mixes capital and operating concerns—which, in most traditional budgeting systems, is like mixing oil and water. Yet the capital versus operating distinction is a false dichotomy; spending categories actually form a more or less continuous spectrum from very short- to very long-term concerns. The boundary between short-term operating items and long-term capital items is arbitrary. Modern financial analysts are quick to find ways to move spending from one side of this boundary to the other when, for example, there are perceived needs for more capital but the debt ceiling has been reached. Leases are simply one mechanism through which this conversion can take place.

The use of leasing to convert capital spending into a series of operating flows not only avoids standard accountability checks but also results in confusion when capital items (in the form of leases) and true operating items must be considered side by side in operating budgets. By what standard can present savings be compared with future costs? This is the fundamental problem of capital allocation, and it has little place in the review of operating budgets. Such a review is designed to ask whether each expenditure in a given period will generate benefits commensurate with costs in that period. Capital projects are evaluated within capital budgets on the basis of how well they trade benefits over time against costs over time. Leases make this trade-off over time but are considered in operating budgets, where those trade-offs are not examined. City Alert's operating budget will list a request for payment of one installment on the ambulance contract. If this is not a capital item and is not treated within the capital budget, then where is the review of the decision about whether the long-term commitment represented by the contract is a sensible investment of public funds?

The fact that leasing can blur the capital-versus-operating boundary creates a serious accountability issue because it can lead to the wrong kind of review. But perhaps the most serious accountability problem created by leasing is that the arrangements involved are so complex that they practically defy accurate analysis; they may make it impossible to agree on *any* review. The Navy's tanker leasing program created so much smoke that virtually no one could see the fire or even agree that there must be one. The dark side of public leasing may be just that—so dark that it shields both good and bad choices from public view.

The accountability problems of public leasing are hardly costless. The Navy belatedly discovered that the cost of leasing is generally higher than that of purchasing. Leasing is, when all is said and done, just a form of borrowing. But it is viewed by the lender as less secure than an authorized bond pledging the full faith and credit of a governmental unit. As a consequence, the lender generally charges a higher interest rate for a lease contract than for a bond.

Moreover, the overhead costs of lease borrowing (the legal and underwriting costs) are generally higher than those of more traditional forms of borrowing. Leasing contracts are complex, they are not codified, and they are difficult to explain to investors, all of which raises their price tag. These costs may be reduced in time, but the complexity of these arrangements will very likely keep leases expensive to develop and market.

The central accountability question for any financial instrument of government is, Whose interest does its use serve? In the case of leasing, the interested parties are numerous. Investors benefit, although the higher interest rates they charge reflect a somewhat higher level of risk than they would bear through bonds. In a number of celebrated transactions (the first MTA sale-leaseback discussed above is one of them), the investors did very well. Underwriters and lawyers profited along with their clients.

The story for state and local governments is mixed, but probably positive on balance. They have gained by transferring costs to the federal government and, on occasion, by opportunities for arbitrage created through leasing. Some have lost by using leases as an end run around capital budget or debt restrictions, paying more than they would have paid for bonds used to raise the same funds.

For hard-pressed state and local officials, leases have sometimes provided temporary and occasionally long-term relief from fiscal stress by moving costs to the future or to the federal taxpayer. Leases have also given many

ublic officials important additional managerial flexibility; this is the plus
de of leases' ability to push aside taxpayer-endorsed restrictions like capi-
al budgeting and debt limitations. The central question is whether the price
aid for this greater managerial discretion—the reduction in the account-
bility of public spending—has been too high.

Leasing operates at an odd combination of accountability levels. The
irect payments under lease contracts are appropriated, but the direct
xpenditures are sometimes little more than a smoke screen concealing
ther spending. When a lease hides a sale that generates proceeds absorbed
vithout scrutiny into the general fund, it undercuts the accountability of
ther programs by providing funds without explicit taxation. When a lease
s so complicated that we can no longer see the cost of what is purchased,
t undermines accountability based on balancing costs against benefits.
Vhen a creative financing package loads local government costs onto the
ederal taxpayer through arbitrage, it cuts the accountability link between
hose who receive and those who pay. And when these transactions sur-
ound flows of public resources with so much fog and technical complexity
hat an interested public cannot reasonably be expected to understand them
—indeed, when that seems to be part of their purpose—they assault even
he prerequisites of accountability.

Improving the accountability of creative financing packages may require
hat they become less creative. Simple lease transactions—tax-exempt lease
urchases, for example—are easy enough to understand. Some more com-
lex deals can be broken down into understandable components. Others
nay have to be avoided completely.

One change in treatment seems crucial to raising the accountability of
eases. Perhaps a lease is a lease is a lease—but it is *also* a debt. Even most
eases that are technically subject to cancellation through nonappropriation
f funds should properly be treated as debts, recognized as obligations, and
ncluded under debt limitations.

Prospects for Change

Noting the high and rising cost to the federal Treasury, Congress signifi-
antly limited the tax benefits available to private lessors when a govern-
nent unit is the lessee. As part of the reforms included in the Deficit
Reduction Act of 1984, most public sale-leasebacks no longer qualify for

any favorable depreciation treatment. The tax benefits from other forms of public leasing are also limited. These changes are likely to turn state and local capital acquisition away from "creative" alternatives and back toward traditional channels. The brief flurry of complex tax-advantaged and tax driven public sector leasing deals may soon die down, and creative financing may become a closed chapter in the evolution of public financing.

But even as it painstakingly disqualified some public leasing, the Deficit Reduction Act carefully left room for a few very fancy creative devices. One of these is a meticulously defined set of "service contracts." Under these arrangements, the public buys services from a private firm rather than buying the facility that produces them. Service contracts allow investor depreciation benefits as well as investment tax credits. Wastewater treatment service contracts seem to be particularly popular; they qualify under the special exemptions for IDB financing as well as depreciation benefit and investment tax credits. Financing schemes that allow depreciation write-offs, investment tax credits, and tax-exempt financing are the flagship of the creative financing fleet.

Service contracts involving government organizations were a target of public finance reformers for years. In a move reminiscent of the adoption of "curbs" for IDBs (curbs that led to massive expansion of private use tax-exempt borrowing), Congress "limited" service contracts between governments and corporations by defining them much more carefully. The Deficit Reduction Act details long lists of conditions that disqualify financing arrangements from being treated as service contracts. The narrower and more careful definition excludes many formerly popular arrangements. But it also studiously creates room for others. For example, wastewater treatment service contracts are still available. The demise of service contracts with public organizations is not yet upon us.

"Simple" leases will also remain. Tax-exempt lease purchase arrangements and true leases by public organizations—less complicated transactions—can be overseen with reasonable accountability.

The leasing experiment, however, offers lessons that extend to the nature of public control and scrutiny of spending. Inadvertently created tax advantages gave rise to the bulk of recent leasing activity. There was pressure from investors to make use of the opportunities. But why did public official go along? Many of the advantages of leasing were not economic but political. Leases are used in spite of their higher cost because they achieve other purposes—like allowing managers to undertake needed spending for which they could not otherwise obtain funds. Where there is opportunity, there is activity—because there is always motivation.

Creative financing approaches in general, and public sector leasing in particular, were responses of hard-pressed public officials to fiscal pressures generated by the forces of the "tax revolt," on the one hand, and the deterioration in public infrastructure, on the other. Public managers sought ways to maintain the level of public investment, as services continued to be demanded by taxpayers reluctant to approve the taxes to pay for them. The very public works spending that officials sought to maintain was a contributing factor in the tax revolt. Taxpayers were suddenly confronted with the dramatically higher full costs of infrastructure construction, all the more shocking because costs had been held artificially low by the bondfall of the 1960s. Many taxpayers object to much of public works spending as wasteful pork barrel expenditures designed more to create jobs than to provide public services. And many perceive that a major problem with public works is inadequate reinvestment and maintenance, not a lack of new construction. If maintenance is the problem, leasing is not the solution.

Leasing sustains the part of public works spending that much of the public considered wasteful when the tax revolt began. It is an end run around the spirit of the movements to limit taxes and spending. This kind of financial gimmickry as a way to maintain spending is not what the public had in mind when it expressed its general displeasure with the level of government spending.

PART II

APPROACHES TO RAISING THE PROFILE OF QUIET SPENDING

Introduction to Part II

CONSISTENT PRESSURES for quiet public spending ensure that it will always be with us. The framers of our Constitution designed the appropriations process—providing checks, balances, and opportunities for review—to foster integrity and orient the government toward broadly shared interests. Appropriations review may not embody all we would like accountability to the "public interest" to mean, but it provides a useful point of reference. Can we achieve similar scrutiny through well-designed information systems outside the appropriations hearing room?

The examples in part I of this book do not provide a basis for optimism about the future effectiveness of information strategies to enhance accountability. Great efforts have been made to strengthen reporting for pensions, credit, and tax expenditures. Yet all still operate materially differently from the way they would if they required appropriations. The appropriations process seems to be not just an additional test but a different kind of test. Public financing through the appropriations process, where actual dollars are involved, may not be fully accountable, but at least it provides some sense of actual spending taking place. Quiet spending programs use real public resources, but they don't seem to make us confront the cost. They give with a flourish but take with a whisper; they disburse checks unbalanced.

These examples pose deep challenges to those seeking to build accountability for any public program. It is hard to know what information is relevant and useful and how it can be understandably presented. It is hard to know whose interests are really being advanced—and whether a program is supported only by those whose direct interests it serves while those it hurts are kept in the dark.

Quiet programs are unlikely to fade away or be converted to appropriations forms of spending. There should thus be continuing efforts to strengthen the meaning of informed consent both by developing more and better information and by proposing different tests of consent. Two major approaches to reduce the level of hidden spending have been advocated and to some extent explored. The first is an "information" strategy: it seeks to make quiet spending less hidden. We can improve accounting, budgeting, and financial reporting about the activities of government, making their coverage more comprehensive and their content more comprehensible. The idea is to reduce the level of hidden spending by bringing it out into the light, and perhaps to reduce the spending itself by putting it under the full force of public scrutiny. An underlying prerequisite to this approach is the development of better—more comprehensive—accounting methods. Any strategy based on this approach would almost certainly have to enlist the cooperation of the accounting profession. The next chapter discusses the prospects for forming a union of interest among accountants and those who would limit hidden spending. The prognosis is not bright.

The second approach is a "consent" strategy. Its focus is on sweeping legislative change rather than on a detailed and specific understanding of the intricacies of each program. The limitation movement proposes to establish broadly defined and general limits on discretionary government spending. This strategy is directed at all spending by governments, not focused on hidden spending. But some of its advocates have pointed to quiet spending programs as important examples of the failure to hold government in check, and it is worth inquiring whether commonly proposed limits would affect quiet spending. The proposed restrictions, discussed in chapters 10 and 11, take many different forms, including tax and expenditure limitations, balanced-budget requirements, and requirements for super-majority votes to authorize new taxes or to approve appropriations. These devices have clearly had an impact—less, probably, than their proponents had claimed, but more than their opponents had hoped. It is not obvious, however, how large an effect this approach can have on quiet spending, much of which is not counted under the advocated limits.

Chapter 9

Accounting

THE MOST natural reaction to discovering the prevalence of quiet spending is that it should not be allowed to be so quiet. We need a more alert watchdog, with sharper eyes and a louder bark. To upgrade accountability we need better information more widely dispersed. We need more-sophisticated, more-comprehensive, but still-accessible reports. The most natural direction to turn is toward the accounting profession. Who better to understand the issues and provide the backbone than accountants? Governmental accountants are professionally dedicated to providing accurate, timely reports to the public and others about the financial activities of government. If we want better records of quiet public spending, why not give accountants a wider charter and more responsibility for helping us understand what governments are actually doing? They are trained for the task. Their code of conduct says they will serve the public. They have more access to detailed, comprehensive information about government activities than any other single professional group.

Historically, governmental accounting has not provided a fully comprehensive review of governmental expenditures. Much of the information available about *on-budget* programs is collected and reported by accountants, and the integrity of the public accounting profession guarantees that it is reasonably accurate. But much remains that accountants do not include in their reports about government. Pension debts are not adequately represented. Tax expenditures at all levels of government elude accountants entirely because they consist of the *absence* of physical flows of funds. Similarly, the hidden cost of credit subsidies lies in interest charges and loan guarantee premiums not collected, and accounting takes little notice of what is *not* done. The quiet cost of private use tax-exempt bonds lands on downy feet at a different level of government in the form of reduced tax payments; accountants concentrate on one jurisdiction at a time. If the public cares to know more about these and other forms of quiet spending, a natural step is to ask accountants to take on extended responsibilities— to expand their charter to include some of the activities currently defined as outside their purview.

Is this a plausible strategy? Probably not. The reasons are deeply rooted in the history and culture of the accounting profession. Government accountants are technically ill-prepared for wider responsibilities. The traditions of the field narrowly focus accountants' attention on the cash flows of government units. Their work is not leavened by much curiosity about the noncash disbursements that make up quiet spending. Adopting a wider view of the domain of government accounting to include these quiet financial activities would require bold and creative conceptual work in building definitions, practices, and methods. Governmental accounting is largely disinclined to propel itself into the forefront of such a venture. Accountants generally do not have reputations for the kind of freewheeling exploration that this stretching of the boundaries of the field will require.

The Evolution of Public Sector Accounting

The rather narrow definition of the responsibilities of public sector accounting is explained, in part, by its historical roots. Public sector accounting was not designed to provide a comprehensive picture of government financial activity. As a consequence, it is unconcerned about most resource flows that are not in the form of money. The profession developed in response to a rising level of public alarm about government corruption in the early years of this century.[1] At the turn of the century, governmental accounting systems consisted of an informal collection of practices, often mirroring private sector accounting in form but rarely in rigor or substance. No widely accepted practices had been established. Each entity reported what it chose in whatever form it wanted. Private sector accounting had by then advanced to a reasonable level of accuracy and acceptance; many of the unresolved issues of that era remain unresolved today. However advanced the state of accounting for private organizations (and critics would say that, then as now, even private accounting was not very advanced), governmental accounting was far behind. Private sector accountants were openly scornful of the poor quality of municipal accounting systems, and they said so regularly in their professional journals. H. W. Wilmot, in a timeless article published in 1906, observed,

> It is generally admitted by students of municipal finance that the accounting methods of most cities of the United States are deplorably behind the times, and that similar methods could not be tolerated for a day in any successful commercial corporation. These methods may possibly have met the local requirements when cities were smaller, but as municipal affairs have become more complex the multiplication of matters to be recorded has rendered these antiquated accounting systems entirely inadequate.[2]

There was a growing perception that these informal accounting practices bred, or at least permitted, widespread governmental corruption and rampant diversion of public funds.[3] Its forms were not subtle. Sweetheart contracts in which the government purchased goods and services at inflated prices, multiple payments for the same item, "graveyard" payroll checks issued to employees long gone, and other gross abuses of public funds were widely reported.

Whether or not poor accounting contributed to corruption, better accounting was portrayed as part of the cure. To a young professional society of private accountants engaged in defining their field, the needs of public accounting were obvious. The foundation—an accurate recording system, reporting what was being purchased, by whom, for how much—was missing. Better "control" systems, through which financial officers could check that expenditures were appropriately authorized and that funds had been appropriated to pay for them, were a necessary prerequisite to gaining real control over public spending.

The profession set about devising standards for processing and recording governmental receipts and expenditures. Improved recording systems were developed and instituted. A system of financial checks—encumbrance accounting—was expanded and widely implemented. Under an encumbrance system, disbursements must be approved by a financial officer before funds are committed. This permits three crucial checks to be carried out: (1) that the expenditure has been approved by a legally authorized executive, (2) that funds have been legislatively appropriated to cover it, and (3) that these funds have not already been spent or committed. When an expenditure is approved, the funds for it are encumbered until the bill for it comes through, ensuring that appropriated funds are not committed more than once. These systems have a "green eyeshade" orientation: they require records and sign-offs ensuring that the necessary approvals have been obtained before funds leave the treasury. Not incidentally, they provide a handy audit trail in cases of alleged fraud or misconduct.

Transactions in which the government was defrauded typically involved an immediate cash payment of public funds. Stealing future payments—for example, counterfeiting a municipal bond or arranging a pension for an unqualified employee—has always been more difficult and less profitable. Thus, public accounting systems designed to protect against fraud intently watched the cash flows in and out of the public till. Accountants tried first to make sure that cash deposits were not diverted before arrival, and then to guarantee that any funds that left the till were for a lawful purpose, appropriately authorized, for goods or services purchased at a fair price. Except for long-term contractual obligations (like the repayment of municipal bonds), considerably less attention was paid to the flows of long-term promises issued by governments. While direct debt was a matter of great interest to accountants (because it resulted in a large volume of inflowing funds), governments' routine promises to current employees that they would be paid after their retirement were a matter of small concern. They involved no current exchange of funds and were therefore unlikely to be a form of stealing. Pension promises were ignored; only pay-as-you-go cash payments were watched. Governments needed systems for keeping track of purchases (like office equipment), so that goods didn't find their way into private hands, but there was little danger that large, immovable objects— roads, bridges, buildings—would disappear. Governmental accounting thus made the recording of fixed "infrastructure" assets optional.

The result was a determined focus on the authorization and disbursement process, particularly on cash flows. Since legislative authorization of disbursements was almost universally on an annual basis, modern public sector accounting began with—and has largely retained—an orientation toward the annual budget. With the exception of explicitly authorized debt issues, the longer-term commitments of public funds are accorded little attention. The focus is narrow, but intense, and it has served the purposes for which it was designed rather well. Direct embezzlement of public funds appears to have decreased, and the occasional remaining scandals seem tame by comparison with those of the early part of the century. This is not to say that governmental recording systems are now completely foolproof. Three recent scandals in a single major metropolitan area testify to faulty financial operating procedures—or to sound procedures being ignored. (One concerned the distribution of payroll checks, one the collection of coins from parking meters, and one the counting of transit fare-box revenues.) Yet these abuses are, on the whole, less common, less profitable, and less systematic than they used to be. The scrutiny designed into the systems of public sector accounting and control ensures a reasonable degree of integrity.

The narrow focus on the cash flows associated with the annual budget cycle also served the professional interests of the new society of public accountants rather nicely. The problem—fraud and theft—could readily be defined and, once the right tracking systems were in place, identified. Private sector accounting had faced many of the same problems, and procedures were at hand to deal with them. Higher procedural standards to safeguard integrity were required in the public sector because the funds being disbursed did not belong to any of the people spending them. (Private sector accounting has always maintained that the presence of financially interested owners is a strong form of accountability in itself, a check largely and unfortunately lacking in the public sector.) The basic procedures had already been developed for maintaining accurate records and for handling cash inflows and disbursements with a minimum of opportunity for untraceable theft. With some strengthening and adaptation, these procedures formed the core of the new field of public sector accounting.

The apparent match between what was required and what accountants could readily provide may have been merely a happy accident. But accountants had a large role in setting the bounds for their responsibilities. They chose the scope of the problem. Their interpretation of how to ensure the integrity of governmental finances—capturing, controlling, and reporting cash flows—focused on the parts of the problem most within their competence to address. This helped shape their mandate—and its limits—and marked the starting point of the evolution of modern governmental accounting.

Beyond the Budget Focus

Originally responsible for stopping unauthorized disbursements from the public treasury, governmental accounting still bears a deep imprint from its early orientation. Attention remains strongly focused on annual operating results—revenues received and expenditures made against them. Funds committed, but not disbursed because of lags in delivery or billing, are generally held in trust at the close of the year; remaining funds are returned to the treasury as "revenues" usable in the next budget cycle. Operating funds roll from cycle to cycle, and scant interest is shown in longer-term obligations or commitments of government. Little attempt is made to present a comprehensive picture of the long-term financial condition of public organizations in official financial reports.[4] Some governmental units now use multiyear appropriations processes, recognizing that budgeted programs often require more than one year to be planned and executed. Procurement is a good example, particularly when it includes research and development of the product to be purchased. But multiyear systems are still in their infancy; and at best they can only slightly extend the time period we examine.

Many forms of public spending are not captured in the narrow definition of resource flows tracked by public sector accounting. Chapter 7 discussed the process of "spending" by failing to maintain the existing public service capital stock, thus freeing current operating funds for other, more-immediate (but not more-important) purposes. Tax expenditures, discussed in chapters 4, 5, and 6 are, in concept, the spending of uncollected taxes. These resources never enter the domain of financial reporting as defined by accountants. Accounting does capture the main dollar flows associated with credit programs, discussed in chapter 3, but not in a way that identifies, computes, or reports the subsidy element these activities often conceal. Similarly, public sector accounting records the receipts, asset management, and disbursement of annual public pension payments, but it generally does not fully measure the cost of promises extended to current workers. Public-employee retirement systems, discussed in chapter 1, and social security, discussed in chapter 2, have deep accountability problems as a result. Leasing, discussed in chapter 8, is one form of quiet spending that current accounting standards capture reasonably well. Public sector accounting recognizes leasing as a form of unofficial borrowing. It often requires "capitalizing" long-term lease obligations, recording them much like explicit debt issued to fund the same acquisitions. But because these obligations are long-term, they show up in a part of financial reports outside the main focus of attention.

These forms of hidden spending and others like them—regulation, inefficient management, and so on—largely escape recognition under current governmental accounting and financial reporting. The problem is caused partly by public accounting's short-term orientation; the system often allows long-term commitments to remain obscure. But in addition to having a short-term focus, public sector accounting is narrowly defined around transactions, and in particular around current cash transactions. Most of the resource flows associated with tax expenditures are immediate; they are missed by public sector accounting not because they are long-term commitments but because they do not involve transactions in which the government actually receives and then disburses cash. Disbursements that are not narrowly financial are often ignored.

The Culture of Accounting

Governmental accounting's narrow definition of what financial activities of government come under its purview reflects its historical origins. It is in keeping with the tendency of professional groups to define problems in terms of questions to which they already know the answers. But a profession's roots need not limit its growth. The original task—reducing public fraud—is still part of the historical evolution and momentum of current practice and its continuing development. If this approach is now too narrow, the profession has presumably had time to grow beyond its original conceptions. What made accountants circumscribe their territory—and why do they stay within it?

Like every profession, accounting needs clear boundaries in order to distinguish members from outsiders. To maintain its professional standing, accounting must be able to assert its expertise within well-defined problems.[5] Professional boundaries and expertise are often defined by a set of technical skills. Accounting is no exception. It has evolved exacting standards that describe the measurement and reporting of the financial affairs of organizations—standards requiring substantial technical skill to understand and to apply. Entrance into the profession requires extensive technical training and the satisfactory completion of a series of examinations. The boundaries of the profession are well guarded by the enforcement of high technical standards.[6]

These boundaries determine what accounting is and what it is not. Accountants circumscribe their domain of responsibility so that within their chosen sphere their expertise will be recognized and respected. Accounting has a long, proud history associated with the self-image that emerges from the choices it has made.

Precision and certainty are core requirements of professional accounting, and they are deeply revered professional virtues in the culture of accounting. Numbers reported by accountants are expected, first and foremost, to be accurate—to be objectively determinable and correct. The responsible accountant or auditor certifies their precision to be within the exacting standards set by the profession, giving assurance that the numbers fairly represent the financial position of the audited organization.

Accuracy is supported in practice by volumes of technical rules specifying methods to be used, dictating required forms of reporting, and prescribing when an auditor must grant only a "qualified" opinion about the accuracy of the image reflected in the financial figures presented. If there is a single historical choice that has left a deep imprint upon the profession, defining its self-image, determining who would be attracted to it, and shaping its operating rules and procedures, it is the profession's allegiance to precision and certainty.

Accounting's continuing struggle about how to represent and treat inflation shows how deeply these principles cut. The traditional rules of accounting specify that fixed assets should be carried on an organization's books at their historical cost, adjusted for depreciation.* This method of valuation has the virtues of precision and certainty; the *exact* historical cost can generally be ascertained. Using an estimate of the current market price, by contrast, would be both imprecise and uncertain; it would be subject to debate and reestimation. There are strong arguments for using market prices, in spite of their imprecision. In particular, market prices provide a more accurate measure of the actual financial standing of the firm. Accountants regularly renew this debate with vigor. They have always resolved it in favor of precision and certainty—rather than accuracy.

The historical-cost approach has its difficulties even in an era of stable prices. In the face of persistent inflation, these faults become critical. Firms own assets purchased in different periods, with dollars of different purchasing powers. Nonetheless, historical-cost accounting requires that purchase prices simply be added to one another in totaling the "value" of fixed assets. In periods of rapid inflation, the results are at best meaningless and at worst a material distortion. They do represent the (meaningless) concept they reflect, however, with perfect precision and certainty, and for that reason they are still prescribed as the standard by the accounting profession.

Scholars of accounting are painfully aware of this flaw and have struggled to develop a better method. Various approaches have been debated; some have been raised for discussion purposes, others have been required as footnotes in the financial statements of certain large companies. But the profession as a whole has been stymied in its attempt to devise a universally applicable standard that accurately adjusts for inflation. A fundamental stumbling block is allegiance to precision and certainty. The effects of inflation cannot be computed precisely from known, certain figures. Trying

*The exception to this rule is that the market price should be used if it is lower than the historical cost. "Lower of cost or market" is the rule of thumb.

to be accurate means estimating inflation adjustments, and this threatens the basic integrity—the precision and certainty—of the system. Of course, the *accuracy* of the current system has *already* been undermined—but it retains its virtues of precision and certainty.

The narrow focus of the accounting profession, while demanding—and permitting—a high level of technical skill and performance, leaves wide gaps in the reported information about the public sector. Against the backdrop of the ingrained culture of the accounting profession, it is easier to see which public financial activities will readily be treated by public sector accounting and which will not. The task of carefully tracking cash transactions of public organizations addresses a central dilemma facing government, provides a solvable accounting problem, and fits easily into the cultural milieu of accounting. Recording systems, mechanical systems designed to control expenditures (like encumbrance accounting), and reporting mechanisms focusing on the legislated annual budget all fit neatly into the cultural tapestry. Transactions can be defined precisely, and magnitudes can be measured with certitude. This is the kind of problem that defines accounting.

By contrast, reporting about the wider disposition of public resources—disbursements that are not necessarily immediate or in cash—is not a natural province for accountants. Estimating the current cost of pension liabilities, for example, requires projections about the future that can be neither precise nor certain. The view that taxes not collected are simultaneously revenues and expenditures is, to accountants, only a mental construct—and a confusing one at that. It has none of the concreteness usually associated with the transactions accountants audit, and it is surely imprecise and uncertain. Economists still argue about how to measure the subsidy element in government loans and loan guarantees; any measure of subsidies is tentative.

Public sector accounting thus presents the profession with both a challenge and an opportunity.[7] A much wider charter is available to accounting, but with it would go substantially wider responsibility, greater controversy, and more risk. Adopting it would stretch the traditional boundaries of accounting, including the core concepts that form such a powerful part of the self-image of accountants.

Government Accounting in Evolution: Reporting about Pensions

The evolution of financial disclosure about public-employee retirement systems provides an interesting illustration of the tensions between the role accountants feel comfortable playing and the role sometimes demanded by the requirements of complete public reporting. The development of standards has been tortuous and slow. It was complicated by conflicts between the public and private sector accounting standard-setting bodies (the National Council on Governmental Accounting [NCGA] and the Financial Accounting Standards Board [FASB], respectively). Generally, the two agencies tried to maintain a similar posture on issues that concerned both. While the NCGA was in the process of revising its pension reporting standards, the FASB issued new guidelines, interrupting the NCGA process. The NCGA decided after a long review that it could not accept the FASB approach. This conflict delayed the promulgation of new accounting standards for public pension systems. (It also exacerbated the conflict between the NCGA and FASB over the establishment in 1984 of a new and universally acceptable public sector standard-setting body, the Governmental Accounting Standards Board [GASB].)

The two central issues in setting standards for retirement system reporting are measuring the liabilities of a system (and, from the annual increment in liabilities, the annual cost) and measuring system assets. The FASB and the NCGA took different positions on both. Arguing that public workers are protected by civil service and other regulations, the NCGA found that public employees had considerably greater claims to continued employment than private sector workers do. This difference in proposed *liability* measurement seemed a sensible recognition of the differing rights of private and public sector workers. It implied that the FASB approach to valuing pension benefits—estimating the value of rights already earned and ignoring anticipated future accruals—would substantially underestimate the public's commitments to its employees. The NCGA prescribed instead that a projected-benefits method of liability estimation (which recognizes that rights already earned will become more valuable as salaries rise) be used to determine the value of public pension liabilities.*

This represented an important break with tradition. The projected-benefits method entails a complex estimation process—the actuarial model-

---

*Chapter 1 discussed the preferred methods of assessing pension costs and liabilities and argued for the methods prescribed by the NCGA.

ing of the future of the pension system. Accountants will not generally be responsible for the modeling process; it will remain the province of actuaries, whose profession is the construction of projections. The change nonetheless forces accountants to use numbers that are neither precise nor certain. It is a minor triumph of serious and accurate representation of the financial condition of pension systems over a blind allegiance to precision and certainty. The projected-benefits standard may represent a precedent-setting first step toward a wider charter and a correspondingly greater responsibility for public sector accountants.

The second major pensions accounting issue dividing the NCGA and the FASB was the measurement of system assets. Here, the action taken by the NCGA moves in a less progressive direction. The vital question in asset measurement is whether the holdings of pension funds—typically, marketable securities like government and high-grade corporate bonds, bank certificates of deposit, and other safe and commonly traded financial assets—should be valued at their market value or at their historical cost. The use of historical cost rather than current values distorts the fund value. For the bulk of pension fund holdings, market values are easy to determine. The market value standard allows an accurate measurement of the fund's current condition—the actual value of its assets. This approach, long advocated by economists, was endorsed by the FASB in its recently issued standard for pension system reporting.

The NCGA, however, did not go along.[8] It argued that market prices fluctuate too rapidly and that the public might be confused and concerned by quick changes in the value of retirement system asset holdings. Perhaps rapid changes in asset values *are* confusing. But is the public served any better by inaccurate and outdated asset values? When market prices of financial securities fluctuate, the value of assets *does* change rapidly. Masking this does not provide a more accurate rendition to the public; it hides the performance of pension administrators.

Historical-cost valuations do, of course, have the traditional virtues of precision and certainty—though not of accuracy. Yet the allegiance to certainty does not seem to have been the dominant influence in the NCGA deliberations. Rather, the decision seems to be an illustration of the best as an enemy of the good. Most members of the committee appear to have agreed that historical cost was a poor basis for the measurement and reporting of asset values. But several alternatives were available, and the NCGA could not reach a general agreement on which new system was best. The outcome was the persistence of the status quo, even though it was well down on nearly everyone's list.

Can—and Will—Accounting Take a Wider Role?

The recent history of setting standards for pension reporting shows some changes in the traditional positions taken by accountants. On the measurement of the pension liabilities side of the balance sheet, some movement away from the comfort of traditional requirements is evident. On the assets side, this trend is less clear. But the accounting profession is struggling to redefine its domain, and it may gradually shift away from its traditional center.

There are several reasons to expect that this shift, if it comes, will be slow. Accounting practices, and accountants themselves, represent the current stage in a continuing evolution. The present members of the accounting profession have not been selected through this evolutionary process for their willingness or ability to boldly redefine the scope of their responsibilities and create new standards based on a different conception of their role. Accounting as a profession is technically unprepared for new tasks of estimation (for example, measuring subsidy elements in loans) and conceptualization (for example, assessing tax expenditures). Training and certification procedures are oriented toward the current self-conception. New technical skills will be difficult to sell and will take a long time to be developed and disseminated. Many accountants are constitutionally disinclined to expand their domain, preferring their current circumscribed duties and responsibilities. Moreover, the profession may be economically discouraged from taking on too broad a definition of its public stewardship role. Accountants ultimately work for those who pay for their services, not for those to whom they report.

Even if the profession does decide to accept broader responsibilities, it may not make much difference in taxpayers' knowledge about the financial activities of government. More information would be available, but it would not be useful unless the public sought and understood it, or unless it was embodied in some way within the appropriations process. Pension reporting offers a telling illustration. The current standards promulgated for public organizations by the NCGA call for precisely the kind of reporting advocated in chapter 1. But the financial statements of pension systems, however accurate, are not widely read and are even less widely understood. The jurisdictions to which these reports are made are not forced by any law or standard to fund their retirement systems according to the reported annual costs, whose calculation is so laborious (and, now, conceptually correct). Funding is a matter of local discretion, and, as we saw in chapter 1, underfunding is common. Reporting, by itself, is unlikely to change this until the implications of the reports are better understood by a wider taxpaying (or bondholding) audience. Even then, taxpayers may find pension borrowing a convenient mechanism for transferring the costs of current services to future taxpayers. Accurate reporting will still have to be better integrated with accountable spending processes, the definitive example of which is the appropriations process. Until that happens, the acceptance of a wider mandate by accountants will have little impact.

Taxpayer inattention to good reporting is not the only impediment to the wider influence of accounting in checking government spending. The behavior of governments may neutralize the impact of proposed changes in public accounting. Sometimes, a system has to be entirely complete to work at all. A dam built across only half of a harbor will not hold back any of the tide. An accounting system that shines a bright light on some activities also necessarily defines an area of deep shadows. Inevitably, many will consciously push their programs toward the dark. We tend to assume that inappropriately treated programs will operate more in the public interest if we can find ways to represent them better. But some of the activities exist in their present forms precisely because they escape notice by our existing accounts. We may stop, slow, or alter specific current practices by designing ways to account for them, but no matter how comprehensive any particular accounting system is, ingenious methods for quiet spending that will not be captured within it may still be found. Accounting reform may be a continuing process of catch-up in which clever subterfuge runs ever ahead of plodding reporting. Will the conflict between accountability and quiet spending always be like antibiotics trying to keep up with new resistant strains of bacteria?

Perhaps not. The picture of ingenious new spending devices always outpacing accountability mechanisms is too bleak. There will always be innovative ways to spend quietly. But many spending devices that accounting is now struggling with have existed for a very long time. Public pensions were established for veterans of the Revolution; tax expenditures have been with us since the inception of taxes; credit programs began in earnest during World War I. We have not witnessed a succession of new ways to avoid increasingly comprehensive accounting; it has simply taken a long time for accounting to develop to the point where it can tackle this wide territory. Government spending practices are not an ever-receding target. Rather, there is a limited number of forms of spending, and some are still not fully treated by public sector accounting. Accounting can eventually encompass them.

There has been only slow progress in that direction. The profession, particularly its public sector wing, is in flux. Congress and the Securities and Exchange Commission (under whose authority the FASB is the self-regulating standard-setting body for private sector accounting) have shown increasing impatience with accountants' continuing fascination with tedious details and existing rules. The FASB has been unable to promulgate bold new standards in areas of controversy on a timely basis.[9] It remains to be seen whether the additional pressure of threats that Congress will move to resolve these issues will embolden or intimidate the private standard-setting process.

The recently established Governmental Accounting Standards Board had an opportunity to clear the field and draw new boundaries for it. Its first challenge, however, was to gain the respect of the existing accounting profession, and its first official act was to adopt all previously promulgated NCGA standards and practices. In one swift, sure stroke, GASB appears to have cast its lot squarely with the past. It relies on many of the same people and emerges from the same intellectual traditions. The GASB will very likely deliberate rules in much the same ways as its predecessor—and achieve similar results.[10]

It is common and natural—and deeply unfair—to lay the problems of governmental financial accountability solely at the feet of public accountants. It is simple first to observe the lack of available information, then to claim that comprehensive information would ensure accountability, and finally to blame accountants for not producing it. But it is useless to blame accountants for not being what they are not and what they did not choose to be nor try to become.

Accountants' reputation for precision and integrity is valuable. One indication of the public's trust in accountants is their having been selected to run the Academy Awards and various sweepstakes competitions. This public trust is an important asset of the accounting profession—one it might jeopardize if it began to take responsibility for more controversial and overtly political judgments. We should not expect the accounting profession to move too quickly toward wider responsibility.

Public sector accounting deliberately narrowed its responsibilities, to be sure. But the task it chose to accept is important. Fraud is always a potential problem in government, and it significantly undermines faith in public institutions. Public sector accounting played an important role in reducing the direct diversion of public resources. The rest of what is needed—a better numerical representation of the other resource flows of government—seems closely related to what accountants already do. Accountants may be the best nominees to accept this wider charge. But given the history of their profession, their disinclination to accept this responsibility, and the characteristics of their professional culture, it is unlikely that accountants will soon choose to accept a larger role in supporting government financial accountability.

Chapter 10

Mechanical Limits on

Government Spending

IN THE LATE 1970s, a great deal of attention was focused on public spending. Long-standing limits on taxes and spending, which constrained virtually all state and local governments, were viewed as insufficient. It became popular to declare that government spending was out of control, that much of the taxpayers' money was being wasted, that tighter budgets would force efficiency improvements in service delivery so that taxes could be cut without a reduction of service levels. A grass roots "tax revolt" took shape and grew almost overnight into a political force to be reckoned with. This wave of genuine middle-class populism cut across geographic and ethnic boundaries. State after state passed legislation and constitutional amendments, many of them voter initiatives, limiting state and local spending, taxes, or both.[1]

If one was predisposed to be against government growth, then there *was* something to revolt against. From 1949 to 1980, combined federal, state, and local expenditures grew from $59 billion to $869 billion, an annual rate of 9 percent. Even measured in inflation-adjusted dollars, the increase was nearly 5 percent per year—and most taxpayers focus on nominal, not real, growth. Ten million new government employees nearly tripled the government work force. The public sector's share of the GNP rose from 23 percent to 33 percent. Every level of government expanded substantially; state and local government work forces grew more than threefold.[2] By any measure, government in the postwar era grew rapidly and, in the view of many, became too large.

Many of the strategists of the tax revolt, however, saw it as more than a move to reduce the size of government. They saw it—or, at least, portrayed it—as a means of reestablishing lost taxpayer control over government activity, a way of making government accountable to the people for its spending. To many advocates of limitation, the distinction between cutting back on size and raising accountability wasn't clear; to others, it wasn't important. They believed that government was too big—that it had grown far beyond what taxpayers had contemplated or were willing to pay for. Making government smaller became synonymous with making it accountable. Tax and spending limits seemed a way to force needed reductions and therefore were accountability devices by definition.

But accountability and scale are not, in fact, the same thing. Many believe that government has been assigned too many tasks, some of which should be done privately and some of which are better left undone. Others think that the current scale is about right or that it is too small. A trend showing that government is an increasing share of the economy does not automatically warrant the conclusion that it is now too big, any more than we can properly conclude that it was formerly too small. Informed people have honest differences about the responsibilities it is desirable to assign to government, and our views of what government should do have changed markedly over time.

Accountability is less value laden than are judgments about the appropriate scale of government activity. Accountability is silent about scale. The task of accountability in government is to ensure that the scale we have is the scale we want. Accountability has to ensure responsiveness to changing aspirations, values, and tastes. If one believes strongly that government is too large because taxpayers want it to be smaller, then it may follow that some breach in accountability has occurred. It does not necessarily follow, however, that making it smaller will make it more accountable.

The Evolution of Mechanical Spending Limits

While the federal government has not been constrained by any mechanical limitation on spending or taxing, and has been only mildly inconvenienced by a self-imposed statutory debt ceiling, state and local governments have traditionally operated under fairly stringent requirements of fiscal balance. Virtually all maintain separate capital and operating budgets. In general, both must be balanced, and borrowing is permitted only to balance the capital budget. Operating expenses cannot be covered by bonding, though all jurisdictions have some short-term borrowing mechanism to roll over unanticipated deficits to be funded in the following budget cycle. All states except Vermont impose some form of balanced-budget requirement, although the stringency of their requirements varies widely. In Massachusetts, the governor must submit a budget in which expected revenues equal anticipated spending, but the legislature is not required to pass a balanced budget. In Missouri, by contrast, the governor and the legislature are obliged to cut expenditures from the current budget if there is reason to believe that there will be a revenue shortfall.

Most states do not require the strict balancing called for in Missouri. Even states with such limits can experience deficits if, in spite of the best projections, there is more of a revenue shortfall than officials were able to foresee. Because most balance rules require equating an estimate of revenues with an estimate of expenditures, there is considerable slack in the budget balance requirement of most state budget processes. Still, some form of limit exists almost universally. Interestingly, Vermont, the only state without any budget balance requirement, has shown no greater proclivity than other states to spend more than it receives.

Traditional state and local fiscal discipline rests on a foundation of estimated-budget balance, careful separation of capital and operating flows, permission to use long-term borrowing only to fund capital expenditures, and ceilings on total debt issues. These combined requirements have been reasonably successful. While the federal government has run a surplus in only five of the last thirty-five years, state and local governments have come close to maintaining balanced budgets even in periods of intense fiscal strain. In fiscal year 1983, at the end of a recession during which state and local governments felt the bite of the taxpayer revolt and a stagnant economy, only eight states ran deficits. The average state had a surplus of about 3 percent of general fund expenditures.[3]

Fiscal discipline requirements do not determine budget size, though they act as a restraint on it. They allow state and local governments to balance their budgets at any chosen level—or, more accurately, at any level their constituents are willing to pay for. Discipline through budget balance limits spending to the level of taxation tolerated by the current constituency. Separating capital from operating funds ensures that current taxpayers do not hand the bill for the services they enjoy to future generations. These structural elements of restraint ensure that taxpayers feel the tax bite of whatever level of services they choose to receive.

Local spending is held down by debt, revenue, and expenditure limitations imposed by states.[4] A rising tide of complaints about property taxation led to a widespread enactment of property tax limitations by state legislatures in the early 1970s. Three states had tax levy limits before 1970; nine more states followed by 1974. By 1976, forty states had imposed some form of local property tax rate or tax levy limitation; four had expenditure limitations. These limitations were imposed by state legislatures concerned about the rapid growth of local spending and about widening expenditure disparities among local jurisdictions, particularly in spending for education. These measures were in the form of ceilings, not floors; they sought to equalize the disparities through restraints at the high end.

Judging from the tax revolt of the late 1970s, however, these forms of restraint had not kept government as small as some taxpayers wanted. Both the proximate and the underlying causes of the revolt have been widely discussed.[5] The proponents of tax and spending limitation asserted that there was "fat" in government spending that would be squeezed out through fiscal austerity, so that reductions would not result in service cuts. Given the choice between the current level of services and taxes, on the one hand, and the same level of services with lower taxes, on the other, taxpayers made the obvious decision.[6]

To claim that the tax revolt was the result of good marketing by advocates of smaller government is to underestimate the level of underlying malaise that fueled the limitation movement. Buffeted by oil price shocks, the U.S. economy stagnated in the 1970s. Accustomed to the general prosperity of the 1960s and early 1970s, taxpayers still expected increases in real income at a time when real income growth was actually declining. Rapid inflation confronted taxpayers with the harsh reality of larger paychecks devoured by larger prices. Inflation psychology is lopsided: workers see wage increases as a well-deserved recognition of their contributions and price increases as an obstacle to their enjoyment of the benefits of justly higher wages. In the late 1970s, taxpayers found themselves on a speeding treadmill. Frustration was palpable. Government provided a natural target, since its price—in the form of taxes—had also been increasing. Taxpayers couldn't vote to lower the price of food or a car, but they could vote to cut the tax bite from paychecks. And they did, in droves.

Recent Tax and Spending Limits

For whatever reasons, taxpayers between 1976 and 1983 approved, or persuaded their legislators to approve, a flood of tax and expenditure limitations (TELs). There had long been movements to reduce government by constraining its revenues, expenditures, or borrowing. Voters' disapproval of fiscal issues put before them—mainly referenda on new debt issues—grew steadily in the 1970s. Advocates of strong, specific, and comprehensive TELs had always been a fringe element on the fiscal scene. Now they moved to center stage. Fiscal limits were introduced into the American political economy. Once started, controls spread rapidly.

In 1976, New Jersey became the first state to enact a general cap on the level or growth of expenditures.[7] The New Jersey statute was proposed and adopted by the legislature; it limited the rate of growth of state expenditures to the growth rate of per capita personal income of state taxpayers. It embodied what became a common form of limit, based on the idea that government should not grow as a fraction of taxpayers' personal budgets. (New Jersey's statute expired in 1983; attempts to resuscitate it have so far been unsuccessful.) In 1977, the legislatures of Colorado and Rhode Island placed similar limits on expenditures; they fixed the growth rate (at 7 percent and 6 percent, respectively) rather than pegging the growth of state spending to the growth in personal income.

The real boom in the limitation movement came in 1978, with California's adoption of Proposition 13. Like taxpayers elsewhere, Californians had been frustrated by continuing increases in the cost of government. They were particularly angry about property tax increases, which result from property value increases that are largely intangible to the homeowner. Taxpayers can see that larger income tax payments at least come out of larger paychecks and that government takes more in sales taxes partly because prices are rising. Property taxes, however, are levied against the value of an item that taxpayers rarely buy or sell. The notion that they should pay more because the value of the house they own is rising is mildly foreign if not downright infuriating. Most taxpayers in any given year hold rather than sell their houses. The fact that some of their neighbors managed to sell their houses at high prices is small comfort to a taxpayer whose property assessment—and tax bill—has been raised because others turn handsome profits in the real estate market. Skyrocketing housing values in parts of California in the 1970s led to rapid increases in property taxes while the state accumulated a large budgetary surplus. The twin frustrations of rising taxes against a base that did not *feel* as if it were growing, and a large accumulation of funds at the state level that could be distributed to localities, propelled Californians into the forefront of the national trend toward TELs. Initiated and approved by voters, "Prop 13" imposed a severe constitutional limit on fiscal discretion at the state and local levels. It restricts property tax collections to 1 percent of fair market real estate values as of 1975–1976 and permits only a 2 percent annual adjustment upward for any unsold property. Properties can, however, be reassessed when sold.* Under Prop 13, no new property taxes are to be instituted. Other new state and local taxes require a two-thirds vote of the electorate.

By all accounts, property taxes in California had grown out of proportion. Prop 13 sought to move them quickly and permanently downward. It succeeded: the limitation on property taxes was estimated to cost local governments in California about $7 billion annually, or nearly 60 percent of their existing revenues.

The successful passage of Prop 13 demonstrated that grass roots tax limitation movements are not a futile exercise. Between 1978 and 1980, fourteen states adopted TELs with limits determined by the growth of personal income, population, inflation, or some combination. By the end of 1982, nineteen states had limits in place; eight were constitutional, nine voter-initiated. Most legislation constraining state spending focused on expenditures; provisions limiting local fiscal discretion generally reduced the level or growth of property tax collections.

Not every limitation proposal was accepted, of course. Relatively stringent proposals like Prop 13 that cut existing tax revenues and imposed severe limitations on further growth have not fared particularly well. Idaho (in 1978, by statute) and Massachusetts (in 1980, by voter-initiated constitutional amendment) adopted limits akin to those of Prop 13, but similar limits have been defeated in nine instances since 1978.[8] A dramatic proposal to cut income taxes by one-half in California was advanced in 1980 by Howard Jarvis, one of the principal architects of the tax reform movement. Dubbed Jaws II, it was defeated in a California already feeling the fiscal strain of operating under Prop 13. In 1983, Ohio voters rejected a citizen initiative that would have rolled back all state tax increases since 1981.

More moderate measures, by contrast, fared much better. Proposals to limit the growth of government revenues or expenditures to that of personal income or some other measure of tax base capacity tended to be accepted.

*This provision implies that a house will often be considerably cheaper (in property taxes) for the preceding owner to hold than for a new buyer. It led to leasing and other schemes to maintain tax ownership in the hands of the former owner while transferring the other rights of ownership to a new occupant. The definition of "change in ownership" was modified by the legislature in 1979 to permit reassessment when any transfer occurred.

Other approaches like indexing income tax rates to remove the "inflation dividend" received by public treasuries with progressive income taxes were also successfully advanced.[9]

In spite of the failure of most proposed stringent limitations after 1978 the message of the tax revolt was clear enough. The powerful grass roots movement to limit government size and cost was felt even in places where no specific limitation was enacted. While most of the limitation activity was carried out through the usual legislative process, not through voter initiatives, the spur to defuse taxpayer frustration before it resulted in simple and strict limitations was powerful.

By 1979, tax cutting was in full swing. Property tax reductions were enacted in twenty-two states, income tax reductions in eighteen, and sales tax cuts in fifteen. A total of thirty-six different states cut property, income or sales taxes or enacted an expenditure limitation.[10] Most tax cuts were discretionary; they were adopted by legislatures rather than forced through voter-imposed explicit tax limits. The net result was a material reduction in the burden of state taxation. State taxes as a fraction of personal income fell from 7.0 percent to 6.5 percent over the period 1978–1982. Local taxes also dropped from 1978 to 1980.[11] Viewed against the trend up to that time this represented a noticeable shift. The tax revolt's main message was to legislatures—that they had better cut state taxes, increase aid to localities to replace revenues lost in local tax cuts, and think very carefully before contemplating any increase in taxes. Not a single state income tax was increased in 1980 or 1981, and only six states raised general sales taxes.[1]

Reality quickly reasserted itself. Retrenchment was forced in part by the successful tax limitation movement at the national level. The election of a conservative administration in 1980 reduced federal support of state-run programs. An economy in deep recession, the accumulating force of state and local tax and spending reductions, and a growing acknowledgment that essential infrastructure investment and maintenance was being deferred combined to put state and local governments under extraordinary fiscal pressure. The collective cumulative state budget surplus declined steadily from nearly $12 billion at the end of fiscal year 1980 to under $5 billion (of which one-third was accounted for by Texas) by the end of fiscal year 1982.[13]

By late 1982, the force of balanced-budget requirements, the accumulating pain of service reductions, the fading direct impact of the tax revolt, and a rebounding economy led to a substantial round of tax increases at the state level. Forty-three state tax increases, with an estimated revenue impact of about $4 billion, were enacted in 1982.[14] The year 1983 saw tax increases of nearly $8 billion, or almost 5 percent of the existing state tax burden.[1]

Mechanical Limits on Government Spending

In nominal dollars, this is the largest one-year increase in state tax burdens ever enacted (though larger increases in inflation-adjusted dollars and as a percentage of state taxes were enacted in 1969 and 1971). These tax increases were widespread geographically (over three-quarters of the states raised at least one tax), and no major state tax base was immune.[16]

State fiscal positions rebounded sharply. Recent estimates suggest that state and local governments had a combined surplus of about $15 billion to $25 billion in 1983 and an even greater surplus in 1984.[17] This was a result of both the 1983 tax increases and the economic expansion in 1983–1984. Tax increases combined with budget surpluses rekindled the latent tax revolt. Legislatures are still conscious of the need to check revenue and spending growth and are under pressure in many states to roll back tax increases and distribute accumulated surpluses. Nine states have already cut taxes or eliminated temporary increases. Reductions are anticipated in four additional states.[18] A $900 million surplus in Minnesota and a $550 million surplus in Wisconsin prompted the elimination of 10 percent income surtaxes that would have raised $225 million in each state. Michigan is debating how much to cut taxes, with proposals running between $150 million and $800 million.

Tax revolt advocates, however, have not been fully mollified by these legislative actions, and the grass roots movement to limit taxes and spending seems to be resurging. In 1984, thirteen states considered the modification of existing limits or the adoption of new rules; six of these proposals were citizen-initiated.[19] The November 1984 ballot in California carried another Jarvis initiative, Jaws IV, to clarify some of the provisions of Prop 13 that its supporters believed have been interpreted too liberally by the legislature and the courts. California voters rejected Jaws IV, which would have forced a rebate of about $1.3 billion in previously collected property taxes. In November, Oregon taxpayers voted down Proposition 2, an initiative similar to Prop 13 that would have rolled back property tax levies to their 1981 levels or to 1.5 percent of market value, whichever was lower. It would have cut property taxes by about $600 million.[20] It was defeated by less than 1 percent of the total vote. Oregon has not shared in recent economic expansion, because it is heavily dependent on the timber industry, which is still depressed. The frustration of its taxpayers may therefore not reflect the general mood across the nation. Highly restrictive initiatives were on the ballot in several other states, however, indicating that tax revolt sentiments are still abroad. Only about one-quarter of the initiatives were successful.

Do Mechanical Tax and Expenditure Limits Hold Down Spending?

The avowed purpose and clear intent of tax and expenditure limitations is to hold down the level or growth rate of public spending. Do they? It is hard to tell. We do not yet have extended experience with the spending patterns of state and local governments operating under these new limits. It is also hard to distinguish the impacts of different limitations. They have taken a variety of forms—some have focused on spending and some on taxes, some have specifically targeted one revenue source, and others are quite general. They have had different override provisions, have embodied differing degrees of limitation, have permitted different levels of escalation, and have started from baselines in different fiscal years.

Moreover, discerning their effects requires us to compare states that have limits with those that do not. But there are many systematic differences between limit and nonlimit states that confound this comparison. Nonlimit states may not have imposed specific limits because their public sectors were relatively small, or their legislatures may consistently restrain spending to avoid having limits imposed. Differences in spending levels between states with limits and those without do not necessarily reflect the effect of the limitations.

Because of the number of different forms limitations have taken and the short time since their adoption, detailed statistical work on their impacts has not yet been done. There are, however, some preliminary findings. First, many of the limits imposed on state spending had no direct impact; a number of states have experienced less growth in revenues or expenditures than their limits would have permitted. This does not mean, however, that the limitations had no effect. Some states faced budgetary constraints more severe than those legally imposed upon them, as recession-battered economies suffered revenue shortfalls. In many other jurisdictions, the power of the tax revolt held spending below authorized limits.

Second, evidence based on the experience with limits in the early 1970s indicates that tax limitations do have some impact on spending levels. These early limits were only a precursor to the more stringent TELs imposed in the late 1970s, and in many cases were quite different in form, but experience with them is nevertheless of some interest. A study conducted by the Advisory Commission on Intergovernmental Relations examined the effects of the early tax limits by statistically comparing limit and nonlimit states.[21] Their study indicated that property tax limits did hold down per capita local

Mechanical Limits on Government Spending

spending. After adjustments were made for interstate differences in urbanization, income, and state and federal aid, the presence of property tax limitations was found to have a statistically discernible effect, lowering spending by approximately 6 to 8 percent.[22]

More recent evidence, however, fails to confirm the anticipated impact of tax limits on spending. In their review of the impact of TELs on state spending, Daphne Kenyon and Karen Benker compared states with TELs to those without.[23] They found that after TELs were instituted, spending relative to personal income grew more rapidly in some years and more slowly in other years than in non-TEL states. Even in states where TELs were tied to the rate of personal income growth, the changes in spending relative to personal income were not systematically different in TEL and non-TEL states. For most states, the limitations were not binding, and it may be that other influences common to all states (like revenue shortfalls due to the recession) were determining spending growth in TEL and non-TEL states alike. The results suggest that the impact of tax and expenditure limitations is not as straightforward as it might seem.

If these general limitations do hold down spending, what spending do they affect most? The effect of tax limitation in Massachusetts has been extensively studied. Massachusetts localities operate under one of the most stringent Prop 13–style measures, and the impact on spending in some jurisdictions has been undeniable. An early assessment of the impacts finds varied community responses, yet some patterns do emerge.[24] First, "ancillary" programs—parks, libraries, street maintenance—were hard hit. Most communities cut deeply into these programs, on average reducing them by more than 10 percent, over twice the average reduction required in all programs together. Since they made up a relatively small share of municipal budgets, however, deep cuts in these programs did not begin to absorb the required budgetary cut. Because school budgets represent a large fraction of local spending, it was clear that adjusting to Prop $2\frac{1}{2}$ would necessarily require extensive cuts in education. On the average, Massachusetts communities reduced school spending by 6.5 percent, somewhat more than the average for all programs. What remains? Basic day-to-day public services with very strong employment constituencies: sanitation, fire, and police programs. All three were cut less than the overall average; police services were hardly cut at all.[25]

The survival of programs in the face of overall budget cuts correlates directly with the strength of their employment constituencies. An exception to this general rule is education; teachers can be a potent political force, yet the cuts in education programs were deeper than average. There are two explanations for this. First, protecting so large a component of local budgets as the education program would force even deeper cuts on the other programs. Second, a portion of the tax limitation drive in Massachusetts stemmed specifically from concern about the growth of school budgets. School boards historically had autonomous control over their budgets; each submitted a total budget figure to its municipality, which was required to raise the taxes necessary to fund the schools as part of its property tax levy. A specific provision of Prop $2\frac{1}{2}$ brought school budgets directly under the control of local legislative bodies. The sentiment that school boards engaged in uncontrolled spending contributed to the schools' absorbing the large fraction of total cuts that they did. Given this explanation of the impact on school spending in Massachusetts, the rest of the cuts follow an anticipated pattern. Tax limitations land most heavily on programs that do not have strong employment constituencies.

The Ancillary Consequences of TELs

If tax limitations do hold down spending, then they have other predictable effects. A major short-run impact is a form of revenue sharing in reverse. State and local taxes are deductible from income before federal income taxes are computed. Thus, the federal taxpayer pays for roughly one-third of all state and local tax-financed spending.* Any reduction in state and local taxes increases federally taxable income and therefore raises federal revenues. The Prop 13 tax cuts in California resulted in a taxfall to the federal Treasury of about $2.5 billion—more than 35 percent of the reduction.[26] In the aftermath of tax limitations, services formerly provided through tax payments may be privately purchased instead. Parents may send children to private schools, for example, and may have to hire private garbage collectors. The cost of these private services is not tax deductible; they must be paid for out of expensive "after-tax" dollars. By contrast, services purchased through deductible state and local taxes are paid for with pretax dollars. The federal Treasury is one of the prime beneficiaries when local tax limitations reduce state and local spending.

The (unanticipated?) short-term flow of funds from states to the federal government is not the only anomaly TELs may cause. Over a long period,

*Obviously, the state or local taxpayer pays for a fraction of this benefit in his or her own federal income tax payment. But from the perspective of each separate jurisdiction, most of it is paid by federal taxpayers elsewhere.

they may result in a rebalancing of public and private economic activity quite different from the one their proponents project. Many TELs explicitly restrict the growth of government as a fraction of taxpayer incomes. What are the implications of checking government growth this way? Why should the cost of government be a fixed component of personal budgets? Presumably, because there is a sense that there is some reasonable size for government, which it may exceed in the absence of limitation. That government has grown continually and considerably is indisputable. The central question is what prompted this growth. Those who propose to limit the scale of government activity argue that government grows automatically, as politicians and bureaucrats seek greater power and rewards. Government is viewed as powerful, intrinsically self-aggrandizing, and in need of limits.

There are many other views about why government has grown. The traditionalist explains that as real personal income rises and basic necessities (largely privately supplied) are taken care of, people have more room in their budgets to purchase services that only governments can provide. This view was put forward elegantly by Adolph Wagner in a classic essay and is still referred to as Wagner's law.[27] According to Wagner, government's evolution as a growing component of the economy reflects the changing economic status of citizens. Artificial limits would be unwelcome. The tax revolt is vociferous testimony that this explanation does not describe all taxpayers, but it may apply to many.

These explanations assume that the level of services provided by government is increasing. It is, but it may not be increasing as fast as simple statistics indicate. Suppose that the price of government services—the dollar cost per unit of service received—is rising more rapidly than prices generally. Maintaining a constant proportion of private and public services will then require a continuing increase in the fraction of taxpayers' budgets devoted to government. This third explanation has been offered for the secular increase in government spending as a fraction of the economy.[28] If it is correct, then TELs that freeze government spending as a fraction of personal budgets will not maintain a constant balance between public and private services; they will steadily diminish the services provided by government.

A number of researchers argue that the postwar expansion of government reflects increasing relative prices of governmentally supplied goods rather than an increase in actual governmental service levels.[29] Even according to conservative assumptions, nearly one-half of the nominal postwar expansion in public spending reflects the increasing relative cost of government, not a real growth in government services.

If this increased cost reflects waste or fraud, it might be a reason to cut the scale of government. But William Baumol has advanced an alternative more benign explanation. He argues that the nature of public services makes them less subject to productivity improvements than private goods and services are.[30] According to Baumol, public services do not often benefit from technological advances like those that reduce the prices of private goods (or, at least, keep them from rising so fast). Therefore, public services gradually become more expensive relative to private services.[31] While this issue is hardly settled, there is evidence tracing increases in government costs to "slow productivity improvement" rather than to waste or excessive wages of government employees.[32]

If the relative price of public services is rising, the impact of TELs could be quite different from what is commonly thought. Freezing government's share of the economy would ensure a declining level of government services relative to private production.[33] It may be that the share of services provided by government should fall as public services become relatively more expensive to produce. Still, some higher-cost services may be worth retaining. Limiting government to a set share of economic activity, something most TELs do, may thus not fix the scale of government as taxpayers perceive it in their lives. If productivity increases more slowly for government services, TELs impose an arbitrary gradual decline in the actual share of public activity, at a rate determined by the growth in relative prices of public services. This is an anomaly even some TEL advocates would not sanction

Supermajority Requirements

Many tax and spending limit resolutions have included a "supermajority" requirement, advocated by proponents as an accountability device. Some of the early initiatives, including Prop 13, required that future tax increases be approved by more than a simple majority of the electorate (two-thirds was a common choice). Kenyon and Benker note in their review of recent limitation activity that supermajority provisions are now much more common than they were in early limitation proposals.[34] Currently, supermajority provisions are in place in six states, and they are being contemplated in a number of other jurisdictions. California already has a supermajority requirement for tax increases; voters defeated a 1984 proposal to extend it to fee increases. A Nevada proposal, also defeated, would have required a two-thirds legislative majority and a popular vote to approve new tax increases. Michigan voters turned down a proposal to require either a popular vote or a four-fifths legislative majority, but retained their two-thirds majority requirement. Some proponents argue that all spending bills should require a supermajority.

Supermajority requirements are certainly a form of limitation; they make it more difficult to secure approval. Do they increase accountability? Again, it depends on what we mean by accountability. If it means reducing the scale of government, then supermajority provisions for spending or taxing probably improve it. If accountability means that government should reflect the wishes of the electorate, supermajority requirements could be a substantial impediment.

Under a simple majority rule, the opposition must itself be a majority in order to block an action. Simple majority rule has the advantage that either one side or the other always has what is required to act—and that if one does, the other cannot.* A supermajority requirement, by comparison, reduces the size of the coalition necessary to block an action. This empowers (infra)minorities to bargain. Small groups can form blocking coalitions and extract concessions from the majority. And there is no limit to the number of overlapping small blocking coalitions that can form.

Consider the problem of assembling a majority to support a legislative action. Each member is induced to join in a series of negotiations by receiving some benefit. This is called logrolling; it is an accountability *problem*—and it is fostered by supermajority rules. Building the action coalition is harder; more concessions have to be granted to attract more members. If a two-thirds majority rule is in effect, *any* group of one-third of the body plus one member can hold up vital legislation. Requiring a supermajority makes blocking groups more numerous and smaller and thus easier to form and more powerful.

Supermajority provisions therefore empower—and where critical issues are at stake, dramatically empower—small minorities.[35] There are places where minorities should have extra power. Constitutional amendments and U.S. treaty ratification require two-thirds majorities. These are unusual events where minority views are given unusual weight. Budgets do not belong in this category. Applying a supermajority requirement to spending bills is likely to spur *more* spending; budget bills will be riddled with concessions. In this context, supermajority rules encourage special interest spending by promoting concessions rather than competition.

---

*Simple majority has two properties for any either-or decision: (a) one side or the other always has it, and (b) both sides cannot. If we define a decision rule as the number of legislators required to authorize an action, then simple majority is the only decision rule with both properties. It is also the decision rule with the *highest* number required that still has property (a) and the rule with the *smallest* number that still has property (b).

This turns the position of tax limitation proponents completely on its head. They portray government as a collection of politicians clamoring for more and larger government. Supermajority provisions are thought to enhance accountability by making it harder to expand government spending. In fact, they make it easier. Individual legislators can threaten to join a blocking coalition and instead accept a favor in return for supporting the action coalition. When more members can threaten to withhold their support, the aggregate price paid for the ability to act goes up. If accountability means permitting small minorities of legislators or voters to hold a large majority hostage over vital legislation in order to extract favors, then supermajority provisions may enhance accountability beyond our wildest expectations.

Accountability for spending bills would be better served under rules that require the *largest* possible blocking coalition to prevent any action. This would have several advantages. First, it makes it harder to hold legislation hostage. Second, favors granted to the last members to join the action coalition need not be as large, for there are more nonmembers with whom the action coalition can bargain. There is thus greater competition. The total cost of coalition building is held down. What is the largest blocking coalition we can feasibly require? It is just short of a majority, which implies that the action coalition should be a simple majority. Simple majority rule may be the best protection available against logrolling in a democratic process.

Supermajority requirements applied to general tax increases, as opposed to budget approval, are a somewhat different matter. While budgets must be approved every year, some taxpayers may want to build in a bias preventing tax increases. Supermajority rules have an inherent bias toward the status quo. There is no guarantee that either side will be able to construct a supermajority coalition. Under simple majority rule, if one side fails to be a majority, the other side succeeds. With a supermajority, this advantage disappears; the government may not be able to act at all. This may be all right, if the default—the status quo—is publicly acceptable. This may more often be true of taxes than of budgets. But supermajority provisions aid *accountability* only if we know that what the public really wants is no change.

Supermajority provisions do not enhance accountability. They are likely to increase the prevalence and the cost of a legislative practice widely criticized as unaccountable. The supermajority requirement is an archetypal example of a limitation that is decidedly not an accountability device. It has a distinct policy bias; anything subject to a supermajority rule is less likely to occur. A supermajority provision acts as a brake on approval. But it serves its function as a limitation at some—and perhaps at a substantial—*cost* in accountability.

Do Mechanical Spending Limits Affect Accountability?

Limitation devices could result in less accountable government actions. Faced with declining financial resources, but filled with expansive (not to mention expensive) aspirations for what government should be doing, public officials might respond to budget limits by moving more public activities off the budget. There is little evidence that they have done so. True, growth rates of spending and revenues excluded from limitation in states with some form of TEL have tended to exceed growth of those captured within them. This might indicate a willingness by public officials to circumvent restrictions where possible. And there are no comprehensive measures of off-budget activity from which to assess any changes, so it is difficult to tell. But the tax limitation movements succeeded in holding many states' spending growth *below* the prescribed limits. They act as a watchdog to prevent any substantial moves to substitute credit programs or increases in tax expenditures (both of which would escape explicit notice under tax and spending limits) for direct spending. The threat of being caught subverting taxpayer desires to limit the scope of government discourages public officials from finding unlimited avenues to fund programs they can no longer afford to support directly.*

The evidence on the impacts of TELs is at best mixed. In many cases, states have not run up against the limits, although TELs may have some restraining effect anyway. In many jurisdictions, they have resulted in substantial cuts, and these are largest for programs with weak employment constituencies. Where TELs do reduce taxes, they provide a windfall to the federal Treasury. Where they limit spending as a proportion of taxpayer budgets, they may, over time, result in a declining level of public services (if the relative price of producing public services continues to rise). They cut government flexibility, making it more difficult to adapt to the public's changing tastes. And some forms of limitation may have perverse effects—

---

*Sales of assets concealed as part of creative financing schemes are a possible counterexample. They hide costs, and their use has been increasing. See chapter 8 for a discussion of the accountability of creative financing. It remains to be seen whether the restraint is permanent or transitory. The pressure to move spending onto the quiet account is constant; resistance to it may not be.

like supermajority requirements, which may encourage spending through logrolling.

But what do TELs have to do with accountability? Proponents argue that they are exclusively about accountability; opponents, that they are exclusively about policy. Proponents, believing government too large, want to restrict its scope to make it more accountable to the people—that is, smaller. Opponents see limitations as an effort to squeeze programs out of the government sphere and as reflecting a series of underlying policy choices. They see little in tax and expenditure limitations that is designed to make government more answerable. Proponents respond that to make government smaller is to make it more answerable, by definition.[36] Most advocates of limits are politically conservative, and their policy preferences are for fewer policies. They firmly believe that government is unaccountably large. Their views about policy and their views about accountability thus point in the same direction and often cannot be distinguished.

In one sense, tighter, more austere budgets *are* more accountable. By limiting government expenditures, we raise the level of conflict over competing policy priorities. Legislatures are forced to choose among alternatives. For governments as well as for people, budget constraints have a way of forcing choices to be confronted instead of finessed. If accountability means open debate about priorities, then tax and expenditure limitations may indeed contribute to it.

Nonetheless, if the problem is accountability, it is not obvious why the solution is smaller government. If government were fully answerable, we would not have to determine in advance how big it should be. Appropriate mechanisms that ensure public financial accountability would establish the scale of total government activity as one among the many features of government that have to be determined. How does an arbitrary device (in the form of a tax or expenditure limit) make government accountable if it is not so already?

Most tax and expenditure limits are *alternatives* to building better accountability, not accountability devices in themselves. If no other way can be found to make government answerable to taxpayers, spending limits may be the best we can do. TELs make government respond to one important feature of taxpayers wishes, their choice of overall scale. But taxpayers' wishes change. TELs do nothing to guarantee that governments can respond flexibly and accountably over time.

Chapter 11

The Federal

Balanced-Budget Amendment

EVERYTHING about the federal government is bigger. It has more employees, more yards of red tape—and more money. The measured part of federal spending is now about $1 trillion annually; its explicit debt is over $1.5 trillion. It employs about four million workers, roughly one of every three who work for some government. The vast sums involved give spending deliberations an ethereal character.

The scale and growth of the federal government made it inevitable that moves to limit the scope of governmental activity would sooner or later tackle federal spending. The federal work force has increased only about 1 percent annually since 1950, but direct federal spending increased an average of 9 percent per year between 1949 and 1980. The federal share of the economy rose from about 16 percent in 1949 to about 23 percent today.[1] As federal activity expanded, so did deficit spending. The federal government has run deficits in all but one of the last twenty-five years. It is now extending an unbroken string of sixteen deficit years. The only obvious sign of change is that budget deficits will be a larger fraction of the GNP. Figure 11.1 shows a moving average of the budget surplus or deficit as a fraction of the GNP. It shows no five-year period in aggregate surplus since 1948–1952. The trend is clear. Until the early 1970s, five-year average deficits were on the order of 1 percent of the GNP or less. Since then they have

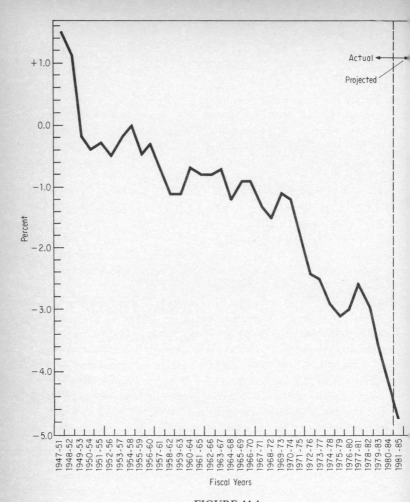

FIGURE 11.1

Five-year Moving Average of the Total Budget Surplus (+) or Deficit (−) as a Percentage of the GNP*

*Total budget surplus or deficit equals the unified budget surplus or deficit plus the deficit from off-budget programs
SOURCES: Congressional Budget Office, *Balancing the Federal Budget and Limiting Federal Spending: Constitutional and Statutory Approaches,* September 1982, fig. 1; updated figures from Office of Management and Budget, *Economic Report of the President 1985* (Washington, D.C.: Government Printing Office, 1985), p. 232; Office of Management and Budget, *Budget in Fiscal Year 1986* (Washington, D.C.: Government Printing Office, 1985), p. 64.

grown steadily; the projected average deficit for 1982–1986 exceeds 4 percent of the GNP.

Continually increasing deficit spending has created a broadly based movement to force some form of budget balance on the federal level.[2] State and local governments have operated under such discipline for years; why should the federal government not face similar limits? This view has long been part of the national temperament. Even during the Great Depression, over 60 percent of those polled wanted to cut federal spending by enough to balance the budget. In 1953, nearly 70 percent preferred balancing the budget to cutting taxes. Similar (or perhaps stronger) support for balancing the federal budget exists today. In a March 1980 Gallup poll, over 80 percent of the respondents favored a constitutional amendment mandating a balanced federal budget. As Alan Blinder and Douglas Holtz-Eakin observe in their review of public opinion concerning federal budget balance requirements, the electorate's response depends on how the question is posed. A CBS/*New York Times* poll that stressed potential spending cutbacks that such an amendment might force (conducted a month after the Gallup poll) found only a two-to-one margin in favor of an amendment.[3] The electorate favors some form of amendment, though the burden it is willing to bear for it is not clear.

Inconsistent responses to questions concerning federal spending are commonplace. A January 1979 Harris poll found nearly 70 percent in favor of a constitutional revision requiring a balanced federal budget and an equal percentage favoring a major cutback in federal spending. Sizable majorities, however, opposed cutbacks in specific program areas, including health, social services, defense, environment, and education. A quick examination of the federal budget will show that there isn't much else. The public wants to balance the federal budget, expand spending in most specific policy areas, and reduce taxes. Happily, these desires are combined with a belief that funds are available to close the gap: wasteful spending can be reduced. Little progress has been made in tapping this supposed reservoir or in proving that it is large enough to matter.

These views, inconsistent as they may be, are strong—and they create broad-based support for constraining federal largess. This sentiment is reflected in calls by thirty-two state legislatures for a constitutional convention to consider a balanced-budget amendment; only two more are needed under Article V of the Constitution. Spurred by the strength and geographic diversity of this grass roots movement and perhaps fearful of losing control of the process, Congress has regularly debated its own version of a balanced-budget amendment in the last four years; the most recent effort was voted down in June 1984.

Congress did pass the Byrd-Grassley statute in 1978, requiring it to enact a balanced budget starting in fiscal year 1981. Neither this statute nor statutory debt limitation has had any appreciable impact on either federal spending or budget balance. Budget deficits of startling proportion began, in fact, the year the Byrd-Grassley statute took effect. Proponents of limitation therefore regard Congress's good-faith efforts (pledged since time immemorial) and statutory limitations as entirely ineffective; they seek constitutional reform instead.

Proposed constitutional amendments generally have two features.[4] First, they would require Congress to balance total outlays and total receipts, with outlays defined to include everything except repayments of debt principal, and receipts defined to exclude the proceeds of borrowing. This provision would prohibit planned borrowing for any purpose other than refinancing existing debt. (Without the exclusion of debt principal from outlays, taxpayers would be required to retire the national debt; under this provision, they would be able to keep it at its current size.) Second, proposed amendments would limit the expansion of federal revenues to the same growth rate as that of national income. The combined effect would require all federal disbursements to fit within a fixed fraction of national income. Exceptions would be permitted in time of national emergency, during a declared war, and at other times when approved by a supermajority of both houses. The limit on revenue growth in many proposals can be overridden by a simple majority, the same number of legislators as is required to pass a tax increase; no more stringent requirement would apply to tax increases than already exists. The proposals would, however, make a tax increase more visible, because the vote authorizing it would be on that issue alone.

As most of the proponents have made clear, these proposals are directed mainly at federal spending, not at the level of federal debt per se. A limit on borrowing is considered a necessary and potentially effective instrument to stiffen resistance to spending. The argument generally advanced for imposing limits of this form is that we need to counterbalance a presumed institutional bias in favor of excessive public spending. It asserts that the benefits of government spending are highly concentrated on the recipients, while the costs are widely diffused. This means that the constituency in favor of any particular spending proposal cares more than those who will be forced to pay for it. In contrast to spending, taxes are viewed as unpopular with the large majority and are thus thought to be more easily restrained. Deficits arise because they permit legislators to yield to the pressure to spend without confronting the pressure not to tax. Proponents of a limit on federal borrowing see deficits as a problem in themselves: they cause inflation and push costs onto future taxpayers. More important, deficits are a symptom of spending more than taxpayers actually want to spend. The balanced-budget idea is to bring spending down to the level taxpayers are willing to pay for. The amendment would transform the pressure lawmakers feel not to raise taxes into a pressure to hold down spending.[5] Proponents argue that this counterforce must have the weight of constitutional authority to stand against the tide of spending for narrow special interests.

Many supporters of the amendment oppose the national debt as an institution and warn about the alleged damage that it does to the economy. But most of the arguments in favor of the amendment have been on the basis that it will restrain spending. David Stockman, in his 1982 testimony expressing support for the House version of the balanced-budget amendment, spoke at length about how concentrated the benefits of public spending are and about how diffuse the costs tend to seem. He presented a series of examples, including the observation that dairy subsidies amount to roughly $7,000 per producer but only $18 per taxpayer, to show the imbalance between the pressure to spend and the pressure to be restrained. He managed to get through eighteen pages of testimony without once mentioning the national debt. He did mention deficits several times, as symptoms of uncontrolled spending.[6] Stockman's is one of many views on the subject; the clear message from most is that the constitutional amendment's major intent is the elimination of federal "overspending."

Anomalies from Forcing Federal Budget Balance

There are many ways to curb spending. Before we choose to take the historic step of using the Constitution to require budget balance, we should look carefully at what we would have forced to balance against what. What would be limited—and what would not? There are several anomalies in the potential impact of budget balance requirements, stemming from what is included or excluded.

First, the inclusive definitions of outlays and receipts contained in most proposed balanced-budget amendments would require the federal government to pay for all direct purchases on a pay-as-you-go basis. This means no borrowing, even to acquire assets that would generate benefits over many years. Current taxpayers, in examining capital acquisition, would decide whether they were willing to pay the full cost of facilities whose benefits will be (largely) enjoyed by future taxpayers. There would be no way to pass along a part of the bill to future taxpayers, who might willingly defray that cost to secure the benefits. This anomaly results because there is no provision for a federal capital budget, which would allow borrowing for investment—that is, to purchase capital assets.

Advocates of federal budget balance frequently draw an analogy to household and business budgets, stating that there is no reason that the federal government should not face the same kind of budget constraints as private individuals do. Individuals, so the saying goes, cannot live beyond their means; why should the government be able to? This view has deep historical and cultural roots. Amendment proponents often quote a passage from Adam Smith, who wrote in *The Wealth of Nations* in 1776, "What is prudence in the conduct of every private family, can scarce be folly in that of a great kingdom."' Smith was referring to free trade policies, arguing that each nation should purchase goods wherever it finds them cheapest, just as every household should. The fact that this passage is not about borrowing has not deterred amendment proponents from using it freely.* Quoted out of context, Smith's phrase stirs a visceral reaction against government borrowing.

This time-tested aphorism may contain great wisdom, but it has virtually nothing to do with whether the federal budget (as currently defined) should be in balance. The existing budget makes no distinction between capital and operating expenses. Households and firms could not possibly operate with budgets balanced on this basis. Under balanced-budget strictures, a household purchasing a home or a company building a new factory would be required to pay the full cost out of receipts in that year. Households and businesses have separate capital and operating budgets: they (try to) keep their operating budgets in balance but often borrow to acquire new assets. Treating the government like any ordinary taxpayer calls for permitting it to borrow for capital purposes, just as households and firms do. Adam Smith's elegant saying—if used with reference to debt at all—should be interpreted as an argument *against* the federal limitation as it is currently proposed.

Treating capital spending incorrectly—confusing it with operating expenditures—is equally wrong whether assets are being purchased or sold. When assets are purchased, treating the expenditure as an operating cost implies that nothing of lasting value was obtained. When they are sold,

*Proponents might do better to quote Mr. Micawber's advice to David Copperfield (which at least has to do with overextending one's resources): " 'My other piece of advice, Copperfield,' said Mr. Micawber, 'you know. Annual income twenty pounds, annual expenditure nineteen six, result happiness. Annual income twenty pounds, annual expenditure twenty pounds ought and six, result misery. The blossom is blighted, the leaf is withered, the God of day goes down upon the dreary scene,—and in short you are for ever floored. As I am!' "

treating the proceeds as revenue makes the same mistake. Either error intensifies myopia in investment decisions. For example, in the fiscal year 1986 budget debate, the Senate claimed $1.7 billion in "savings" for putting a moratorium on purchases of oil for the Strategic Petroleum Reserve.[8] The administration proposed to go further, "reducing" the deficit by selling materials from strategic commodity stockpiles. Perhaps the oil reserve is big enough and the commodity stockpiles are too large. Then these actions are appropriate. But their appropriateness should not be misjudged by thinking they have any impact on the deficit, properly defined. A failure to separate capital from operating expenditures is a fundamental anomaly in federal budgetary accounting that encourages this kind of error.

When we treat the federal government's capital spending correctly, separating it from operating expenditures, the operating budget comes considerably closer to being in balance. Because the federal government has never had a separate capital budget and has not maintained distinctions between capital and operating spending, figures on the level of net federal investment are difficult to construct. The level of investment should be determined by subtracting the deterioration of existing assets (depreciation) from new investment spending. Since the federal government keeps no books on its stock of assets, depreciation estimates are at best guesses, particularly since historical purchase prices must be adjusted to current dollars when current depreciation is computed. The OMB estimates that in fiscal year 1984 *gross* federal investment spending amounted to about $175 billion.[9] This includes part of the defense program and some research and development investment as well as capital acquisition by the federal government for its other programs and by states using federal funds. Depending upon how large the depreciation of federal assets was, the net investment component of the federal deficit—the portion even fiscal conservatives might regard as "legitimate" borrowing—could amount to a significant portion of the total.[10] Removing the net investment part of federal spending (for which we should allow borrowing) would bring the remainder—the operating part of the budget—much closer to being in balance over most of the period since World War II.[11]

An accurate view of capital spending points out that the operating budget is not so far out of balance as it might seem—and that the pressure to spend has not necessarily extended federal largess past the point of taxpayers' willingness to pay. Current taxpayers in fact pay a good deal more than it first appears of the costs of services they are currently receiving. They also pass along to future taxpayers (including themselves) a bill for future benefits. To a much greater extent than is obvious from looking at the size of the national debt, current services are matched to current payments. If this were all there were to the story, it would constitute sound public financial management. There are several important forms, however, in which the cost of current spending is being handed on to future taxpayers. A balanced-budget amendment would do little to restrain them.

Leasing, discussed in chapter 8, is one way to pass capital costs on to the future. Proposed federal balanced-budget amendments would make purchasing assets extremely expensive; the whole purchase price would have to come from the current year's receipts. But what about leasing? A long-term rental is a form of borrowing; the lessor provides financing for the asset and passes the capital costs along to the lessee as part of the rental charge. *Balanced-budget amendments would permit this form of capital borrowing by the federal government.*

This point is vital to an understanding of the impact of a balance requirement. Issuing debt is a way of "leveraging" currently available funds. Instead of paying the whole price today, the debt issuer pays interest on the debt and a portion of the purchase price in each year of the loan. A small annual flow of funds can thus provide "debt service" adequate to the acquisition of an asset costing far too much to buy in one year; the annual flow of funds is "leveraged" to obtain the services of the asset. The same leveraging can be obtained through a lease. An annual rental fee provides access to an asset costing many times the rent. The only difference is that when funds are borrowed explicitly in a debt issue they are spent directly on the purchase, whereas in a lease the borrowing and purchase are done by a third party.

Under the proposed balanced-budget requirements, this difference becomes crucial. Explicit federal borrowing is ruled out, because the funds would be spent directly. Borrowing through a lease is allowed, because the borrowing and purchase would be carried out by some other entity. As now written, the balanced-budget amendments do not prohibit asset acquisition through borrowing. They allow the federal government to borrow—but *only* through leases. As was discussed in chapter 8, leasing is generally more costly than explicit borrowing, and there are in addition many accountability reasons not to prefer it.

One response to this realization might be to forbid leasing as well. This would be thoroughly untenable. Long-term, explicit leases could be prohibited on the theory that they are debts. But if we prohibit short-term rentals, the federal government would have to own every asset it uses, from office buildings to typewriters. It could no longer rent temporary office space or purchase time on a time-shared computer. If we did try to prohibit leasing by the federal government, it could still procure the use of assets owned—

and financed—by someone else by hiring the services, together with their office space and equipment.* For example, the government might contract out keypunch services to an operator with keypunch equipment. Nearly every service the government buys embodies some services from capital; any long-term purchase of services therefore includes some borrowing. Trying to distinguish different levels and forms of borrowing is likely only to enrich lawyers who write contracts transmuting one form into another. To rule out the use of assets borrowed through rentals and leases would be infeasible.

Balanced-budget requirements thus contain a peculiar message. Explicit borrowing is ruled out, not because of the borrowing per se but because it provides freely spendable funds; it disconnects spending from taxing. Borrowing through leasing does not cause this disconnection. The borrowed funds are not freely spendable; they can be spent only on the leased asset. Leasing also forces the government to raise revenues to cover its current cost for use of the asset. This form of borrowing is inherently better controlled, and it is therefore permitted.

The anomaly in this position is that the defense of borrowing through leases applies equally to explicit borrowing to acquire *any* capital asset. Budget balance proposals permit leases to be used to move the purchase cost of capital assets out from under the current revenue ceiling. Explicit borrowing for the same asset, for the very same purpose, is not permitted. This distinction is unreasonable. If we are willing to allow lease financing of a separate capital budget, little can be said for not allowing it through explicit borrowing as well.†

Leasing is not the only form of borrowing a balanced-budget requirement would miss. Another major form, discussed in chapter 1, is public pension programs. Federal retirement systems are not funded on a current basis. The entire social security system represents a very large, conceptually similar example. Promises to pay future retirees accumulate, but no corresponding resources are set aside. This is a form of borrowing. Accumulated quiet pensions borrowing is now approaching $1.5 trillion; if social security is added, the total is close to $6 trillion. It accumulates as current costs, incurred to secure current benefits, are not paid by current taxpayers. These accumulating liabilities may be cases where the pressure to spend has

---

*Hiring freezes often have this impact, when agencies first lay off workers and then hire them as consultants, generally at higher salaries (but with lower benefits).

†We have not seen any great volume of leasing activity by the federal government (except in a few recent highly publicized cases in the Department of Defense; see chapter 8). On the other hand, there has not been any great incentive for it to date. It would flourish if a balanced-budget amendment that permits leasing and rules out explicit borrowing were implemented. Perhaps, to save the taxpayers money, the federal government would establish an off-budget federal entity to acquire assets to be leased to the rest of the government.

outpaced the pressure not to tax by avoiding current payment. Current budget rules and accounting overlook them, for the most part. They would not be noticed under a balanced-budget amendment, either.

Nor would a federal balanced-budget requirement constrain federal tax expenditures. The amendment would not touch them even if they were made an explicit party of outlays and receipts: since they represent both taxing and spending, they would not affect budget balance. But if the central purpose of a balanced-budget amendment is to restrain the aggregate activity of government, then failing to capture tax expenditures could be a serious liability. Holding revenues fixed, the federal government could influence the allocation of resources in the economy by raising tax rates on some activities and lowering them on others. The scale of federal activity could still be expanded by increasing tax expenditures and recouping revenue losses through higher tax rates. Since the budget would remain balanced, proposed amendments are silent on the desirability of such a change.

Requiring a balanced budget without permitting a separation of capital and operating outlays would result in one further anomaly. Freezing the explicit debt in nominal terms would lead to a gradual diminution of the national debt as a fraction of national wealth. Many advocates of limitation regard this as a major side benefit, believing that the national debt is an insurmountable roadblock to private investment and economic expansion. The debt would be gradually phased out, in real terms.

By forcing gradual repayment of the national debt and by making current expenditure dollars expensive, a budget balance requirement would intensify competition for available federal revenues. This could raise the level and profile of the debate, increasing taxpayer interest and validating the claims that budget limitation is a spur toward greater accountability.

There is, unfortunately, another edge on this sword. A bright light casts a deep and inviting shadow. A balanced-budget amendment would not limit other forms of federal intervention at all. They would become relatively less expensive and more attractive instruments of federal policy. Regulation is a telling example. Unable to spend its own funds to achieve purposes it favors, the federal government may be more disposed to issue orders to others. Whether it raises air quality standards and adds to the costs imposed on firms, mandates standards for training programs run by state and local governments, or specifies costly procedures for handling its own nuclear waste, the federal government has considerable power to require spending by others (and itself). It is hard to set definable limits on this power.

Born of taxpayer frustration with the remote but vast power of the federal government and its increasing impact on their own budgets, the federal balanced-budget movement enjoys widespread support. The proposal to limit federal discretion has a number of serious drawbacks. It is designed to limit spending, and it would quite likely do so. But in the absence of a separation of capital and operating funds, it could seriously distort the pattern of federal investment. At a minimum, the federal acquisition of capital assets through leases would be dramatically encouraged. Little or no limitation on total borrowing would be created, both because the amendment (wisely) disregards leases and because it fails to limit spending in the form of pension and other unfunded obligations. It would not control the scope of government, since tax expenditures and regulation would be unrestricted.

If the intent of a balanced-budget amendment is to force balance in the (correctly defined) operating budget, then it probably isn't needed—we are closer to balance than it seems. If it is to eliminate capital spending, then we don't want it. And if it is to control the broadly defined scope of government, then it won't work. If the intent is to improve the accountability of federal spending, other mechanisms—with fewer exclusions and anomalies—might serve us better.

Mechanical Limits—Conclusion

The movement to control government is still active. The late 1970s saw an enormous outpouring of taxpayer energy directed at reducing tax burdens. Much of it was couched in terms of cutting costs without cutting services. Such a choice, if available, is easy to make. The resulting pressure on all levels of government is still felt. Even in jurisdictions with no limitations, government spending has been restrained. The message, for all its diversity in specific form, has rung loud and clear.

Many of the specific proposals for limiting government—tax, expenditure, and debt limitations, supermajority requirements, balanced-budget provisions, and so on—have been presented as ways to enhance government's accountability, not merely to reduce its size. Because many advocates of limitation were politically conservative and viewed government as too large to start with, the concept of accountability was easily confused with smaller scale. Limitations would make traditional forms of spending more difficult and would thus effectively limit the scale of government. A closer examination, however, suggests that at least some of the proposed mechanisms—such as the supermajority requirement, which would increase logrolling—might actually reduce accountability. The willingness of proponents to endorse proposals that would limit spending but reduce accountability makes it clear which is regarded as more important. The target of mechanical limits is scale, not answerability or responsiveness.

Tax limitations do enhance accountability in one way. Every level of government seems more sensitive now than it was a decade ago about controlling spending. Efforts have been and continue to be made to eliminate waste. The power of the tax revolt to hold spending below authorized limits in many jurisdictions suggests new legislative sensitivity. So does the fact that no state or local government has yet made an obvious attempt to move a large portion of its spending off the budget.

Limiting federal spending is another matter altogether. Spending avenues that would fall outside any financial-limit mechanism—regulation, tax expenditures, pensions and other long-term unfunded promises—are more important at the federal level than at other levels of government. Requiring a balanced federal budget seems the more likely to create considerable distortion, diminishing the prospects for effective reform.

The real impact of mechanical spending limits may be their expression of frustration. The limits remind legislators of the broad interests of the public. In that role, limitations may be more of a force for accountability than their specific form and legal impact might suggest.

Conclusion

Accountability, Value,

and Quiet Spending

IN THE 1980s, practically everyone wants more financial accountability for public organizations—more-responsible financial conduct and enhanced accountability at all levels of government. But what does that mean? In a free society, the apparatus of accountability is, by design, the same thing as the apparatus of decision making. The gauntlet that proposed government actions run in order to gain approval—what tests of assent we impose, under what access by whom to what information about program designs and effects—both renders a decision and constitutes a review. The accountability system thus becomes logically inseparable from the decision-making process.

This creates confusion between accountability, on the one hand, and the results of accountable decisions, on the other. Government exists to create value—to produce or procure valuable goods and services its citizens cannot obtain without it. Accountability mechanisms are the answers we give to the question of how to keep the engine on track—how to improve the chances that government actions *do* create value. Value and accountability are thus linked, but they are not the same. Value is the intended result of the actions we take. Accountability is a desired characteristic of the processes through which we choose to act. Two judgments are therefore required. First, did the process force balanced deliberation—is it accountable?

Second, does the action advance broad interests of the general public—is it value-creating?

Government seeks to create value for a variety of principals with conflicting, often poorly defined and ill-perceived interests. It is difficult to determine who the principals are and what their interests are. Moreover, the motives of the agents will never exactly match those of the principals. The effectiveness of even painstakingly designed monitoring and incentive structures will be limited. It will sometimes even be hard to see whose interests are winning and whose are losing. Because its authority is potentially so broad, its purposes so important, and its scope so great, government will necessarily be an arena of conflict among disparate interests.

Accountability mechanisms set the terms for this competition. They determine what we know about what is being done. They make it easy to observe some government actions and difficult to see others. They shelter some programs and expose others to intense scrutiny. They make it easy or difficult to pay attention, and they thus raise or lower the public's attentiveness. They profoundly influence the allocation of the most critical and scarce resource of public accountability—the public's informed attention.

Accountability mechanisms are the operational surrogates for informed public consent. They force a balanced consideration of whether each use of governmental authority is value-creating. Accountability is conferred by successfully confronting a series of hurdles in the public decision-making process. We have established elaborate reciprocal checks on the power of government institutions to make, enforce, and interpret laws and regulations, to create and use police or military force, to intervene by purchase, taxation, or subsidy in private transactions. The specific checks on authority differ in each case, but each device for the use of government power is tied to a mechanism to watch and to check its use.

The presumption is that exposure to these checks improves the odds that authorized actions advance broad interests of the general public. Furthering these interests is the end; accountability is but one of the means. The two are conceptually distinct—but the close association of accountability and decision making, on the one hand, and of decisions and the value they produce, on the other, often leads to confusion between accountability and value.

When we allow accountability and value-creation to become indistinguishable, we set a velvet trap. If the creation of value is the same thing as accountability, arguments that a program has valuable results seem to override demands that it survive confrontation with accepted accountability mechanisms. Any program with plausible political support serves interests of some part of the public and can be presented as creating value. All programs can thus ask to be excused from traditional reviews. It is easy to argue that because a given program is valuable and important, it should be allowed to run quietly, bypassing accountability mechanisms. But then what are those procedures for? Why did we establish them?

Quiet spending programs are caught squarely in this trap. They evade the standard test for permission to use the public's financial resources—the appropriations process. When the evasion is defended at all, it is often with the argument that a program advances interests too precious to be subjected to the rough-and-tumble competition of direct spending through appropriation.

The fatal flaw in these arguments is that accountability mechanisms are precisely the tests we established to prove assertions that a program produces value. The hand is best played in no-trump; arguments that a program is valuable should not automatically overwhelm the presumption for subjecting it to our best tests. Accountability leads to value—not the other way around.

Many quiet spending programs are presented as ways to protect sensitive and critical interests. Several, for example, are said to protect the future. People often make poor judgments, undervaluing future consequences. Many believe government should redress the imbalance. Because people undervalue the future, it is argued, a program that protects the future is at a disadvantage in competing against short-term interests in the appropriations process. Economic development programs are supposed to foster continuing prosperity. Creative financing schemes are said to be necessary to build the infrastructure required for future growth. These schemes are frequently presented as a necessary end run around bureaucratic systems and myopic taxpayers.

But when we scratch the surface of these programs, what do we find? Economic development programs, for the most part, don't work. They advance the agendas of local political factions, usually by spending someone else's money. Many infrastructure financing schemes hide the cost of public works programs largely because their alleged constituencies really do not want them. If anything, the quiet spending programs we examined have a bias *against* the future, not in favor of it. Unfunded pensions allow us quietly to enjoy benefits now and pass costs along to those who come later. Deferred maintenance lets us use up a legacy, leaving those who follow less well off. Public credit programs pile up debts for future taxpayers to pay.

Many quiet spending programs do engage vital public purposes. Tax expenditures to encourage saving for retirement by way of individual retirement accounts and private pension plans may be an example. These spending programs use quiet avenues to achieve important public goals that (arguably) cannot be achieved through more-visible means or that are better achieved through inducing private activity than through direct public spending. Some infrastructure financing schemes that hand the costs of current construction to future taxpayers will also supply them with clean water and safe transportation—a bargain they might well accept voluntarily.

Some quiet spending programs can legitimately claim to advance critical public interests—and that is exactly what makes establishing standards of accountability difficult. The problem is that virtually all quiet spending can be alleged to aid some otherwise underserved but critical public purpose. There is no easy way to judge the validity of these claims. We don't want to let accountability mechanisms obstruct the creation of value, but we also can't let all claims of value prevail over procedural requirements. Whether value is created is, in the end, a matter of judgment. Accountability mechanisms can only act as a surrogate for consent and provide the information supporting that judgment. The ultimate test, in our system, is a test of public acceptance—and the problem, if there is one, is a problem of public perception.

If this is the central accountability issue, then what do the broad approaches examined in the second part of this book have to do with it? The strategies discussed in chapters 9 through 11—expanding the role of accountants and imposing mechanical limits on spending discretion—represent divergent approaches to improving the accounting of spending programs. Reliance on accounting focuses on the details of individual spending programs, searching for comprehensible information to transmit to an attentive public. Reliance on mechanical limits spreads the focus, treating all spending as similar and increasing competition within a fixed budget to provide attention and accountability. Neither strategy appears particularly promising by itself, though each might be an effective component of a more comprehensive approach. Each contains the kernel of a useful suggestion —and each falls prey to a critical weakness.

Improving accounting is an "information" strategy. We have examined a variety of examples where current information leaves much to be desired and where better information might materially enhance accountability. Comprehensible information is surely a prerequisite to accountability; in this sense, improved accounting must necessarily be a part of any solution. The weakness of this strategy lies in the difficulty of getting the established profession to engage it. The established order of the accounting profession is content with its current responsibilities. Reliance on a change in the predilections of an existing profession to address a wider problem is probably a low-return strategy—and it has already been tried.

Tax and expenditure limitations are "consent" strategies. Their strength

ies in forcing trade-offs, in constraining totals so that component parts must be evaluated against each other rather than each separately on its own merits. Political demands must then be balanced against resource costs. But ax and expenditure limitations have two fundamental weaknesses. First, they are more about the scale of government—a broad policy choice—than about its accountability. This illustrates a common problem in the politics of accountability. Accountability is a popular cause. This makes it handy to associate any even vaguely related initiative with improving government accountability. It is a useful banner that other causes can easily pick up—and many do.

The second weakness of mechanical-limit strategies is that they may be not only *un*productive but even *counter*productive. Unless all of the relevant usable resources are counted—and all of the counting is done right—constraining the total will be of little use. In the face of strong political demands, the government will act. If it cannot use direct spending, because of a mechanical constraint, it may substitute other, and often less efficient, forms of influence like regulation.

If not these strategies, though, then what? Or if not these alone, then what else? What do the weaknesses of these approaches to augmenting accountability tell us about how we *should* proceed?

Accountability in the Small: Building the Mechanics

We can never know with certainty which programs truly serve interests of the general public. This implies that we cannot make completely confident judgments about whether specific changes in the mechanics of accountability will be enhancements. Where we do wish to see accountability tightened, the examples we have examined suggest some directions worth pursuing.

IMPROVE ACCOUNTING, BUDGETING, AND FINANCIAL REPORTING

Whatever else we choose to do, we need better accounting and information disclosure. In spite of the continuing efforts of professional accountants and budgeters to represent noncash spending programs accurately, much remains to be done. We have no comprehensive fixed-asset reporting system for governments, largely because there has been no perceived need for one.

To address the infrastructure investment problem, we need one now. Th new accounting standards for evaluating pension fund liabilities cou prompt more intelligible reporting about the liability side of public retir ment systems. The value of pension fund holdings (the asset side), howeve is still not appropriately measured or represented. We can make much mo precise estimates of social security liabilities. The subsidy element of cred programs should be assessed even though doing so requires considerab effort and ingenuity.

We have been in the process of improving the accounting and budg representations of public programs for a long time. The tax expenditu budget is a classic example. It is an attempt to provide understandab information about a low-profile spending program in a form roughly con parable to that of budget documents. TEBs were first bound separately, the bound in the same volumes as the direct spending budget, and now final presented side by side with direct spending in the budget for each progran The process of credit budgeting begun under the Carter administration- bringing the inflows and outflows of credit program dollars into the budg documents—is a second case in point. Over a long period, Congress ha debated improvements in the "unified" budget, which attempts to incorpo rate credit programs. A more comprehensive representation of feder spending is now provided, and these programs are better represented tha they used to be. Improvements at the margin can and should continue t be made.

These examples—the tax expenditure budget and the credit budget, i particular—are double-edged, however. They point out that informatio does not necessarily ensure accountability. The federal tax expenditur budget is a well-thought-out, well-constructed representation of an impo tant low-profile program. The TEB successfully raised that profile, but remains relatively low, all the same. A vast array of tax subsidy programs sti operate at the federal level. In spite of better, more-visible information, th fact that these programs remain outside the appropriations process mater ally weakens their accountability. Even the most overt quiet programs woul operate differently if they were forced into the appropriations proces Information is necessary for accountability but does not guarantee it.

MOVE QUIET SPENDING CLOSER TO, OR INTO, THE
APPROPRIATIONS PROCESS

What does it take to give information real clout in the political proces The movement to limit the scope of government emphasizes the importanc of competition for resources within a fixed budget. For these limitations t bind hidden spending programs, they must first be brought closer to, or into, the appropriations process.

For some forms of hidden spending, this is a simple matter. The visibility of defined-benefit pension programs can be enhanced by requiring them to be fully funded on a current basis. This would require the appropriation of the current cost each year. Congress has legislated this requirement for private plans, in the Employee Retirement Income Security Act of 1974. It has regularly considered, but has so far failed to enact, a similar limit for state and local government retirement systems. Moreover, it has shown no inclination to impose the requirement on itself. But if we want to make it, this is a simple technical change. We could further enhance accountability by shifting to defined-contribution pension plans (similar to IRAs or Keogh plans). Defined-contribution plans are automatically fully funded and would require an annual appropriation. This change would, however, be more complicated—it requires establishing whole new sets of pension plans, not just putting more money aside for existing ones.

An institutional bias favoring direct grants instead of hidden subsidies could bring several other quiet spending programs through the door of the appropriations hearing room. Credit programs could be handled this way. Tax expenditures could be as well, but not without substantial administrative complications. As they are operated now, tax subsidies are entitlements, and decisions are completely decentralized; anyone who wants to engage in the subsidized behavior may file an income tax form and recieve the subsidy. No approval need be granted in advance. Reformulating tax expenditure programs as direct grants would require an approval and monitoring process. This would upgrade accountability but would by no means be a trivial administrative burden.

It is equally hard to imagine requiring appropriations for many other forms of hidden spending programs. Some creative financing schemes make new funds available by selling old assets but obscure the fact that a sale has taken place. Better information—recognizing the sale—might bring public opprobrium down on public officials who sanction such arrangements. But it is not obvious how these sales could be represented in a form that would require appropriations. Similarly, accurate fixed-asset records would convert depreciation into a recordable item, but not into an item that required an appropriation.

DEVELOP A NEW PROFESSION OF PUBLIC SECTOR AUDITING

One of the reasons that the accounting solution to the problem of reducing hidden spending is unappealing is that it is incremental. We are already engaged in it; progress is slow. Public accounting was not designed to measure and report comprehensively the financial—and particularly the low-profile financial—activities of government. The accounting profession has, naturally enough, developed an institutional capacity to address only those problems it has defined as its responsibility. These involve mainly the cash transactions of the government, with some attention to other significant obligations like pensions. Many of the kinds of hidden spending discussed here—subsidies in credit programs, tax expenditures, and so on—lie well outside the boundaries within which the current accounting profession works and is likely to keep working. Accountants resist being stretched over these broader problems for good reason: they have a hard enough task, and enough work to do, as it is.

Accounting is not a solution for the problem of quiet spending; it is an answer to a different question, focusing on less subtle matters. Rather than trying to change existing accountants into a different breed, we should establish a profession with a distinctly different purpose. Its task would be to provide an integrated representation of all the financial activities of government. Many of the basic tools could be provided by accounting. But the members of this new group will have to be prepared to go well beyond the boundaries of precision and certainty that constrain accountants. They must seek accuracy before precision.

The traditional public sector budget is a good place to start. Our current budgets fail in a variety of ways to present fairly and comprehensively the actual financial activities of the government. They sometimes exclude readily measurable programs. They often measure only current cash commitments and fail to estimate current total costs. Pension programs, again, are the classic example; budget documents often contain only pay-as-you-go representations. Most of these flaws stem from the strength of budget documents as appropriations laws: they are designed to capture—for the purpose of authorizing—the actual, largely cash, transactions of a public organization. They cannot act as legal documents and still serve the wider interest of comprehensive reporting.

The task of the new profession of public sector auditing would be to borrow the best of accounting and budgeting and, where those left off, to devise new, intelligible, comprehensive descriptions of public financial activities. The standards for this profession will take a long time to develop. It cannot afford the luxury of the accounting profession, which defined its public sector responsibilities around the problems it knew how to solve. The new public sector auditors must be free of the constraints that bind accountants. Rather than precision and certainty, their profession must have as its core values accuracy, comprehensiveness, and intelligibility.

The Larger Challenge: Building Value-Supporting Accountability Mechanisms

The defining purpose of government is to procure or produce publicly valued goods and services that cannot be obtained through private efforts. Among a vast panoply of conflicting claims for public attention, discerning what the public values is no small task. How can accountability mechanisms help ensure that a program achieves the purposes it is actually designed to advance?

CLARIFY STATEMENTS OF PURPOSE IN PUBLIC PROGRAMS

We need to have a clear idea of what our "real" public priorities are. We cannot judge whether government programs are producing value—or whether we are providing appropriate scrutiny to make sure they do— unless we have a well-formed idea of what public value is. Thus, the articulation of purposes becomes part of the accountability process.

Conflict over purposes is central to the political process; it is what the political process is designed to contain. It is therefore not surprising that purposes are often left unclear; an ambiguous statement of purpose is frequently the result of compromise and a means of reducing conflict. As a matter of political strategy, this is perhaps inevitable in the political process. But the articulation of goals is not just a part of the political process; it is also a part of the accountability process. Sharpening accountability may require an insistence on more-definite statements of purpose.

TEST REAL EFFECTS AGAINST ADVERTISED EFFECTS

Even if purposes are clarified, we may never be certain that the right accountability balance has been struck—but we may sometimes be certain that it has *not*. One sure indication might be that a program does not actually do what it is said to be doing. If a program is supported on the basis of incorrect claims about its costs or effects, it has not passed the reference test of accountability—a specific form of consent by an informed electorate. Testing perceptions against reality is a key component of an effective accountability structure.

Many quiet spending programs are promoted on the grounds that they serve important purposes that otherwise will not receive sufficient attention. All too often, though, the alleged legitimate purpose bears little relation to what the program actually does. Pensions are justified as hidden compensation because it is said the public will not buy enough public services if their whole cost is paid out of appropriated funds. But then why do they *transfer* costs to later taxpayers rather than just hide them? If the purpose is really to increase the consumption of current public services by current taxpayers, pensions could still be paid by current taxpayers. Why are they now paid mostly by future taxpayers? Perhaps because this is the only quiet way to raise current consumption. A less contrived explanation is that taxpayers find it convenient to have a portion of their current service bills paid by others. When the justification for a quiet device bears little relation to what the device is actually doing, the mechanism may be part of the problem and not part of the solution.

APPLY MORE-STRINGENT CHECKS WHEN COSTS ARE NOT BORNE BY BENEFICIARIES

Accountability is also jeopardized when there is no connection between the beneficiaries of a program and those who pay for it. This problem is difficult enough when it arises in direct spending programs, and many legitimate reasons might justify decoupling beneficiaries from payers. But when those on whom costs are imposed have no vote—as when we pass costs to future taxpayers—the accountability question is particularly salient.

When we carry out trades over time directly, by borrowing money against an explicit promise that future taxpayers will repay it, we invoke special bounds on how the funds can be spent, trying to ensure that those who pay will also receive some benefits. Parallel precautions should apply to quiet programs that push costs from one group to another.

SEEK WAYS TO FORCE REGULAR REVIEW OF QUIET SPENDING PROGRAMS

Many quiet spending devices proceed by default. Once under way, they tend to continue unabated until a positive action is taken to halt them. The basic elements of the tax code are rarely altered; once an expenditure program is built in as a tax expenditure, it can quietly disburse funds with no mandatory annual review. Infrastructure assets deteriorate unless we take costly and visible positive actions to maintain them. When salaries are increased, so are pensions—but unlike the salary increase, the pensions adjustment requires no vote. Our system constructs accountability checks on affirmative uses of government power. It often ignores actions that take place in the absence of affirmative decisions. Where *in*action spends public resources, it needs just as much attention as action.

SET CONSTRAINTS ON PROGRAM SCALE TO HEIGHTEN COMPETITION

You don't have to choose what you want when you can have it all. Resources in many quiet spending programs seem unlimited—and hence virtually costless. Quiet costs create a bias for more spending rather than less; beneficiaries know there is a benefit, but payers don't know there is a cost.

Competition for resources heightens the sense that they are costly. This form of balancing is a defining characteristic of the appropriations process; the spending ambitions of each program face counterbalancing pressures from other programs competing for the same resources and from taxpayers seeking to retain them. This appropriations form of competition is absent, by definition, from quiet spending programs, but this does not imply that all competition for resources must be absent. Quiet spending programs can be confronted with limits on how much there is to spend. Once a limit is set, a program seeking to expand its spending must displace the spending of another. The money may seem free, but the fight to get it is definitely not. Scarce resources seem more precious.

What limits might we construct to constrain quiet spending? Tax and expenditure limitations would seem to be in the spirit of enhancing competition, but they are not generally sharply enough defined to serve the purpose. It is too hard to fit the myriad different ways governments spend within a single comprehensive set of definitions and restraints. Precisely because they seek to constrain the broadest aggregates, TELs may have little force at the level of specific programs. To enhance competition at that level, we should set limits in the small rather than in the large.

The history of improvements in the accountability of some quiet programs illustrates the important role that constraints can play in forcing greater deliberation. Tax expenditure budgets have tended to be more effective when intense pressures to raise revenues made even tax-side expenditures seem expensive. The history of the credit budget shows a halting movement toward increasing constraints, but no effective aggregate credit limitation has yet been implemented. Recent debates about direct spending have been framed in terms of what cuts to make to reach spending targets. We have heard a great deal about having to cut either defense spending or social programs to meet spending constraints. When will we hear about having to cut either housing or small business credit to stay within a total borrowing constraint? Most individual credit programs have ceilings on loan disbursements—but little holds down the ceiling of any one program, and even less pushes down the total to make individual programs compete.

Industrial development bonds provide an example of a quiet program whose expansion eventually made it so visible that a limit was imposed. If the newly established IDB cap becomes a genuinely binding constraint, it may force real choices—deliberative determination by state and local officials of which development projects they most prefer. The result may not be perfect accountability, but this program's accountability has so far to go that any added deliberation will almost certainly be an improvement.

IMPROVE THE AUDIENCE

The best orchestras and theater companies are in New York, London, and Paris. Asked why, their members universally respond that the audiences in those cities are better. To get a better orchestra, an audience must be discerning and demanding. The same is true of government.

Whether quiet programs create value is a matter of judgment, and this implies a crucial reliance on those who judge. The mechanics of accountability ultimately do nothing more than set the terms of the debate. They determine what the judges bring to the task of making decisions. But when the mechanics are in place, and the information has been collected and presented, the true burden of accountability lands on the only place it can —on the electorate. If we are serious about upgrading accountability, treating only the mechanisms—and not the people—may miss the most crucial link.

It is often said that to be effective, information about what the government does must meet the "grandparent test": it must make sense to the average grandparent. Government is a complicated business. It has always been so, and it seems more so today. We are beginning to be able to represent some of government's more intricate financial activities, but these representations are and will remain complex. They involve complicated assumptions about the future, describe sophisticated financial contracts, reflect intricate exchanges of rights and responsibilities. If our best efforts at providing simple representation still cannot pass the grandparent test, then the time has come to work on the grandparent. The first step is admitting that we have met the grandparents and that they are us.

Noticing that the audience must ultimately take responsibility for the government's performance brings us back to the twin issues of avoidance and obfuscation. Obfuscation is done *to* us; avoidance is done *by* us. We can and will continue to work to reduce obfuscation, but only the audience can stop avoiding.

Two responsibilities of the audience for public spending programs are fundamental. First, the audience must demand accountability. The accountability system won't exist without effort, won't persist without support, and won't operate itself. In our society *the agents themselves create and operate the system of accountability, and it is not always in their best interest to have it work too well.* It may be in the long-term interest of those who govern to provide, maintain, and operate a strong system of accountability. But it does not follow that their short-run interest is served by systems that hold *them* to account. Of course, we have appointed multiple sets of referees, and they can (and do) advance their own interests and the public's by blowing the whistle on each other. Still, if the audience doesn't care, ultimately no one will.

The second fundamental and unavoidable responsibility of the audience of government spending programs is to judge whether they are valuable. In the final analysis, do the benefits justify the costs? All other tests are surrogates.

We have discussed many ways to strengthen the surrogate tests. But the most obvious and most common suggestion for improving government accountability is conspicuously absent from this list. We tend to blame things on the politicians, to call on public officials to behave better, more responsibly, more like statesmen. Waiting for politicians who have seen the light—or, rather, the dark—to eschew special interests for the good of the many, has long been a bankrupt strategy. And no wonder. We created, and continue to support, a system that provides politicians with ample incentives to respond to special interests. It is useless, though natural, to blame them for doing what we have given them incentives to do. But we find it easy to lay the problem at their feet, criticizing them for not behaving responsibly.

For the most part, they do behave responsibly. They react to the real forces and incentives they face. They respond much the way the agency theory of government would lead us to expect. If the results are not always what we would like, it is hardly the exclusive fault of the agents. They work under incentives we constructed for them. The structure is designed to provide a set of balances of general against narrow interests. The framers of the constitution were keenly aware that even the most widely articulated interests were narrow, the benefits of public spending concentrated, and the costs of public actions diffused. They left us with a system that has some checks and balances, and some room for checks unbalanced.

The agency structure of government is an enduring problem of democ racy. Any particular form of hidden spending can, with sufficient effort, b brought into public view. But we will never be able to capture all forms c low-visibility financial activity within any one accountability system.

These lessons from quiet spending programs reach well beyond spendin in the narrow sense. Every government action uses public resources—n least, the limited allegiance and tolerance of those governed. Quiet spendin is carried out in many forms and currencies. Wherever it is hard to tell ho much of what resource has been used, the lessons of these examples ma apply. Where we cannot easily assess totals, it is hard to impose a budge and force trade-offs. It is therefore harder to pose the question of whethe on balance, value is being created or used up. Whether the specific questio at hand is using military force, imposing trade sanctions, making treat commitments, or quietly borrowing money, the root issues of accountabilit are the same.

What do we get in return for the effort spent on enhancing accountabi ity? If accountability leads to value, stronger accountability should be surer guide in deciding which government actions are valuable. That is th hoped-for result. We have no independent test for whether governmen performance is truly improved, but it should be. Certainly, we can b assured that we have brought government conduct more in line with th established constitutional order. When government action departs too obvi ously from the established norms, it corrodes the foundations of the com pact. Quiet spending programs run that risk. Better accountability woul reduce it.

We should devote more effort to making all forms of quiet spending mor visible and more accountable. This book has explored the major curren examples and advanced both specific and general suggestions. However, i poses an important caution. Shining a bright light helps us to see, but it als defines the dark. Quiet spending is not an accident; it is a fundamenta attribute of the agency structure of our system. Providing a more brightl lit public financial arena will make the shadows beyond it deeper—an more alluring. As in all civilized endeavors, the problem is to find the righ balance.

Notes

Introduction

1. Woodrow Wilson, "The New Meaning of Government," *Woman's Home Companion,* November 1912, cited in Charles T. Goodsell, "The Grace Commission: Seeking Efficiency for the Whole People?" *Public Administration Review* 44 (May/June 1984): 196–204.

2. See, for example, Annemarie Hauck Walsh, *The Public's Business: The Politics and Practices of Government Corporations* (Cambridge: MIT Press, 1978), and James T. Bennett and Thomas J. DiLorenzo, *Underground Government* (Washington, D.C.: Cato Institute, 1983).

3. Other authors have constructed "regulatory budgets" showing the costs imposed through various kinds of regulation. Regulatory budgets generally reflect the notion that such costs are a form of quiet spending by the public. For a discussion of the techniques involved, see David A. Garvin, and Robert A. Leone, "Regulatory Cost Analysis: An Overview," *Environmental Impact Assessment Review* 2, no. 1 (1981), 39–61. For a discussion of the difficulties of the concept in theory and in practice, see Christopher C. DeMuth, "The Regulatory Budget," *Regulation* 4, no. 2 (March/April 1980): 29–43.

4. I am indebted to Bob Leone for this image.

5. There have been many attempts to define the "public interest." What that term can usefully capture is not a central concern of this book, nor will it be concerned with judging what actions are in the public interest. An excellent discussion is given by David Bicknell Truman, *The Governmental Process: Political Interests and Public Opinion,* 2d ed. (New York: Knopf, 1971).

6. "Consent" is construed broadly, to include acquiescence or tolerance in the face of government action. No presumption that consent must be active and unanimous is intended. For an extended discussion, see Alexander M. Bickel, *The Morality of Consent* (New Haven: Yale University Press, 1975).

7. An excellent and accessible treatment of the major elements of agency theory is John W. Pratt and Richard J. Zeckhauser, "Principals and Agents: An Overview," in Pratt and Zeckhauser, eds., *Principals and Agents: The Structure of Business* (Boston: Harvard Business School Press, 1985), 1–35.

8. An extensive discussion of the concept of accountability as it applies to uses of public authority presented in the language of the agency model is given by Mark H. Moore and Margaret J. Gates, "Junkyard Dogs and Wise-Old Dogs: A Preliminary Investigation of Inspectors General in the Federal Government" (Cambridge: John F. Kennedy School of Government, May 1985), unpublished MS, 8–33.

Chapter 1

1. General Accounting Office, *An Actuarial and Economic Analysis of State and Local Government Pension Plans* (Washington, D.C.: GAO, 1980); Laurence Kotlikoff and Daniel Smith, *Pensions in the American Economy* (Chicago: University of Chicago Press, 1983), 352.

2. Most economists use some variant of this "spot contract" approach to the study of pensions. See, for example, the papers in David Wise and John Shoven, eds., *Pensions, Labor, and Individual Choice* (Chicago: University of Chicago Press, 1985).

3. The assumptions underlying these estimates are that inflation will be 5 percent annually and that plan experiences, general real-wage growth for federal workers, and real rates of return on fund assets will all continue at historical levels. See Herman B. Leonard, "The Federal Civil Service Retirement System," in Wise and Shoven, eds., *Pensions, Labor, and Individual Choice,* and Herman B. Leonard, "Investing in the Defense Workforce," in David Wise, ed., *Public Sector Payrolls,* forthcoming 1986.

4. For an extended discussion of these results, see the studies cited immediately above. See also J. Peter Grace, *War on Waste: President's Private Sector Survey on Cost Control* (New York: Macmillan, 1983); Department of Defense, "Executive Summary," *Fifth Quadrennial Review of Military Compensation* (Washington, D.C.: DOD, 1984); Office of the Actuary, Defense Manpower Data Center, *Valuation of the Military Retirement System* (Washington, D.C.: Department of Defense, 1982); and U.S. Civil Service Retirement System, *Annual Report* (Washington, D.C.: Office of Personnel Management, 1984) (prepared by Compensation Group, U.S. Office of Personnel Management).

5. For an interesting discussion of the history of local pension plans, see GAO, *Actuarial and Economic Analysis.*

6. Bureau of the Census, *Finances of Employee-Retirement Systems of State and Local Governments in 1979–80* (Washington, D.C.: Bureau of the Census, 1981).

7. For the definitive summary of data on state and local pension plans, see Kotlikoff and Smith, *Pensions in the American Economy,* chaps. 6 and 7. See also Alicia H. Munnell and Ann M. Connolly, "Financing Public Pensions," *New England Economic Review,* January/February 1980, pp. 31–32, tables 2 and 4.

8. For interesting examples of this trend, see Donaldson Lufkin & Jenrette Securities Corporation, *Municipal Bond Credit Commentary,* October 1978, devoted to "Perception of State and City Pension Liabilities"; Nuveen Research, *Public Employee Pension Funds: Impact on State and Local Credits,* July 1, 1976; and Ronald M. Copeland and Robert W. Ingram, "Municipal Bond Market Recognition of Pension Reporting Practices" (Working Paper 18–15, College of Business Administration, Northeastern University, 1983). Attention to unfunded liabilities by bond-rating agencies and securities analysts provides some pressure for accountability in pension spending.

9. John E. Petersen, *Public Pension System Financial Disclosure* (Washington, D.C.: Government Finance Research Center, Municipal Finance Officers Association [now the Government Finance Officers Association], 1980) contains an excellent inventory of financial disclosure practices by existing public pension systems. For a good discussion of these data problems and an excellent summary of the financial condition of state and local plans, see Munnell and Connolly, "Financing Public Pensions," 30–44.

10. Frank S. Arnold, "State and Local Public Employee Pension Funding: Theory, Evidence, and Implications" (Ph.D. diss., Harvard University, 1983). These results are also summarized and discussed in Kotlikoff and Smith, *Pensions in the American Economy,* 393–405.

11. Kotlikoff and Smith, *Pensions in the American Economy,* 405.

12. Robert P. Inman, "The Funding Status of Teachers' Pensions: An Econometric Approach" (Working Paper no. 1727, National Bureau of Economic Research, Cambridge, Mass., October 1985).

13. Ibid., p. 17, table 5.

14. This literature is ably summarized in Ronald G. Ehrenberg and Joshua L. Schwartz, "Public Sector Labor Markets" (Working Paper no. 1179, National Bureau of Economic Research, Cambridge, Mass., August 1983).

15. Robert S. Smith, "Compensating Differentials for Pensions and Underfunding in the Public Sector," *Review of Economics and Statistics* 63 (August 1981): 463–68.

16. Robert S. Smith, "Salaries and Pension Funding: Are Public Safety Officers Given Preference over Taxpayers?" in Werner Z. Hirsch and Anthony M. Rufolo, eds., *The Economics of Municipal Labor Markets* (Los Angeles: UCLA Press, 1983).

17. Robert P. Inman, "Wages, Pensions, and Employment in the Local Public Sector," in Peter Mieszkowski and George Peterson, eds., *Public Sector Labor Markets* (Washington, D.C.: Urban Institute, 1981).

18. Ibid.

Notes

19. This argument and the debate concerning it are well summarized in Arnold, "Pension Funding."

20. House Committee on Education and Labor, *Pension Task Force Report on Public Employee Retirement Systems,* 95th Cong., 2d sess., March 15, 1978, p. 158, table 62, cited in Munnell and Connolly, "Financing Public Pensions," 37.

21. Office of Management and Budget, *Budget of the United States Government, Fiscal Year 1986—Appendix* (Washington, D.C.: OMB, 1985), I-V3.

22. See Leonard, "Investing in the Defense Workforce," and Howard L. Frant and Herman B. Leonard, "Promise Them Anything: The Incentive Structure of State and Local Pension Plans," in Wise, ed., *Public Sector Payrolls.*

23. See, for example, the results from a survey conducted by Louis Harris and Associates and reported in *A Study of American Attitudes toward Pension and Retirement: A National Survey of Employees, Retirees, and Business Leaders* (Washington, D.C.: Johnson & Higgins of Washington, 1979), 77.

24. For example, short-term public employees in South Dakota recently indicated this preference. See *Report on State Pension Commissions, 1983* (Washington, D.C.: E. H. Friend, 1983), 2.

25. Ibid.

26. See Frant and Leonard, "Promise Them Anything."

Chapter 2

1. George J. Church, in *Time,* May 24, 1982, pp. 16–27, cited in Jason Berger, ed., *Saving Social Security* (New York: H. W. Wilson, 1982), 18.

2. Treatments of both the ancient and the modern history of social security and the power of its political foundations are given in Ernest R. May and Richard E. Neustadt, *Thinking in Time: The Uses of History for Decision-Makers* (New York: Free Press, 1986), chaps. 2, 6, and 12. An excellent concise history of the formation and operation of the social security system from 1935 to 1981 is given by Megan Jones, and Richard E. Neustadt in *Social Security (B),* John F. Kennedy School of Government Case C14-77-198, 1983. This section follows their treatment. I am also indebted to their work for references to a number of the sources cited below and for a variety of particularly salient quotations.

3. For a detailed review of the status of the elderly prior to social security and of the political forces that grew around this problem, see Carolyn L. Weaver, *The Crisis in Social Security: Economic and Political Origins* (Durham, N.C.: Duke Press Policy Studies, 1982). Weaver reviews the history leading up to the establishment of the social security program, the development of the social security legislation, its progress through Congress, and its later evolution.

4. Press release, statement by President Roosevelt on signing of the Social Security Act, August 15, 1935; in "Social Security Bill Is Signed," *New York Times,* August 15, 1935, p. 1, cited in Rita Ricardo Campbell, *Social Security: Promise and Reality* (Stanford: Hoover Institution Press, 1977), 4.

5. This passage is variously quoted and cited. See Frances Perkins, *The Roosevelt I Knew* (New York: Viking Press, 1946), 293–94, cited in Jones and Neustadt, *Social Security,* 7.

6. Weaver, *Crisis in Social Security,* 77–101, provides a detailed review of the legislative progress of the Social Security Act.

7. The history of the postlegislative challenges to the concepts of social security is ably summarized, ibid., 106–10.

8. Ibid., 108.

9. One more reverse twist followed. The social security staff had purged the word "insurance" from its literature during the period when constitutionality was in doubt. Now the term returned in force. Arthur Altmeyer, the chairman of the Social Security Board, was later asked why. He observed, without explanation, that the fact that the Supreme Court upheld all of the act's titles indicated that "Titles II and VIII were inseparable and formed a single plan . . . [and] clearly established that in the opinion of the Court both the contributions and the benefit titles made a single whole which . . . can be properly described as an insurance system." Arthur J. Altmeyer, *The Formative Years in Social Security* (Madison: University of Wisconsin Press, 1968), 226, cited in Weaver, *Crisis in Social Security,* 225 n. 35.

10. "Congress Looks at Social Security," *Congressional Digest* 18 (May 1939): 140–41, cited in Weaver, *Crisis in Social Security*, 112.

11. *Congressional Record*, 75th Cong., 1st sess., 1937, 81, pt. 2:2324, cited in Jones and Neustadt, *Social Security*, 12.

12. Arthur M. Schlesinger, *The Coming of the New Deal* (Boston: Houghton Mifflin, 1959), 308.

13. Interview with Luther Gulick by Michael McGreary, Institute of Public Administration, New York, February 28, 1980, cited in Jones and Neustadt, *Social Security*, 23.

14. An excellent review of the political difficulties, and mishaps, experienced by social security reformers in the 1977–1983 period is given in May and Neustadt, *Thinking in Time*, chap. 2.

15. For an intriguing treatment of why this commission was so effective, see ibid.

16. National Commission on Social Security Reform, *Report of the National Commission on Social Security Reform* (Washington, D.C.: Government Printing Office, 1983).

17. For a discussion of the balance between the value of contributions (with interest) and benefits for new participants, see Anthony Pellechio and Gordon Goodfellow, "Individual Gains and Losses from Social Security before and after the 1983 Amendments," *Cato Journal* 3 (Fall 1983): 417–42. Their calculations suggest that the generation now entering the system will contribute, in present-value terms, about what it can expect to draw out. The "money's worth" of the system is thus close to one, substantially smaller than it used to be.

18. Board of Trustees of the Federal Old-Age and Survivors Insurance and Disability Insurance Trust Funds, *1984 Annual Report* (Washington, D.C.: Government Printing Office, 1984), 78.

19. For a discussion of this debate, see Laurence J. Kotlikoff, "Taxation and Savings: A Neoclassical Perspective," *Journal of Economic Literature* 22 (December 1984): 1576–1629. Research on the effects of social security was inspired by Feldstein. See Martin Feldstein, "Social Security, Induced Retirement, and Aggregate Capital Accumulation," *Journal of Political Economy* 82 (September/October 1974): 905–26.

20. Martin Feldstein, "The Optimal Financing of Social Security" (Discussion Paper 388, Harvard Institute of Economic Research, 1974).

21. Department of the Treasury, Financial Management Service, *Statement of Liabilities and Other Financial Commitments of the United States Government As of September 30, 1984* (Washington, D.C.: Department of the Treasury, 1985), 14 n. 4.

22. For discussions of this issue, see A. Haeworth Robertson, *The Coming Revolution in Social Security* (McLean, Va.: Security Press, 1981), 81–100, and Peter J. Ferrara, *Social Security: The Inherent Contradiction* (Washington, D.C.: Cato Institute, 1980).

23. The General Accounting Office, the audit arm of Congress, is designing an annual report on the financial status of the federal government that would report magnitudes of this kind. Reporting methods for social security liabilities and the annual increment to liabilities are still being debated. The GAO prototype is still in draft. At this point, social security liabilities are omitted.

Chapter 3

1. The history of federal credit activities is sketched briefly in Temporary Subcommittee on Federal Credit, *Report to the Committee on the Budget, United States Senate*, 97th Cong., 2d sess., December 1982, chap. 2.

2. See Herman B. Leonard and Elisabeth H. Rhyne, "Federal Credit and the 'Shadow Budget,'" *The Public Interest*, no. 65 (Fall 1981): 40–58. In that discussion, support of state and local borrowing through the tax exemption of bond interest is treated as a fourth form of federal credit activity. In this work, the issue will be discussed in chapter 4, on tax expenditures, and with reference to state and local economic development policies in chapters 5 and 6.

3. General Accounting Office, *Catalog of Federal Credit Programs and Their Interest Rate Provisions* (Washington, D.C.: GAO, 1982), p. 1.

4. Office of Management and Budget, *Budget of the United States Government, Fiscal Year 1985* (Washington, D.C.: OMB, 1984), Special Analysis F, p. F-5, table F-1.

Notes

5. Congressional Budget Office, *Conference on the Economics of Federal Credit Activity*, pt. 1, *Proceedings*, and pt. 2, *Papers*, Special Study (Washington, D.C.: CBO, 1981).

6. See, for example, the papers by Plantes and Small; Kaufman; Silber and Black; and Barth, Cordes, and Yezer, ibid., pt. 2.

7. For a discussion of other credit programs and their politics, see Dennis S. Ippolito, *Hidden Spending: The Politics of Federal Credit Programs* (Chapel Hill: University of North Carolina Press, 1984).

8. An excellent discussion of the Eximbank and its history can be found in Barry Bosworth, Andrew Carron, and Elisabeth Rhyne, "Credit for Business," in "Economic Effects of Government Credit" (unpublished MS, 1985), chap. 5. I have drawn heavily on this work, on conversations with Elisabeth Rhyne, and on Eximbank annual reports in preparing this section. A more complete description and analysis of the Eximbank is given by David P. Baron, *The Export-Import Bank: An Economic Analysis* (New York: Academic Press, 1983).

9. Eximbank, *Annual Report,* 1982, p. 35.

10. Cited in Bosworth, Carron, and Rhyne, "Credit for Business."

11. Hendrik Houthakker, in testimony at congressional hearings about financing the Clinch River breeder reactor through a private syndicate under federal loan guarantees, made an argument along similar lines.

12. Eximbank, *Annual Report,* 1982, p. 26; 1983, p. 27.

13. Bosworth, Carron, and Rhyne, "Credit for Business."

14. Ibid.

15. *Budget of the United States Government, Fiscal Year 1985,* Special Analysis F, p. F-14.

16. Bosworth, Carron, and Rhyne, "Credit for Business."

17. The best treatment of the SBA, including its history and an analysis of its program performance, is contained in Elisabeth Rhyne, "An Evaluation of the Small Business Administration's Business Loan Guarantee Program" (Ph.D. Diss., John F. Kennedy School of Government, Harvard University, 1985). See also Bosworth, Carron, and Rhyne, "Credit for Business." A short history is contained in Temporary Subcommittee on Federal Credit, *Report to the Committee on the Budget.*

18. *Budget of the United States Government, Fiscal Year 1985,* p. I-W2.

19. Bosworth, Carron, and Rhyne, "Credit for Business."

20. Ibid.

21. *Budget of the United States Government, Fiscal Year 1985,* Special Analysis F, p. F-34, table F-12.

22. Bosworth, Carron, and Rhyne, "Credit for Business."

23. Rhyne, "Evaluation."

24. For a related discussion of the evolution of credit accounting in the federal government, see Leonard and Rhyne, "Federal Credit," 50–51.

25. John D. Shillingburg, *The Federal Financing Bank and the Budgetary Treatment of Federal Credit Activities* (Washington, D.C.: Congressional Budget Office, 1982), p. 26.

26. This issue is discussed in a report by the CBO on the FFB. See Shillingburg, *Federal Financing Bank,* 40–41.

27. Finance theorists have studied the problem of estimating the cost of "contingent liabilities" of the government, particularly loans and loan guarantees. See E. Philip Jones and Scott P. Mason, "Valuation of Loan Guarantees," in CBO, *Economics of Federal Credit Activity,* 349–77. An interesting application to FHA mortgage insurance is given by Donald F. Cunningham and Patric H. Hendershot, "Pricing FHA Mortgage Default Insurance" (Working Paper no. 1382, National Bureau of Economic Research, Cambridge, Mass., June 1984).

28. See Carliss Baldwin, Donald Lessard, and Scott Mason, "Budgetary Time Bombs: Controlling Government Loan Guarantees," *Canadian Public Policy* 9, no. 3 (1983): 338–46.

29. These are presented in *Budget of the United States Government, Fiscal Year 1985,* Special Analysis F, p. F-28, table F-9.

Chapter 4

1. This concept was popularized by the late Stanley Surrey when he was assistant secretary of the Treasury for tax policy in 1968. For an extensive discussion of the concept and its applications, see Stanley S. Surrey and Paul R. McDaniel, *Tax Expenditures* (Cambridge: Harvard University Press, 1985).

2. The proposal would reduce or eliminate existing preferences for banking, insurance, mining, timber, and oil and gas; quash tax exemptions for interest on nongovernment bonds; curtail "tax shelters"; and raise taxes on businesses while reducing taxes on individuals. See *The President's Tax Proposals to the Congress for Fairness, Growth, and Simplicity* (Washington, D.C.: Government Printing Office, May 1985).

3. See Ronald F. King, "Tax Expenditures and Systematic Public Policy," *Public Budgeting and Finance* 4 (Spring 1984): 23.

4. For an extended discussion and additional data, see Congressional Budget Office, *Tax Expenditures* (Washington, D.C.: CBO, November 1982), appendix C. The historical figures that follow are from table C-1.

5. The OMB's effort this year is printed as Special Analysis G of the *Budget of the United States Government, Fiscal Year 1986* (Washington, D.C.: OMB, 1985); the CBO prints a special study each year detailing its estimates of tax expenditures.

6. To see that the three goals are inconsistent, consider two single taxpayers earning the same income, x. Let the tax they each pay, if single, be $T_s(x)$. If they are married, their combined income is 2x and their tax is $T_m(2x)$. Progressivity requires that $T_s(2x) > 2T_s(x) = T_s(x) + T_s(x)$, which is the combined tax they pay if single. To avoid a marriage penalty, we want $T_s(x) + T_s(x) > T_m(2x)$, so we have $T_s(2x) > T_m(2x)$. But households with the same income are supposed to pay the same tax: $T_s(2x) = T_m(2x)$. The three goals are thus inconsistent. For a discussion see Harvey S. Rosen, *Public Finance* (Homewood, Ill.: Richard D. Irwin, 1985), 363–65.

7. The major tax reform package unveiled in December 1984 by the Treasury proposed to adjust for inflation along the lines of the suggestion made here. This suggestion has already been modified in the package submitted to Congress by the President. At best, it looks as though this approach would not be phased in until after 1990.

8. *Budget of the United States Government, Fiscal Year 1985,* Special Analysis G, p. G-5.

9. *Budget of the United States Government, Fiscal Year 1986,* Special Analysis G.

10. The Congressional Budget Office, in its October 1983 report on tax expenditures, discusses the strains that might appear if more reliance were placed on TEBs as a device for controlling expenditures. See CBO, *Tax Expenditures* (October 1983), 9.

11. *Budget of the United States Government, Fiscal Year 1985,* Special Analysis G, p. G-43, table G-2.

12. The Congressional Budget Office has provided an excellent discussion of options for bringing the TEB more fully into the budget process. See CBO, *Tax Expenditures* (November 1982), chap. 3.

13. Ronald King, in an intriguing essay on the political economy of tax expenditures, pursues a similar theme. He argues that tax expenditures are the device of preference when Congress wants to advance a public purpose but "is uneasy about the entailed interference with the private sector." See King, "Tax Expenditures and Systematic Public Policy," 14–31.

14. For a good discussion of their use internationally, see CBO, *Tax Expenditures* (October 1983), chap. 3. Their use by states is discussed in the National Conference of State Legislatures' *The Fiscal Letter* 6, no. 5 (November/December 1984): 10–11.

Chapter 5

1. This literature is ably summarized by Karl E. Case, Leslie Papke, and Susan Koenigsberg, "Interstate Business Locational Decisions and the Effect of the State's Tax Structure of After-Tax Rates of Return of Manufacturing Firms" (Preliminary unpublished working paper of the Legislative Commission on the Modernization and Simplification of Tax Administration

Notes

and the Tax Law, State of New York, December 1984), 9–31. A public version of Case, Papke, and Koenigsberg is given in their final report to the Legislative Commission, entitled "Taxes and Business Location," August 15, 1983. There are some recent studies that find small impacts. For example, see Timothy J. Bartik, "Business Location Decisions in the United States," *Journal of Business and Economic Statistics* 3 (January 1985): 14–22.

2. Tax Foundation, *Facts and Figures on Government Finance,* 21st ed. (Washington, D.C.: Tax Foundation, 1981), 234.

3. Department of Commerce, Bureau of the Census, *State Government Finances in 1983,* 6–12.

4. Roger J. Vaughan, *State Taxation and Economic Development* (Washington, D.C.: Council of State Planning Agencies, 1979), 74–75.

5. Price Waterhouse & Company, *State Tax Comparison Study* (1978), cited in Michael Kieschnick, *Taxes and Growth* (Washington, D.C.: Council of State Planning Agencies, 1981), 42.

6. This study was conducted by David Winkler of the University of Southern California and was funded by the Los Angeles Taxpayers Foundation. Reported in the *Public Administration Times* 7, no. 12 (Washington, D.C.: American Society of Public Administration, June 15, 1984), 8.

7. Delaware is excluded because of its special status as a corporate headquarters state, which makes it difficult to assess business income for the state meaningfully. Wheaton measured its ratio of business taxes to business income at 20.2 percent. If fees are excluded, it falls to 10.2 percent, while the ratio for Michigan falls negligibly, to 12.6 percent. See William C. Wheaton, "Interstate Differences in the Level of Business Taxation," *National Tax Journal* 36 (March 1983): 91.

8. See Case, Papke, and Koenigsberg, "Interstate Business Locational Decisions," 41 n. 57.

9. These figures are from G. Cornia, A. Testa, and F. Stocker, "State and Local Fiscal Incentives and Economic Development" (Urban and Regional Development Series no. 4, Academy for Contemporary Problems, Columbus, Ohio, 1978), cited in Kieschnick, *Taxes and Growth,* 43.

10. These and several other reasons why the effect of state and local tax policies is expected to be relatively slight are discussed in Vaughan, *State Taxation,* 77.

11. The literature is summarized in depth in Case, Papke, and Koenigsberg, "Interstate Business Locational Decisions," 9–31. Their report contains an extensive bibliography. A good set of references is also presented in Roger W. Schmenner, *Making Business Location Decisions* (Englewood Cliffs, N.J.: Prentice-Hall, 1982).

12. Schmenner, *Making Business Location Decisions.*

13. Kieschnick, *Taxes and Growth,* tables 22, 23, and 24.

14. Ibid., table 25.

15. Coopers & Lybrand, "Report to the State of Illinois on HB 2588," in *Tax Notes,* October 11, 1982, cited in Case, Papke, and Koenigsberg, "Interstate Business Locational Decisions," p. 10n19.

16. Schmenner, *Making Business Location Decisions,* 46.

17. Ibid., 45.

18. Robert Newman, "Industry Migration and Growth in the South," *Review of Economics and Statistics* 65 (February 1983): 76–86.

19. Several recent surveys have summarized the many empirical studies that attempt to separate tax effects from other location influences. Particularly careful—and carefully worded —reviews can be found in Case, Papke, and Koenigsberg, "Interstate Business Locational Decisions," esp. 12–25, and in Kieschnick, *Taxes and Growth,* 35–63. The brief review presented here closely follows the former's review.

20. Dennis Carlton, "Why New Firms Locate Where They Do," in William Wheaton, ed., *Interregional Movements and Regional Growth* (Washington, D.C.: Urban Institute, 1979), and Dennis Carlton, "The Location and Employment Choices of New Firms," *Review of Economics and Statistics* 65 (August 1983): 440–49.

21. His data consisted of individual records on several million start-up and expanding businesses. See David Birch, *The Job Generation Process* (Cambridge, Mass.: MIT Program on Neighborhood and Regional Change, 1979).

22. Kieschnick, *Taxes and Growth,* 74–78 and appendix 3.

23. Ibid., 78.

24. Advisory Commission on Intergovernmental Relations, *Regional Growth: Interstate Tax Competition,* Report A-76 (Washington, D.C.: ACIR, 1981).

25. Case, Papke, and Koenigsberg, "Interstate Business Locational Decisions," 51–74.

26. Bennett Harrison and Sandra Kanter, "The Political Economy of States' Job-Creation Business Incentives," *Journal of the American Institute of Planners,* October 1978, reprinted in *State and Local Tax Revolt: New Directions for the 80s* (Washington, D.C.: Conference on Alternative State and Local Policies, 1980), 277–88.

27. Commonwealth of Massachusetts, *Tax Expenditure Budget* (Boston: Massachusetts Executive Office of Administration and Finance, May 25, 1984), II-21–II-28. Figures are for tax expenditures listed under "Economic Development and Commerce." Revenue losses for tax preferences for in-state banks are not included.

28. Kieschnick, *Taxes and Growth,* 16, tables 8 and 9. Kieschnick defines a general incentive program as "a conscious and automatic feature of the tax code, which is conditioned upon a hiring, purchase, or investment decision."

29. National Association of State Development Agencies, National Council of Urban Economic Development, and the Urban Institute, *Directory of Incentives for Business Investment and Development in the United States: A State by State Guide* (Washington, D.C.: Urban Institute, 1983).

30. Vaughan, *State Taxation,* 100.

31. Ibid., 95 (emphasis in original).

32. Elliot Schwartz, *The Federal Role in State Industrial Development Programs* (Washington, D.C.: Congressional Budget Office, 1984), 66–67.

33. Commonwealth of Massachusetts, *Tax Expenditure Budget,* May 25, 1984, II-25.

34. They may also have believed that the benefits would be low. For a discussion see Rhode Island Strategic Development Commission, *The Greenhouse Compact* (Providence: The Commission, 1984).

35. States may be leaping ahead with UEZ programs simply so that they have legislation in place to take advantage of any program the federal government eventually decides to offer. Their apparent enthusiasm may not reflect a real commitment to the program or belief that it will work. When they put serious amounts of money of their own down, the indication of their support will be more meaningful. The recent history of state UEZ programs, and a description of existing state programs, is provided in Lawrence Revzan, "Enterprise Zones: Present Status and Potential Impact," *Governmental Finance* 12, no. 4 (December 1983): 31–37. This discussion draws on Revzan's presentation.

36. State UEZ programs are described in Revzan, "Enterprise Zones," table 1.

37. A General Accounting Office report on UEZ legislation voiced similar concerns. See GAO, *Revitalizing Distressed Areas through Enterprise Zones: Many Uncertainties Exist* (Washington, D.C.: GAO, 1982).

38. Revzan, "Enterprise Zones," 36.

39. A recent study by the National Conference of State Legislatures found that very few states have done a comprehensive analysis of their tax expenditures: only twenty-three had done *any* analysis, and only thirteen had a legislative requirement for periodic reporting. See its *The Fiscal Letter* 6, no. 5 (November/December 1984): 10.

40. See Schmenner, *Making Business Location Decisions,* 54–59.

41. Vaughan, *State Taxation,* esp. 19–31.

42. See Roger Vaughan, Robert Pollard, and Barbara Dyer, *The Wealth of States: The Political Economy of State Development* (Washington, D.C.: Council of State Planning Agencies, 1985).

Chapter 6

1. Good summaries of the history of IDBs can be found in Sheryl J. Lincoln, "Is There —and Should There Be—a Future for Industrial Revenue Bonds?" *Journal of Housing,* November 1981, and Charles P. Edmonds and William P. Lloyd, "Industrial Development Bond Financing," *Financial Executive,* April 1981 (both are reprinted in John Matzer, ed.,

Notes

Capital Financing Strategies for Local Governments [Washington, D.C.: International City Management Association, 1983]), and in James T. Bennett and Thomas J. DiLorenzo, *Underground Government* (Washington, D.C.: Cato Institute, 1983).

2. The challenge in Mississippi was brought in state court, on the theory that the borrowed funds were not being used for a public purpose. The Mississippi Supreme Court held that they were. The U.S. Supreme Court had previously held, in 1914, that it would not review definitions of "public purpose" developed by states—that it was up to each state, within constitutional restrictions, to determine what purposes were legitimately public. See John L. Kraft, "Control of Tax Exempt Financing," *National Civic Review,* October 1981, reprinted in Matzer, ed., *Capital Financing Strategies.*

3. This section draws on a summary of the legal history covered ably in Charles P. Edmonds and William P. Lloyd, "Industrial Development Bond Financing," *Financial Executive,* April 1981, reprinted in Matzer, ed., *Capital Financing Strategies.*

4. Philip J. Fischer, Ronald W. Forbes, and John E. Petersen, "Risk and Return in the Choice of Revenue Bond Financing," *Governmental Finance,* September 1980, reprinted in Matzer, ed., *Capital Financing Strategies.*

5. Edmonds and Lloyd, "Industrial Development Bond Financing," 94. The states were Alabama, Arkansas, Georgia, Kentucky, Mississippi, and Tennessee.

6. Pearl Richardson, *Small Issue Industrial Revenue Bonds* (Washington, D.C.: Congressional Budget Office, 1981).

7. Some of these uses have since been ruled out through unusually specific requirements in the Tax Equity and Fiscal Responsibility Act of 1982. IDBs were limited for retail food and beverage outlets, automobile dealerships, and recreation and entertainment facilities. They were explicitly banned for golf courses, country clubs, massage parlors, tennis and racquetball clubs, skating, hot tub, and suntan facilities, and racetracks. For an interesting discussion of the politics of the specific bans, see James Verdier, "Advising Congressional Decision-Makers," *Journal of Policy Analysis and Management* (1984): 421–38.

8. Office of Management and Budget, *The United States Budget in Brief, Fiscal Year 1985,* (Washington, D.C.: OMB, 1984), table 4. The international affairs budget does not include defense spending.

9. *Budget of the United States Government, Fiscal Year 1985,* Special Analysis G, table G-1.

10. For a detailed examination of the trends in the interest rates of tax-exempt bonds and their relation to interest rates on taxable securities, see Michael D. Hernandez and Darcy Bradbury, Kidder Peabody & Company, *An Analysis of Tax-Exemption for State and Local Debt,* September 1984.

Chapter 7

1. Pat Choate and Susan Walter, *America in Ruins: Beyond the Public Works Pork Barrel* (Washington, D.C.: Council of State Planning Agencies, 1981).

2. Estimates of this order of magnitude were presented to a congressional group. *U.S. News and World Report,* September 27, 1982, p. 57, discusses how this persistently quoted figure was constructed.

3. "Special Report on State and Local Government Trouble," *Business Week,* October 26, 1981, pp. 135–81; "The Decaying of America," *Newsweek,* August 2, 1982, pp. 12–19; "To Rebuild America—$2,500,000,000,000 Job," *U.S. News and World Report,* September 27, 1982, pp. 57–61.

4. An early government report was *The Condition of Urban Infrastructure in the New York–New Jersey Region: A Survival Issue for the 1980s,* by the Regional and Economic Development Task Force, Port Authority of New York and New Jersey, May 1979. For more-recent studies, see *California's Infrastructure: Rusty Hinges on the Golden Gate,* by the Assembly Office of Research, State of California, January 1984; *Report to the Governor and General Assembly,* by the Environmental Facilities Study Commission, State of Georgia, December 1982; *Boston's Infrastructure,* by the Boston Redevelopment Authority, April 1984;

and *Infrastructure Report and Recommendations,* by the Infrastructure Review Task Force, State of California, April 1984.

5. Congressional Budget Office, *Public Works Infrastructure* (Washington, D.C.: CBO, 1983), 9; "Study Says $53 Million [*sic*] a Year Is Needed for Public Works," *New York Times,* April 27, 1983, p. A19.

6. Department of Commerce, Bureau of Economic Analysis, cited in *U.S. News and World Report,* September 27, 1982, p. 60, and in *Business Week,* October 26, 1981, p. 142. This figure excludes schools and hospitals, which also are aging on the average.

7. An excellent review of these trends and the composition of public works spending through 1977 is given by Nazir G. Dossani and Wilbur A. Steger, "Trends in U.S. Public Works Investment: Report on a New Study," *National Tax Journal,* 33 (June 1980): 123–48.

8. See, for example, Roger Vaughan, *Rebuilding America: Financing Public Works in the 1980s* (Washington, D.C.: Council of State Planning Agencies, 1983), chap. 4. Vaughan is one of the principal advocates of the user fee approach.

9. See, for example, Touche Ross & Company, *The Infrastructure Crisis: Roundtable,* 1983; Lehman Brothers Kuhn Loeb, *Public Infrastructure: Problems, Priorities, and Financing Alternatives,* 1983; Dillon Read & Company, *Infrastructure Financing: An Overview,* 1983; Jeffrey C. Carey, Merrill Lynch Capital Markets, *Financing Alternatives for Wastewater Systems,* 1984; and Kidder Peabody & Company, *Infrastructure Finance,* 1984.

10. *Hard Choices: A Report on the Increasing Gap between America's Infrastructure Needs and Our Ability to Pay for Them* (Washington, D.C.: Government Printing Office, 1984).

11. *Newsweek,* August 2, 1982, p. 13.

12. Ibid.

13. Standards for public asset accounting, and their role in accountability, are discussed in Herman B. Leonard, "Measuring and Reporting the Financial Condition of Public Organizations," *Research in Governmental and Non-Profit Accounting,* 1 (1985): 117–48.

14. National Council on Government Accounting (NCGA) Statement 1, pp. 9–10. The NCGA is the predecessor of the GASB, which superseded it in 1984. The GASB's first official action was to reaffirm all existing NCGA standards; Statement 1 thus remains in force. A different set of rules applies to assets of public enterprises—business conducted by the government, for which charges are levied (a municipal power company, for example). These organizations are accounted for much the way they would be in the private sector; asset valuations are supposed to be recorded, and depreciation is taken as a cost.

15. A proposal of this form is being considered by the Governmental Accounting Standards Board. Whether it can be practicably implemented, and made acceptable to the accounting profession, remains to be seen. A similar idea has been discussed by Michael A. Pagano, "Notes on Capital Budgeting," *Public Budgeting and Finance,* 4, no. 3 (Autumn 1984): 35.

Chapter 8

1. Literature on the benefits of public leasing under ERTA considers whether it is generally desirable as a matter of state, local, and federal policy. For a view critical of the use of leasing, see Herman B. Leonard, *Creative Financing for New York City Projects* (New York: Office of Economic Development, 1984), and Herman B. Leonard, "Financing the Reindustrialization of the Public Sector," in Neal A. Roberts and H. James Brown, eds., *How Can Local Governments Finance Capital Improvements in the 1980's?* (Cambridge: Lincoln Institute of Land Policy, 1982). For more-favorable treatments, see John E. Petersen, and Wesley C. Hough, *Creative Capital Financing* (Chicago: Municipal Finance Officers Association, 1983), and John Matzer, Jr., ed., *Capital Financing Strategies for Local Governments* (Washington, D.C.: International City Management Association, 1983). The best-known, most heavily used public-leasing provision was the "safe harbor" treatment allowed for leases of mass-commuting vehicles. This permits transit authorities to enjoy the tax benefits of both accelerated depreciation and tax-exempt bond financing. For a description of transit vehicle safe harbor leases, see Leonard, *Creative Financing for New York City Projects,* 16–19.

2. John E. Chapoton, transcript of hearing before the House Committee on Ways and Means, HR3110, 98th Cong., 1st sess., June 8, 1983, *Government Leasing Act of 1983* (Washington, D.C.: Government Printing Office, 1983), 24.

Notes

3. This transaction has been widely discussed. A detailed treatment is given in Judy Bunnell, *New York City Leaseback Case Series* (New York: Office of Economic Development, 1984).

4. See Bunnell, "MTA Safe Harbor Lease, Part A," ibid., and Howard L. Frant, "Public Sector Leasing and Federal Tax Policy" (unpublished mimeo, 1982).

5. This is similar to a problem with the IRS's arbitrage restrictions on individuals. Taxpayers are not allowed to borrow money (on which they could deduct the interest payments as investment costs) to invest in tax-exempt municipal bonds. But suppose a woman has a house with unused mortage capacity and money in the bank for a vacation. She wants to purchase tax-exempt bonds. If she borrows to buy the municipal bonds, this is arbitrage. If she borrows against the house to buy bonds, it is likely to be determined to be arbitrage unless the timing is very carefully arranged. But if she buys the bonds with the money in the bank, then borrows against the house for the vacation, it is not arbitrage, even though the net transaction is the same.

6. This transaction has been widely discussed. For a good, short description, see David E. Dowall, and David Shiver, "Case Studies on Property Development: Oakland Museum Sale and Leaseback," in Roberts and Brown, eds., *How Can Local Governments Finance Capital Improvements in the 1980s?* 34–61.

7. "Oakland Sells the City Jewels," *Western City* magazine, the official publication of the League of California Cities. This article was adapted from the report of the city manager, Henry L. Gardner, to the Oakland city council. It is reprinted in Matzer, ed., *Capital Financing Strategies*, 88.

8. Edward A. Dyl, and Michael D. Joehnk, "Leasing as a Municipal Finance Alternative," *Public Administration Review*, 1978, reprinted in Matzer, ed., *Capital Financing Strategies*, 66–76.

9. Ibid., 76 n. 1.

10. Jacques Schlenger, testimony before the House Committee on Ways and Means, 98th Cong., 1st sess., June 8, 1983 (*Federal Leasing Practices* [Washington, D.C.: Government Printing Office, 1983]), 87.

11. Over the years, this issue has generated reams of Congressional testimony and analysis. A good summary of the issues is provided in testimony before the Subcommittee on Oversight of the Committee on Ways and Means of the House of Representatives, 98th Cong., 1st sess., February 28, 1983, *Federal Leasing Practices*.

12. The definitive—and correct—analysis, together with a good history of the ebb and flow of the argument, is provided by Geoffrey White, *DoD Leasing Policy: Memorandum for the Director, Program Analysis and Evaluation* (Washington, D.C.: Office of the Secretary of Defense 1984).

13. Senator Howard Metzenbaum, in particular, denounced Navy leasing practices. See his testimony before the Subcommittee on Oversight of the Committee on Ways and Means of the House of Representatives, 98th Cong., 1st sess., February 28, 1983, *Federal Leasing Practices*, 7–25.

14. White, "DoD Leasing Policy," 3.

Chapter 9

1. A discussion of this history, and of how little has changed, can be found in Sidney Davidson, et al., *Reporting by State and Local Government Units* (Chicago: Center for Management of Public and Non-Profit Enterprise, 1977).

2. H. W. Wilmot, "Municipal Accounting Reform as Illustrated in the City of Minneapolis," *Journal of Accountancy*, June 1906. Wilmot was a member of the firm that audited Minneapolis's financial reports. Many observers believe that the finances of governmental units have become complex faster than governmental accounting, so that Wilmot's comments apply with greater force today. Cited in Davidson et al., *Reporting by State and Local Government Units*, 5.

3. See Herman B. Leonard, "Measuring and Reporting the Financial Condition of Public Organizations," *Research in Governmental and Non-Profit Accounting* (1985): 117–48.

4. For an extended discussion of what changes in public sector accounting would be required to capture financial conditions comprehensively, see ibid.

5. For a discussion of the problem of defining a profession, see R. Dungwall and P. Lewis, eds., *The Sociology of the Professions* (New York: Macmillan, 1983). For a more extended discussion of its relevance to governmental accounting, see Leonard, "Measuring and Reporting."

6. For a detailed discussion of the accounting profession and its difficulties, see Stanley Charles Abraham, *The Public Accounting Profession* (Lexington, Mass.: D. C. Heath, 1978).

7. This is not unique to the public sector; it also applies to many aspects of private sector accounting. To date, the accounting profession has not demonstrated any great affinity for challenge, but it now shows some signs of being more adaptable. It has recently extended its domain to report some estimates that previously would have seemed rather avant-garde.

8. For a discussion of the appropriate methods of public-employee retirement system asset valuation, see Leonard, "Measuring and Reporting."

9. An example is the controversy over interjurisdictional tax issues. FASB has consistently been unable to define coherent standards for the geographic allocation of income for organizations operating across jurisdictional boundaries. In frustration, many jurisdictions have legally adopted simple allocation schemes.

10. For a discussion of standards that the GASB could adopt to improve comprehensive governmental accounting, see Leonard, "Measuring and Reporting."

Chapter 10

1. The tax revolt has spawned a wide, if not deep, literature, including descriptions, analyses, and advocacy documents. Some of the more interesting, widely read, and useful books on the subject are Norman Walzer and Glenn W. Fisher, *Cities, Suburbs, and Property Taxes* (Cambridge, Mass.: Oelgeschlager, Gunn, and Hain, 1981); Arthur B. Laffer and Jan P. Seymour, eds., *The Economics of the Tax Revolt: A Reader* (New York: Harcourt Brace Jovanovich, 1979); Howard Jarvis, with Robert Pack, *I'm Mad as Hell* (New York: Times Books, 1979); Alvin Rabushka and Pauline Ryan, *The Tax Revolt* (Stanford: Hoover Institution, 1982); Lester A. Sobel, *The Great American Tax Revolt* (New York: Facts on File, 1979); and Robert J. Dworak, *Taxpayers, Taxes, and Government Spending* (New York: Praeger, 1980). A good collection of popular articles is in *State and Local Tax Revolt: New Directions for the 80s* (Washington, D.C.: Conference on Alternative State and Local Policies, 1980).

2. Figures compiled by the Advisory Commission on Intergovernmental Relations, presented in *Significant Features of Fiscal Federalism* (1981), cited in Henry J. Raimondo, "State Limitations of Local Taxing and Spending," *Public Budgeting and Finance,* 3, no. 3 (Autumn 1983): 35.

3. These figures were computed by Daphne A. Kenyon and Karen M. Benker in "Fiscal Discipline: Lessons from the State Experience" (Paper presented at a National Tax Association —Tax Institute of America conference, May 1984).

4. The history of these limits and evidence of their impacts up to 1976 is provided by the Advisory Commission on Intergovernmental Relations, *State Limitations on Local Taxes and Expenditures* (Washington, D.C.: ACIR, February 1977).

5. See, for example, Helen F. Ladd and Julie Boatright Wilson, "Who Supports Tax Limitation: Evidence from Proposition $2\frac{1}{2}$," *Journal of Policy Analysis and Management* 2 (Winter 1983): 256–79.

6. Ladd and Wilson's data are particularly interesting on this point. Most who voted for tax limitation in Massachusetts believed that resulting service cuts would be small; those who voted against it reported that they did so largely because they believed that cuts in services they used would be severe. Ibid., 268 and 270.

7. See Kenyon and Benker, "Fiscal Discipline," 2–6, for a good brief history of the development of state TELs.

8. Steven Gold, "State Tax Increases in 1983," *National Tax Journal* 37 (March 1984): 9–11.

9. A good summary is provided ibid, 9–14.

10. Based on a survey by the National Conference of State Legislatures and the Coalition of American Public Employees, Washington, D.C., 1979, reported in Roger Kemp, *Coping with Proposition 13* (Lexington, Mass.: Lexington Books, 1980), table 1–1.

Notes

11. Gold, "State Tax Increases," 12.

12. Ibid., 13.

13. Ibid. Gold presents a list of causes for state and local fiscal distress in the early 1980s similar to that discussed here.

14. James Papke, "The Response of State-Local Government Taxation to Fiscal Crisis," *National Tax Journal* 36 (September 1983): 401.

15. Figures compiled by the National Tax Foundation, cited in Gold, "State Tax Increases," 14.

16. Gold, "State Tax Increases," 15–17.

17. Figures from a survey by the Morgan Guaranty Trust Company, October 1983, cited ibid., 15. See also Department of Commerce, Bureau of the Census, *State Government Finances in 1983,* 1.

18. "States Roll Back Taxes as Economy Improves," *Public Administration Times,* May 15, 1984, p. 8, summarizes recent state tax cut activity.

19. Kenyon and Benker, "Fiscal Discipline," 11–14. A seventh citizen proposal in a fourteenth state (Florida) was removed from the ballot by the state supreme court.

20. "West Coast States Set Anti-Tax Initiative Votes," *Public Administration Times,* August 1, 1984, p. 1.

21. See ACIR, *State Limitations,* 21–32 and appendix.

22. Tax rate limits were found to have more impact than levy limits. Ibid., 21 and appendix, table A-2.

23. Kenyon and Benker, "Fiscal Discipline," 7–11.

24. A good summary of the impacts is provided by Jerome Rothenberg and Paul Smoke, "Early Impacts of Proposition $2\frac{1}{2}$ on the Massachusetts State-Local Public Sector," *Public Budgeting and Finance* 2, no. 4 (Winter 1982): 90–110 (the figures presented here are contained in the summary, 100–102). See also Lawrence E. Susskind and Jane Fountain Serio, eds., *Proposition $2\frac{1}{2}$: Its Impact on Massachusetts* (Cambridge, Mass.: Oelgeschlager, Gunn, and Hain, 1983).

25. The averages conceal wide variation, and the largest impacts were very large indeed. Boston, already under financial stress before Prop $2\frac{1}{2}$, faced several consecutive years of 15 percent reductions in property tax revenues. Capital spending was eliminated. Maintenance not critical to public safety disappeared. Tremendous political capital was expended at the statehouse to raise state aid to offset local revenue losses.

26. Karl E. Case, "Proposition 13 and the Distribution of Income" (unpublished mimeo, 1979).

27. See Wagner's essay in Richard A. Musgrave and A. Peacock, *Classics in the Theory of Public Finance* (London: Macmillan, 1958). Musgrave discusses the Wagner hypothesis in "Leviathan Cometh—Or Does He?" in Helen F. Ladd and T. N. Tideman, eds., *Tax and Expenditure Limitations* (Washington, D.C.: Urban Institute Press, 1981), 77–120.

28. This argument, and its relation to tax and expenditure limitations, is presented by David Lowery, "The Hidden Impact of Fiscal Caps: Implications of the Beck Phenomenon," *Public Budgeting and Finance* 3, no. 3 (Autumn 1983): 19–32. The discussion here follows his argument closely.

29. This is commonly referred to as the "Beck" phenomenon. See Morris Beck, "The Expanding Public Sector: Some Contrary Evidence," *National Tax Journal* 29 (March 1976): 15–21. The issue has also been examined by Elliott Dubin, " 'The Expanding Public Sector: Some Contrary Evidence'—A Comment," *National Tax Journal* 30 (March 1977): 95, and by A. F. Ott, "Has the Growth of Government in the West Been Halted?" in W. Samuels and L. Wade, *Taxing and Spending Policy* (Lexington, Mass.: Lexington Books, 1980), 3–16. This research is ably summarized in Lowery, "Hidden Impact of Fiscal Caps," 21–22.

30. William J. Baumol, "Macroeconomics of Unbalanced Growth: The Anatomy of Urban Crisis," *American Economic Review* 57 (June 1967): 415–26.

31. Baumol's original argument is rephrased in the form of public and private services in Beck, "Expanding Public Sector." For a discussion, see Lowery, "Hidden Impact of Fiscal Caps," 22.

32. See W. D. Berry and David Lowery, "The Measurement of Government Size: Implications for the Study of Government Growth" (Working paper in public administration, PA–28–1982, Martin Center for Public Administration, University of Kentucky, 1982). Cited in

Lowery, "Hidden Impact of Fiscal Caps." Lowery reviews conflicting evidence on the level and causes of productivity improvements in the public sector and notes that lack of productivity improvement is one form that waste could take, intertwining the two explanations. Ibid., n. 3.

33. Richard Musgrave observes that this is appropriate if we wish to fix the ratio of government to private value of services, and if costs reflect values. Consider an economy in which half the services are public and half are private. Suppose the cost of public services doubles: we have to buy less of one or both services. If we continue to spend equal amounts on public and private services, the level of private services remains unchanged and the level of public services falls by one-half. If we continue to purchase equal amounts of public and private services, each will fall by one-third, but the share of the public budget would rise to 67 percent. Musgrave observes that if costs reflect values, then the public sector's share of the dollar budget will correctly indicate the public share in production of value to consumers. See Musgrave, "Leviathan Cometh," 85.

34. Kenyon and Benker, "Fiscal Discipline," 15.

35. The Congressional Budget Office warns of this danger in its study of options for limiting federal spending. See John W. Elwood, *Balancing the Federal Budget and Limiting Federal Spending: Constitutional and Statutory Approaches* (Washington, D.C.: CBO, 1982), 59. Kenyon and Benker also discuss it, with reference to the increase in proposals including it, in their "Fiscal Discipline," 16.

36. The issue of whether the public sector is over- or underexpanded appears to be timeless, and perhaps cyclical. The built-in biases of political, social, and economic institutions for too large and for too small a public sector have been debated since time immemorial. An excellent summary is given in Musgrave, "Leviathan Cometh."

Chapter 11

1. Henry J. Raimondo, "State Limitations of Local Taxing and Spending," *Public Budgeting and Finance* 3, no. 3 (Autumn 1983): 35. An interesting discussion of these trends is given by Al Ullman, "Federal Spending and the Budget Crisis," in C. Lowell Harriss, ed., *Control of Federal Spending* (Montpelier, Vt.: Capital City Press, 1985), 38–46.

2. The history of popular support for a federal balanced-budget requirement is traced by Alan Blinder and Douglas Holtz-Eakin in "Public Opinion and the Balanced Budget" (Working Paper no. 1234, National Bureau of Economic Research, Cambridge, Mass., November 1983). A summary of the recent history is provided in John W. Elwood, *Balancing the Federal Budget and Limiting Federal Spending: Constitutional and Statutory Approaches* (Washington, D.C.: Congressional Budget Office, September 1982). The survey results referred to here are summarized in these papers.

3. Blinder and Holtz-Eakin, "Public Opinion," 2–3.

4. A variety of specific amendments have been suggested. The summary presented here is based on S.J. Res. 58, adopted by the Senate in August 1982.

5. This argument has been presented in a variety of forums. See, for example, James M. Buchanan and Richard E. Wagner, *Democracy in Deficit* (New York: Academic Press, 1977); Richard E. Wagner et al., *Balanced Budgets, Fiscal Responsibility, and the Constitution* (Washington, D.C.: Cato Institute, 1982); and Milton Friedman and Rose Friedman, "Constitutional Amendment to Limit the Growth of Spending," in Harriss, ed., *Control of Federal Spending,* 132–36. The issue of whether our institutions are biased toward an over- or an undersupply of public services is the focus of a long-standing debate. Richard Musgrave provides a good summary in "Leviathan Cometh—Or Does He?" in Helen F. Ladd and T. N. Tideman, eds., *Tax and Expenditure Limitations* (Washington, D.C.: Urban Institute Press, 1981), 77–120.

6. David A. Stockman, testimony before the House Subcommittee on Monopolies and Commercial Law, Committee on the Judiciary, May 19, 1982.

7. Adam Smith, *The Wealth of Nations,* ed. Edwin Cannan (New York: Random House, 1937), 424.

8. *Wall Street Journal,* June 14, 1985, p. 1.

9. Office of Management and Budget, *Budget of the United States Government, Fiscal Year 1986* (Washington, D.C.: OMB, 1985), Special Analysis D, pp. D-19–D-24.

Notes

10. There have been heated debates recently about whether the federal government should have a capital budget. These discussions are not new. Fiscal policy advocates generally recoil from the view that the operating and capital budgets should be separated, because doing so might constrain using surpluses or deficits to cool off or stimulate the economy. See Francis M. Bator, "Budgetary Reform: Notes on Principles and Strategy," *Review of Economics and Statistics* 45 (May 1963): 115–20.

11. A variety of researchers have tried to refigure the federal budget, separating capital and operating expenditures and estimating depreciation and other noncash costs and receipts. It is extremely difficult to do so accurately. A number of other adjustments, including deficits in the current funding of social security, pensions, and other obligations, are also required to put the federal budget fully on an "accrual" basis. A good brief description of what is involved is given by William Nordhaus, "The Imperfections of the Budget," *New York Times,* March 22, 1981, p. F2. More detailed discussions are in Michael J. Boskin, "Federal Government Deficits: Some Myths and Realities," *American Economic Review* 72 (May 1982): 296–303, and in Robert Eisner and Paul J. Pieper, "A New View of Federal Debt and Budget Deficits," *American Economic Review* 74 (March 1984): 11–29. A popular discussion of this and other adjustments is given by Susan Lee, "Of Course I'm Sure, I Read It In . . .," *Forbes,* November 19, 1984, pp. 39–40.

Index

Index

Index